Data Science for Beginners

Samir Dey
Dean (R&D) and Head
Department of Mathematics, JIS University, Kolkata

Dibyendu Banerjee
Senior Architect & Data Scientist, Global IT Company
and
Member, BoS, Department of Mathematics, JIS University, Kolkata

Sourav Kairi
Software Engineer & Data Science Expert, Global IT Company
and
Guest Lecturer, IIT Jodhpur

PHI Learning Private Limited
Delhi-110092
2026

*In fond memory of **Shri Asoke K. Ghosh** (October 1942 – February 2024), Founder Chairman and Managing Director of PHI Learning, whose vision endlessly inspires.*

The Legacy Continues....

Published by Pushpita Ghosh, PHI Learning Private Limited, Rimjhim House, 111, Patparganj Industrial Estate, Delhi-110092 and Printed by Multi Colour Services, 92, DSIDC Sheds, Okhla Industrial Area, Phase-I, New Delhi-110020.

₹ **595.00**

DATA SCIENCE FOR BEGINNERS
Samir Dey, Dibyendu Banerjee and Sourav Kairi

ISBN-978-81-997576-8-4 (Print Book)
ISBN-978-81-997576-4-6 (e-Book)

The export rights of this book are vested solely with the publisher.

Contents

Preface

Data Science for Beginners has been written with one clear intention—to make the world of data science approachable, practical, and engaging for learners at every stage. This book is not about grand discoveries or exhaustive coverage of every emerging technology. Instead, it focuses on building a strong foundation—connecting essential theory with hands-on practice, and offering insights into the developments that are shaping the field today. This book is designed first and foremost for beginners—students, fresh graduates, and curious learners who want clear explanations, simple foundations, and practical guidance while keeping the learning journey simple and clear. The work is the result of collaboration among educators, practitioners, and researchers who share a common vision to bridge the gap between theory and practice, and to make data science accessible for everyone. The chapters are structured to guide readers step by step—beginning with the fundamentals of data science, probability, and statistics, moving through tools, data types, and visualization, and then advancing into machine learning, deep learning, natural language processing, and time series analysis. We conclude with a discussion on ethics, privacy, and responsible AI, because technical knowledge must always be paired with accountability. Our aim is not to overwhelm but to empower. Whether you are a student taking your first step, a professional expanding your skill set, or a leader seeking clarity in a rapidly evolving field, this book is designed to serve as a companion and a practical resource. Ultimately, this book is as much yours as it is ours. We hope it helps you take your first steps navigate through the exciting world of data science. If it sparks curiosity, provides clarity, or inspires exploration, we will consider it a success.

The analyses, interpretations, and perspectives presented in this book are solely those of the authors. They do not reflect, nor should they be construed as representing the views, positions, or policies of their organizations, institutions, or employers.

Acknowledgements

The creation of this book has been an immensely rewarding journey, made possible through the generous support, guidance, and encouragement of many individuals and institutions. We extend our deepest gratitude to all who have contributed to its successful completion.

We are especially indebted to the Department of Mathematics, JIS University, Kolkata, for their invaluable academic and technical support. Their expertise and insights have been instrumental in refining the concepts presented here.

Our sincere appreciation goes to Prof. Dr. Diptendu Sinha Roy, National Institute of Technology, Meghalaya; Dr. Dakshina Ranjan Kisku, Associate Professor, National Institute of Technology, Durgapur; and Dr. Dharmpal Singh, Professor, JIS University, for their thoughtful suggestions and constructive feedback.

We are also grateful to PHI Learning Private Limited, Delhi, for their support in transforming our manuscript into its published form.

A special note of thanks goes to the students and research scholars whose curiosity, questions, and enthusiasm have continually inspired us. Their engagement has not only enriched our perspectives but also motivated us to refine and clarify the ideas presented in this book.

This work has further benefited from the valuable feedback of numerous dignitaries and experts—many of whom we cannot name individually—but whose contributions have been vital in shaping the final outcome.

Finally, we owe a heartfelt thanks to our colleagues, friends, and family members for their unwavering encouragement, patience, and belief in this project.

Their support has been constant source of motivation. This book stands as the collective result of many contributions, and we remain profoundly grateful to everyone who played a part in making it possible.

Samir Dey
Dibyendu Banerjee
Sourav Kairi

1

FUNDAMENTALS OF DATA SCIENCE

1.1 UNDERSTANDING DATA SCIENCE

1.1.1 Definition and Scope of Data Science

What is Data Science?

The term Data Science means the scientific processing of very big amounts of both structured and unstructured data, mostly through the application of various tools and methods borrowed from other sciences like computer science and application domain, and statistical analysis, with the objective of making informed decisions and turning strategies.

The term 'data scientist' was first popularized in 2008 by DJ Patil and Jeff Hammerbacher, who noticed their roles didn't fit traditional job labels.

Evolution of Data Science as a Field

Data Science can be traced back to the fields of statistics and data analysis that became common in the early years of the 20th century. However, the past 20 years have drastically changed the landscape due to the digital technology, Internet and the introduction of large-scale data storage impacting every area of business. The Data Science domain has incorporated machine learning, big data technology and cloud computing as skills. Thus, we are currently in the midst of the Data Science ecosystem, which is often referred to as "modern" Data Science.

Importance of Data-Driven Decision-Making

Modern organizations encounter multiple intricate problems which demand well-informed choices. Data-driven decision-making uses data to eliminate uncertainty while detecting patterns and maximizing operational efficiency and forecasting upcoming results. From improving supply chains, crafting products tailored to customer needs, and even crafting data-driven public health policy-making; **Data-Driven Decision-Making** is an industry leader in both operational and cross industry excellence. Because of Data-Driven Decision-Making, businesses can timely adjust to market fluctuations and minimize associated risks while creating strategies that are verifiably calculable.

1.1.2   The Role of Data Scientists

Responsibilities of a Data Scientist

A Data Scientist's responsibilities include identifying data-driven opportunities, collecting and processing data, developing models and algorithms, visualizing results, and communicating insights.

Their goal is to solve problems through data and guide business decisions using analytics.

The following diagram explains and highlights Sills and Roles for a Data Scientist.

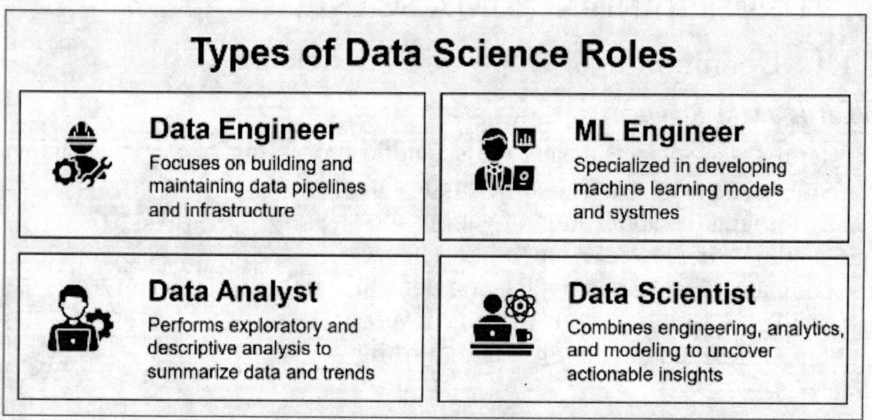

1.1.3   Real-World Applications of Data Science

Data science is revolutionizing various industries by enhancing decision-making and process optimization. In healthcare predictive analytics improves disease diagnosis, personalized medicine enhances treatment, and AI-powered image diagnosis enhances radiology precision. In banking and finance, credit risk modeling and real-time fraud detection systems improve lending safety. Retail and e-commerce thrive through recommendation engines, dynamic pricing, and customer segmentation.

1.2   DATA SCIENCE LIFECYCLE

Data Science life cycle follows the below steps:

- **Problem Definition:** Identify the business challenge to address with data.
- **Data Collection:** Gather structured, semi-structured, and unstructured data.
- **Process and Clean Data:** Prepare data by transforming, cleaning, and removing inconsistencies.
- **A Exploratory Data Analysis (EDA):** Examine data distributions, trends, and relationships using statistical and visualization techniques.
- **Modeling:** Train machine learning models for predictions or classifications.
- **Visualization and Interpretation:** Present insights using dashboards and charts.
- **Decision and Deployment:** Apply findings to real-world applications and improve strategies.

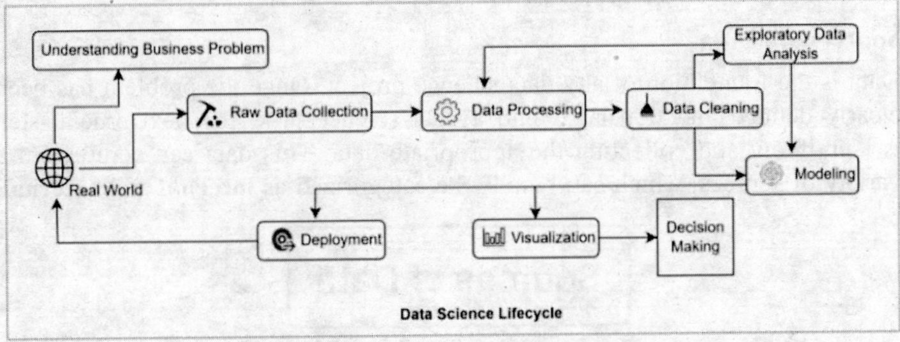

Data Science Lifecycle

1.2.1   Problem Definition

Understanding Business Problems

The first step towards success in the field of data science is correctly identifying a business problem, which is a requirement for all data science projects. The reason for this is that even the most advanced techniques will be useless in solving a problem that is not well defined. If the right data science solutions are to be implemented, it is necessary to fully comprehend the business problems, which are the organization's objectives expressed in a different language.

The data scientist has to be on the lookout for business signals from the stakeholders, and these will most likely include clarifying questions such as:

- What is the precise desired result from the business's side?
- What are the measurements that will indicate success or failure?
- Are there any limitations (e.g., on time, budget, legal or ethical reasons)?
- Which decisions will be based on the data science results?

A profound comprehension of the problem's "why" is essential. For instance, let us consider an e-commerce site that is facing a drop in user engagement. The most rational action to take is to enhance the website's user interface. Nevertheless, if we go further into the matter, we may discover that the real reasons behind this are delayed shipping or poor customer support. This comprehension, in turn, transforms the problem-solving from web design to operations optimization and thus necessitates a different data approach altogether.

Moreover, there are times when the issues are so enormous or intricate that it would be impractical to handle them all at once. In such cases, it is better to decompose the problem into a number of smaller, more manageable components to be addressed one by one.

1.2.2 Data Collection

Sources of Data

Data is the foundation of any data science project. Once the problem has been clearly defined and translated into a data science task, the next crucial step is identifying and collecting the appropriate data. This data can come from a variety of sources, which can broadly be categorized as **internal** and **external**.

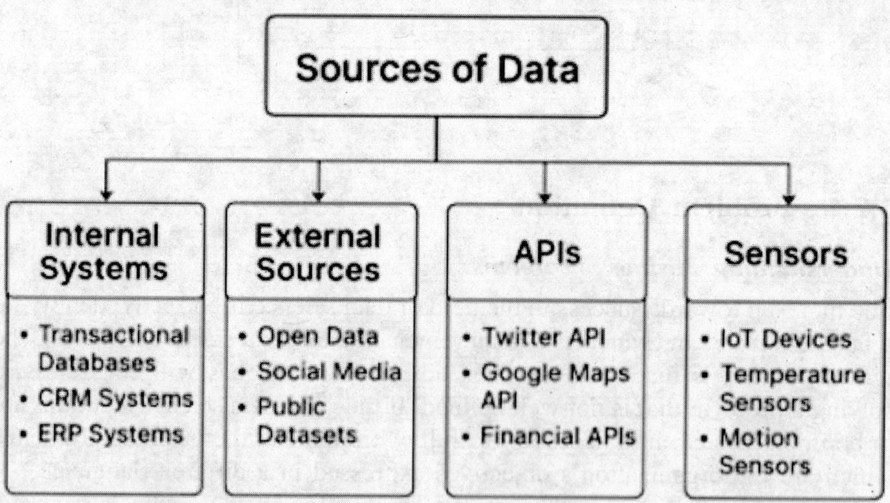

1. **Internal Data Sources:** These are data sources that are generated and maintained within the organization. Examples include:

- **Transactional Databases:** Sales records, payment histories, order logs.
- **Customer Relationship Management (CRM) Systems:** Customer profiles, interaction history, support tickets.
- **Enterprise Resource Planning (ERP) Systems:** Inventory levels, supplier details, employee records.
- **Operational Logs:** Application logs, server logs, audit trails.

There are several advantages using internal data source, which are listed below:

- High relevance to the business problem.
- Typically well-documented and structured.
- Easier to control for privacy and compliance.

2. **External Data Sources:** External data complements internal data and often provides broader context.

- **Open Data Repositories:** Government census data, environmental data (e.g., data.gov, World Bank).
- **Social Media Platforms:** Public comments, posts, trends from Twitter, Reddit, LinkedIn, etc.
- **Public Datasets:** Academic datasets or industry-specific datasets (e.g., Kaggle, UCI Machine Learning Repository).
- **Websites:** Information extracted using web scraping.

3. **APIs (Application Programming Interfaces):** APIs enable access to live dynamic and formatted outside data. APIs are exposed by most systems so that data can be programmatically consumed by developers.

Some of the popular APIs are–Twitter API, Google Maps API, OpenWeather API, Financial API etc.

4. **Sensors and IoT Devices:** In manufacturing, agriculture, healthcare, and smart cities, data is often collected using physical sensors.

Examples:

- Temperature Sensors in cold storage.
- Heart Rate Monitors in wearable health devices.
- Motion Sensors in autonomous vehicles.

This type of data is typically **real-time**, **high-frequency**, and **high-volume**, often forming the basis for time-series or streaming data analysis.

Structured Unstructured and Semi-Structured Data

In data science, one of the key distinctions made when collecting and processing data is between **structured** and **unstructured** data. Understanding this distinction is crucial because it determines the methods used for storage, processing, analysis, and the types of tools required to handle each data type. The following Table shows a comparative view of the 3 types of data:

	Structured Data	**Unstructured Data**	**Semi-structured Data**
Data Type	Quantitative, Categorical	Text, Audio, Images, Videos	Tags, Audio, Multi-media
Data Analysis Complexity	Low	High	Medium
Searchability	Easy to search	Difficult to search	Moderately search-able
Use Cases	SQL tables, spread-sheets	Social media, docu-ments	Web data, logs
Examples	Relational databases, Excel sheets	Emails, videos, posts	XML, JSON, HTML

1. **Structured Data:**   Structured data refers to highly organized and easily searchable data that is stored in a predefined format, typically in **rows and columns**. This type of data is often found in **relational databases** and is easy to manage, analyze, and process using traditional data tools.

Characteristics of Structured Data:

- **Well-defined schema:** Each column in a structured set of data demands a data type, such as integers, characters, or dates.
- **Easy to query:** Structured data are queried under SQL (Structured Query Language) for simple retrieval and manipulation.
- **Predictable:** It follows a format consistently to make it easy to analyze and be used in machine learning models.

Examples of Structured Data:

- **Customer databases:** Containing fields such as name, address, and purchase history.
- **Financial data:** Consisting of transactions and balance sheets, as well as stock market prices.
- **Survey responses:** Stored in a tabular format, such as Excel or CSV files.

Advantages of Structured Data:

- **Efficient storage and retrieval:** Due to its organized format, structured data is easy to store and access.
- **Ideal for traditional analysis:** Well-suited for basic statistical analysis, business intelligence, and machine learning tasks.

2. **Unstructured Data:** Unstructured data does not take any set format or structure. Most of the data have text or multimedia contents and cannot be conveniently placed into made-for-purpose arrays or other database elements. Unstructured data has an irregular and varied nature that makes processing and analyzing it a little more complex.

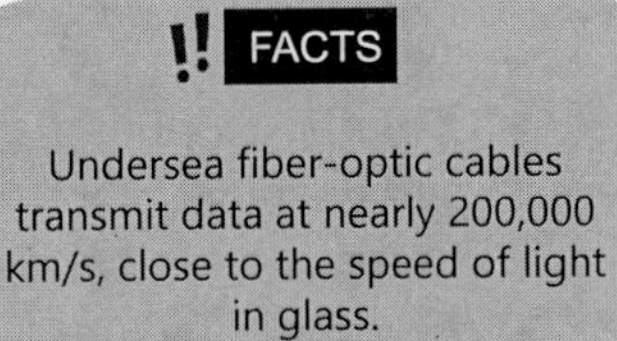

Characteristics of Unstructured Data:

- **No predefined structure:** There is no set format or organization for unstructured data, hence making it hard to handle.
- **Variable:** It can occur as text, images, video, social media posts, audio files, etc.
- **Needs special treatment:** Usually unstructured data require additional tools and methods to extract meaningful information from it, such as Natural Language Processing (NLP) for most texts, Computer Vision for images, and so on.

Examples of Unstructured Data:

- **Text:** Can be emails, social media posts, comments from users, or simply web pages.
- **Multimedia:** Could be images, videos, audio recordings, or photos.
- **Web data:** HTML documents, blogs, forum discussions, etc.

Challenges of Unstructured Data:

- **Storage and querying:** Unlike structured data, unstructured data can't be queried using some traditional query languages, such as SQL. Therefore, one would require special systems for its storing and retrieval.
- **Analysis:** Sometimes unstructured data contains noise and some kind of extra, non-useful information. Usually, it really requires the extraction of the insights using advanced techniques as well as more computing power to do so.

3. **Semi-structured Data:** Semi-structured data lies between structured and unstructured data: it has some organizational structure yet does not conform to any specific schema, as opposed to strictly structured data. Semi-structured data may contain tags or markers to separate various elements of data, these markers being optional in their use and never being fixed in their format.

Examples of Semi-structured Data:

- **ML and JSON files:** Data exchange formats utilized in web services and APIs.
- **Emails:** Applying a mechanism that marks header fields like a subject and recipient in a structured format while an unstructured format applies to the message body.
- **Log files:** Include structured time stamps for events and event codes for events that describe unstructured text.

Challenges of Semi-structured Data:

- **Parsing complexity:** Semi-structured data contains some markers or tags that allow information extraction but often proves challenging and requires custom parsers.
- **Inconsistent structure:** The variations in format can hamper the analysis unless some preprocessing is done.
- **Storage and scalability:** With increases in volume, semi-structured data would tend to create problems in managing and scaling infrastructural storage and processing.

Advantages of Semi-structured Data:

- **Flexible structure:** Semi-structured data is more flexible than structured data. It does not require a fixed schema, yet it retains a certain level of organization through tags, keys, or markers. This makes it highly suitable for real-world scenarios where data formats frequently change or do not strictly follow predefined standards.
- **Rich in information:** Semi-structured data often contains more detailed and contextual information than structured data. Since it can store complex and nested attributes, it provides a richer representation of real-world entities and relationships.

Ethical Considerations in Data Collection

Data generation, storage, and utilization must always involve ethical considerations; any activity that collects data should always be considered in the lens of ethics. Ethical data collection is essential for safeguarding privacy, challenging bias, and remaining stewards of the data correctly, especially in highly sensitive domains such as healthcare, finance, and education.

1. **Privacy and Informed Consent:** Consent must be sought from individuals when collecting data, particularly if it is personal or sensitive information. This would imply that:
   - Users must be aware of what information is collected and how it is used and to whom it might be disclosed.
   - Consent must be voluntarily given and not coerced.
   - The individual must have the right to withdraw consent at any stage.

Healthcare providers need permission from their patients to allow their medical data to be used for research or AI models with explicit consent. Website users, on the contrary, should be made aware of what data is being collected through cookies or any other tracking technology.

2. **Data Minimization:** Data minimization in ethical data collection promotes collecting only the data needed to achieve a certain goal. The objective of this principle is to reduce unnecessarily large amounts of personally identifiable data that might be used improperly.

   - **Limit data scope:** Only collect data necessary for your analysis or research.
   - **Anonymize or pseudonymize data:** When possible, remove personally identifiable information (PII) to safeguard.

3. **Transparency and Accountability:** This involves:

   - **Clear privacy policies:** Ensuring that users can easily access and understand the organization's data policies.
   - **Explaining data practices:** Informing users about how long their data will be stored, who will have access to it, and the security measures in place to protect it.

4. **Security and Protection of Data:** Ethical data collection comprises:

   - **Implementing strong security measures:** Protecting data via encryption, secure storage, and regular security audits.
   - **Limiting access to the data:** Only managers or individuals requiring it for a legitimate purpose should be allowed access.
   - **Retention policies:** Clear policies are set down to govern how long data will be stored and does ensure that such data is deleted securely when it is no longer required.

5. **Compliance with Legal and Regulatory Standards:** Focus here is on jurisdictions having certain sets of laws and/or regulations that regulate the collection and use of data. Some of them are:

   - **GDPR (General Data Protection Regulation):** Throughout the European Union, the GDPR controls the processing, storing, and sharing of personal data.
   - **CCPA (California Consumer Privacy Act):** California residents are granted by this Act the rights to know what data about them are collected; to opt out from data sales; and to request deletion of personal information.

   A good organization must keep track of local laws pertinent to their operations and ensure compliance to avoid legal penalties and embrace public goodwill.

1.2.3 Data Cleaning and Preprocessing

In any data science work, data is hardly ever perfect. It must be pre-conditioned before one can implement any kind of analysis or predicted model creation. This preparation has to be undertaken upon any data-driven project and is generally known as data cleaning and preprocessing.

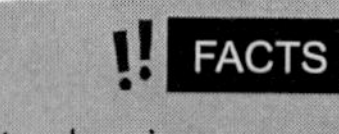

Such unclean data reminds one of a cracked jigsaw with some pieces missing, some duplicates thrown in, and some pieces that belong to another jigsaw altogether. The insight or prediction given by a model on such data would be misleading, or in some cases, outright false.

Why is this Step Important?

- Enhances accuracy and reliability of results
- Ensures fairness and consistency in analysis
- Makes the data ready for exploratory analysis and modelling

Let's now explore the key steps involved in this phase.

Identifying Missing, Inconsistent, and Duplicate Data

Missing Data

Missing values occur when information is not recorded. This could happen for many reasons: maybe a customer left a form field empty, or a sensor failed to record data. Look at the below data for example:

Name	Age	Email
Raj	24	raj@email.com
Sita		sita@email.com
Aman	22	

Here, **Sita's age** and **Aman's email** are missing.

Inconsistent Data

Inconsistencies appear when similar data is entered in different formats. **Example:**

Gender	Country
Male	India
M	INDIA
male	Bharat

The entries should be standardized so that they are treated as the same value.

Duplicate Data

Duplicate records are repeated entries, which can distort statistics and outcomes. Which should be removed.

Example:

Name	Age	Email
Raj	24	raj@email.com
Raj	24	raj@email.com

Techniques for Cleaning Data

Once we've identified problems, we need to clean the data. Here are common techniques used:

Removing or Filling Missing Data

- **Deletion:** Remove rows or columns with too many missing values (if data is small or missing values are excessive)
- **Imputation:** Fill in missing values using:
  - The mean, median, or mode
  - A default or estimated value (like "Unknown" or 0)
  - Using the value from similar entries (peer comparison)

Standardizing Inconsistent Data

- Decide on a standard format and convert all entries accordingly
  - Convert "M", "male", "MALE" → "Male"
  - **Standard**ize date formats (e.g., "01-05-25" → "2025-05-01")
- Use lookup tables to replace ambiguous values

Removing Duplicates

- Compare entries using identifiers like email ID, customer ID, etc.
- Remove repeated rows manually or using tools

Data Normalization and Standardization

To ensure fairness during analysis and modeling, numeric data often needs to be **scaled**. Different features may use different units—such as height in centimeters and income in rupees—and their ranges can vary greatly.

Normalization

- Rescales values between 0 and 1
- Good for algorithms sensitive to magnitude (e.g., k-NN)

Example:

Marks (Before)	Marks (After Normalization)
30	0.3
50	0.5
100	1.0

Standardization

- **Converts values into z-scores:** how many standard deviations they are from the mean
- Good for algorithms assuming data is normally distributed (e.g., SVM, Logistic Regression)

Basics of Feature Engineering

Feature engineering is the art of transforming raw data into meaningful input for models. It improves performance and allows algorithms to better understand patterns.

Common Methods:

- **Creating new features:** E.g., extract "Year" from a "Date of Birth" to get "Age"
- **Combining features:** E.g., combine "City" and "State" into "Location"
- **Encoding categories:** Convert text labels into numbers using techniques like one-hot encoding or label encoding
- **Binning:** Convert continuous data into categories, such as age ranges (e.g., 0–18: Child, 19–60: Adult)

1.2.4 Exploratory Data Analysis (EDA)

The process of Exploratory Data Analys is to examine your dataset through visual and numerical methods in order to understand its structure, find patterns, and see if there are any issues. This is like getting to know your data before relying on it.

EDA is one of the most **important steps** in any data science project, as it lays the groundwork for modeling and decision-making.

Purpose and Importance of EDA

EDA helps answer key questions such as:

- What does the distribution of the data look like?
- Are there any outliers or extreme values?
- Is there any missing or inconsistent data?
- Are variables related to each other?

EDA is **not about building models**—it's about understanding what you're working with.

Objectives of EDA

Objective	Description
Detect anomalies	Identify outliers, unusual patterns, and data errors
Understand distributions	Find out how each variable is spread (e.g., normal, skewed)
Spot relationships between variables	Check if features are correlated or influence each other
Guide data cleaning and modeling	Reveal preprocessing needs and modeling strategies

Tools for EDA (Using Tables and Visual Concepts)

You do not need to code in order to perform basic EDA. You can use spreadsheet software such as Excel or visualization tools such as Tableau or Power BI. Data scientists often use programming tools such as Python (Pandas, Seaborn, Matplotlib) or R instead, but we will keep the discussion conceptual.

Common Techniques: Histograms, Correlation Matrices, Boxplots

1. **Histograms—Understanding Distribution:** Histograms show how values of a single variable are distributed.

   Example: Imagine a class of 50 students. You count how many students scored between:

Score Range	Number of Students
0–20	2
21–40	5
41–60	15
61–80	20
81–100	8

   This tells you that most students scored between 41 and 80—a bell-shaped distribution.

2. **Correlation Matrix—Relationship between Variables:** A correlation matrix shows how much two variables move together. Values range from:

   - +1 (perfect positive relationship)
   - 0 (no relationship)
   - −1 (perfect negative relationship)

Example:

	Age	Income	Spending Score
Age	1	0.4	–0.6
Income	0.4	1	0.7
Spending	–0.6	0.7	1

- **Positive correlation:** Income → Spending
- **Negative correlation:** Age → Spending

This insight is crucial when choosing features for modeling.

3. Boxplots—Spotting Outliers

Boxplots visually represent:

- The median
- The interquartile range (IQR) (middle 50% of the data)
- Outliers (values far from the rest)

Example: If most people's monthly expenses are between ₹10,000 and ₹25,000 but one person reports ₹1,00,000, a boxplot will highlight this outlier.

1.2.5 Model Building

Once data has been cleaned, explored, and understood, the next step in the Data Science Lifecycle is **modeling**. This is where we teach machines to learn from data and make predictions or decisions based on it.

Think of modeling as training a smart assistant—you show it enough examples (data), and it begins to recognize patterns and respond accurately.

Introduction to Predictive Modeling

Predictive modeling refers to building a mathematical or statistical model that uses known data (input) to predict unknown or future data (output).

Simple Real-World Examples:

- Predicting the price of a house based on its size and location
- Forecasting sales for the next month using previous months' data
- Classifying emails as spam or not spam

Types of Problems Models Can Solve

Problem Type	Output	Example Task
Regression	A number	Predict temperature for tomorrow
Classification	A category	Identify whether a review is positive or negative
Clustering	Groups (no labels)	Segment customers based on purchasing behavior

Overview of the Model Building Process

Building a model involves several steps. Here's a simplified version of the process:

Let's say you have the following data about houses:

Area (sq. ft.)	Bedrooms	Price (₹ in lakhs)
1000	2	50
1200	3	60
1500	3	70
2000	4	90

Your goal is to **predict the price** of a house. You can train a **regression model** using this dataset. The model learns the relationship between area, bedrooms, and price—and can then predict the price of a new house with similar features.

Choosing the Appropriate Model Based on Problem Type

Here is a simplified guide to choosing models:

Task Type	Example Problem	Recommended Models
Regression	Predicting house prices	Linear Regression, Decision Tree Regressor
Classification	Predicting whether a customer will buy or not	Logistic Regression, Decision Tree, Random Forest
Clustering	Grouping customers by behavior	K-Means Clustering, Hierarchical Clustering

Keep in Mind:

- No single model is best for all problems.
- Try multiple models and compare their performance.
- The quality of data is often more important than the complexity of the model.

1.2.6 Model Evaluation and Deployment

Once a model has been trained, the job isn't done. A model is only valuable if it performs well on **real-world data** and can be **integrated into a usable system**. This section covers how to evaluate and deploy models effectively.

Importance of Model Evaluation

Model evaluation helps us **measure how well** a model is performing and whether it's suitable for production use.

Why Evaluate?

- To avoid overfitting (model performs well on training data but fails on new data)
- To compare different models
- To decide if the model is ready for deployment

Train vs. Test Performance

Term	Description
Training Data	Data used to teach the model
Testing Data	Data used to check how well the model performs on unseen examples

A good model performs well on both.

Evaluation Metrics (Accuracy, Precision, Recall, F1-Score)

For Classification Problems (e.g., spam or not spam):

Metric	Meaning	Best Used When...
Accuracy	% of total correct predictions	Classes are balanced
Precision	% of predicted positives that were correct (True Positives/Predicted Positives)	False positives are costly (e.g., email spam)
Recall	% of actual positives correctly predicted (True Positives/Actual Positives)	Missing positives is risky (e.g., fraud detection)
F1-Score	Harmonic mean of Precision and Recall	You need balance between precision and recall

Quick Example:

Actual Value	Predicted Value
Positive	Positive
Negative	Positive
Positive	Negative
Positive	Positive

- **True Positives (TP):** 2
- **False Positives (FP):** 1
- **False Negatives (FN):** 1
- Accuracy = (TP + TN)/Total
- Precision = TP/(TP + FP) = 2/3
- Recall = TP/(TP + FN) = 2/3
- F1-Score $\approx$ 0.66

For Regression Problems (e.g., predicting house prices):

Metric	Description
Mean Absolute Error (MAE)	Average of absolute errors
Mean Squared Error (MSE)	Average of squared errors (punishes large errors more)
R-squared (R²)	Proportion of variance explained by the model

Basics of Model Deployment (*APIs, Cloud Deployment Overview*)

Once a model performs well, it must be made available to users or systems — this is **model deployment.**

Ways to Deploy a Model:

Method	Description
Local Deployment	Running model on a personal computer or internal server
Cloud Deployment	Hosting the model using platforms like AWS, Azure, or Google Cloud
API Deployment	Expose the model as a service via REST API, so other applications can send data and receive predictions

1.3 APPLICATIONS OF DATA SCIENCE IN VARIOUS INDUSTRIES

Data Science is revolutionizing industries across the world by enabling businesses to make informed decisions, optimize operations, and predict future trends. By analysing large datasets, organizations can uncover hidden patterns, improve customer experiences, and even predict outcomes. Some key sectors where Data Science is having a transformative impact are given below:

Domain	Use Case	Description
Healthcare	Disease Prediction and Diagnosis	Predict diseases or disorders using patient data, improving early diagnosis and outcomes.
	Personalized Treatment Plans	Develop customized treatment strategies tailored to individual patient data and health history.
	Medical Imaging	Enhance accuracy of imaging analysis using computer vision and deep learning.
	Predictive Analytics for Epidemics	Forecast the spread of diseases to assist in proactive healthcare planning.

(Contd.)

Domain	Use Case	Description
Finance and Banking	Fraud Detection	Identify and prevent fraudulent financial transactions in real-time.
	Credit Scoring	Evaluate customer creditworthiness using predictive models.
	Algorithmic Trading	Optimize stock trading decisions using data-driven models and AI algorithms.
	Customer Segmentation	Categorize customers based on financial behavior for targeted services.
Retail and E-commerce	Recommendation Systems	Suggest relevant products to customers using purchase and browsing patterns.
	Customer Sentiment Analysis	Analyze feedback and reviews to gauge customer satisfaction.
	Inventory Optimization	Forecast product demand and optimize inventory levels.
	Churn Prediction	Identify customers likely to stop purchasing and plan retention strategies.
Social Media and Sentiment Analysis	Sentiment Analysis	Evaluate public sentiment on products, services, or brands using text data.
	Fake News Detection	Detect misinformation and fake news by analyzing text authenticity.
	Targeted Advertising	Use user data and preferences to deliver personalized ads.
	Social Network Analysis	Study user interactions and relationships for improved engagement.
Education and Learning	Personalized Learning	Customize educational content and learning pace for individual students.
	Student Performance Prediction	Anticipate academic performance to provide timely support.
	Automated Grading Systems	Grade assignments and exams using AI-driven assessment tools.
	Intelligent Tutoring Systems	Provide adaptive guidance and feedback to enhance learning outcomes.

(Contd.)

Domain	Use Case	Description
Transportation	Route Optimization	Determine the fastest or most efficient travel routes using real-time data.
	Fleet Management	Monitor and manage fleet behavior, usage, and maintenance.
	Demand Forecasting	Predict future transportation needs to plan efficiently.
Manufacturing and IoT	Predictive Maintenance	Anticipate machine failures and schedule maintenance to reduce downtime.
	Quality Control	Detect and correct production issues using data-driven quality checks.
	Supply Chain Optimization	Optimize logistics, inventory, and material flow using predictive analytics.
	Digital Twins	Create virtual models of physical systems to simulate and optimize performance.

1.3.1 Summary

	Industry	Key Data Science Applications
	Healthcare	Diagnosis, imaging, treatment recommendations
	Finance and Banking	Fraud detection, credit scoring, algorithmic trading
	Retail and E-commerce	Recommenders, customer insights, inventory management
	Manufacturing and IoT	Predictive maintenance, quality assurance
	Transportation	Route planning, fleet tracking, demand prediction
	Social Media and Sentiment Analysis	Fake news detection, targeted advertising, social network analysis
	Education and Learning	Personalized learning, student performance prediction, automated grading systems

1.4   KEY SKILLS AND TOOLS IN DATA SCIENCE

The design elements of the graphics through color and font modifications while providing information to the pictures Data Science needs students who excel in computer science and information technology and statistics and business knowledge together. Machine learning together with traditional research and software development serve as necessary components for effective artificial intelligence implementation. The field of study involves various technical abilities and analytical capabilities combined with domain expertise while programming languages serve as the core operating system.

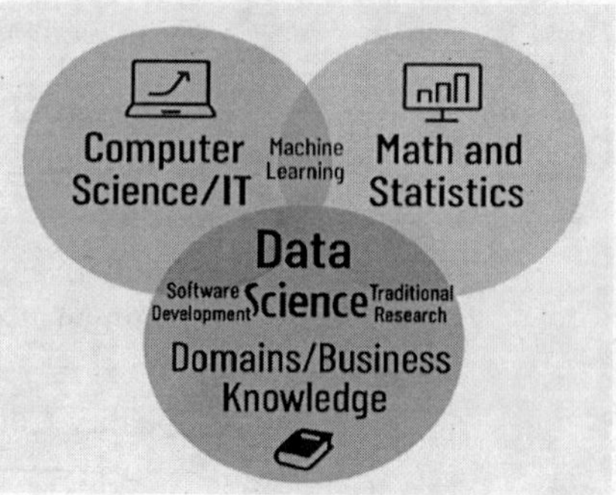

1.4.1   Programming Languages in Data Science

Data Science depends entirely on programming as its fundamental element. To perform data cleaning and analysis and machine learning model construction you must understand appropriate programming languages. Data Science professionals primarily use Python along with R and SQL programming languages.

Python: The Most Popular Language for Data Science

Python became the leading programming language in Data Science because of its simplicity in learning together with the extensive library system it offers. The language Python serves multiple functions in Data Science operations through activities such as data cleaning and data manipulation and development of advanced machine learning models. People prefer Python as a programming language because it combines simplicity with the ability to connect easily to various tools and technologies.

Why Python is Popular in Data Science: Ease of Learning and Use: Python is often praised for its easy-to-read syntax that makes it more accessible for beginners. It also simplifies the coding process so that Data Scientists can focus on analytics and solving problems rather than worrying about compelling syntax.

- **Wide Range of Libraries:** Python provides an extensive library for virtually any task including:
    - NumPy and Pandas for data manipulation and analysis.
    - Matplotlib and Seaborn for data visualization.
    - Scikit-learn for machine learning.
    - TensorFlow and Kera's for deep learning.

- **Community Support:** Python has a very active community which is global in scope. This provides for a lot of tutorials, resources, and forums for Data Science or Data Science related issues for learning and professionals alike.
- **Versatility:** Not only is Python used for Data Science and similar applications, it is actively used in web development, automation, and many more fields, making it really useful to have in many industries.

R: Statistical Analysis and Data Visualization

Although Python is used extensively, R is still the language of choice for those in statistics and visualization. R has greater specialization in statistical computing and data visualization, which is often extremely helpful in bioinformatics, economics, and healthcare.

Role of R in Statistical Analysis and Data Visualization:

- **Statistical Power:** R was developed by statisticians, for statisticians, and its syntax still reflects such a design. It has a wide variety of statistical tests and methods, ranging from basic regression to time series and tests of hypotheses.
- **Data Visualization:** R's ggplot2 package is one of the most powerful and flexible packages to make informative, visually appealing, and high-quality data visualizations. Other packages, such as plotly and lattice also support presenting your data visually in R.
- **Comprehensive Data Analysis:** R has many functions that enable data manipulation, cleaning, and transformation, so it is somewhat of an all-in-one platform for analyzing data.
- **Integration with Other Tools:** R works well with other languages, databases, and platforms. In particular, R plays along with Python, making it easy for professionals to facilitate, and bounce between the many positives of R and Python.

SQL: Essential for Data Querying and Manipulation

SQL (Structured Query Language) is the universally accepted language for the management and manipulation of relational databases. Regardless of the data analysis tool that is being employed, SQL is nearly always a prerequisite for getting and treating data stored in databases.

Role of SQL in Data Querying and Manipulation:

- **Data Retrieval:** SQL provides the means for the database to be queried and for the data necessary for the analysis to be returned. The commands SELECT, FROM, WHERE, and

- **Data Manipulation:** Besides the data being fetched, SQL can also be used for altering the data itself. Command set of INSERT, UPDATE, DELETE allows wide open access to the database by adding new data, changing existing data or erasing data.

- **Efficient Handling of Large Datasets:** SQL has been made capable of handling large datasets. That assures data scientists of quick data retrieval even in the case of the biggest databases.
- **Integrating with Data Science Tools:** Picture Python, R and Tableau—data engineering through SQL is the common thread that connects them all.

Soft Skills and Domain Knowledge

While technical skills are essential, **soft skills** and **domain knowledge** play a crucial role in the effectiveness of a Data Scientist. Some of the key soft skills and domain-specific expertise include:

Soft Skills

Communication: The capacity to communicate complex technical issues to non-technical stakeholders is important. Data Scientists should be able to interpret their findings and explain what the data insights mean mostly to non-technical stakeholders.

Problem-solving: Data Scientists usually need to solve business problems using data sets, which requires creative critical thinking to identify and solve the problem.

Collaboration: Data Science usually consists of collaborative products. Good people skills allow Data Scientists to work collaboratively with other professionals, i.e., engineer, business analyst, or other scientists.

Domain Knowledge:

- **Industry-specific awareness:** Domain knowledge allows Data Scientists to apply their technical skills in a meaningful way. For example, knowledge of healthcare data would be beneficial for developing predictive models in patient outcomes from data analysis, while knowledge of finance is needed to assess credit risk when performing data analysis.
- **Specific awareness of the problem:** Being aware of the problem allows Data Scientists to ask the right question and create data science tasks that successfully address business needs.

Skill	Key Features	Common Uses
Python	Simple syntax, powerful libraries (e.g., Pandas, Scikit-learn, TensorFlow)	Data cleaning, analysis, machine learning, deep learning

(Contd.)

	Skill	Key Features	Common Uses
	R	Statistical computing, visualization (e.g., ggplot2, dplyr)	Statistical analysis, data visualization, research
	SQL	Powerful querying and data manipulation capabilities	Retrieving and manipulating data from databases
	Soft Skills	Communication, problem-solving, collaboration, critical thinking	Presenting findings, collaborating with teams, addressing business problems
	Domain Knowledge	Industry-specific understanding, problem-specific expertise	Applying data science techniques in healthcare, finance, marketing, etc.

Wrap-up

Data science is the process of converting unstructured and raw data into meaningful insights that support decision-making across various industries. This chapter introduces the concept of data science, explains the role of a data scientist, and outlines the **Data Science Lifecycle**, including key stages such as problem definition, model development, and deployment. It also provides an overview of the essential tools, skills, and real-world applications that form the foundation of the field. This introductory discussion prepares readers to understand how data-driven thinking influences and shapes the modern world.

QUESTIONS FOR PRACTICE

1. Define Data Science. Explain the difference between descriptive, predictive, and prescriptive analytics.   *Anna University, 2022*

2. What is the role of a Data Scientist? Give three real-world examples of how a Data Scientist adds value in an organisation.

    Vellore Institute of Technology, 2021

3. Describe the full Data Science Lifecycle, drawing a diagram. For each phase, provide a short example relevant to the retail industry.

    SRM Institute of Science and Technology, 2023

4. Discuss the importance of problem definition in a Data Science project. What are the risks of skipping this step?   *IIT Bombay, 2022*

5. Explain the process of data collection. What are common sources of data, and what challenges an analyst might face while collecting data from each source?   *Amity University, 2021*

6. Why is data cleaning and preprocessing critical in Data Science? Identify at least four types of data quality issues and how you would remediate them.
   Anna University, 2020

7. What is Exploratory Data Analysis (EDA)? Describe two EDA techniques you would use on a dataset of customer transactions and justify your choice.
   Manipal University, 2022

8. After building a model, what aspects must you consider during model evaluation and deployment? Illustrate with an example from the healthcare industry.
   IIT Delhi, 2023

9. Across different industries (finance, manufacturing, retail), list and explain three distinct applications of Data Science, showing how they differ in scope and methods.
   BMS College of Engineering, 2021

10. What essential skills should a Data Scientist have (including programming languages, soft skills and domain knowledge)? Rank these skills in order of importance and justify your ranking for an entry-level data science role.
    Amrita Vishwa Vidyapeetham, 2022

2

Essential Mathematics for Data Science: I Probability

2.1 BASICS OF MATHEMATICS

2.1.1 Vectors

A vector is just a list of numbers in a specific order. You can think of a vector as a row or a column of numbers.

In data science, a vector can represent:

- A single data point with features (height, weight, age)
- A direction in space
- A row of data in a dataset

2.1.2 Matrices

A matrix is a collection of vectors arranged in rows and columns—a table of numbers.

Example:

$$A = \begin{bmatrix} 1 & 6 & 4 \\ 3 & 5 & 1 \\ 2 & 1 & 3 \end{bmatrix}$$

In data science, a matrix is often used to represent:
- A dataset where each row = data point, each column = feature
- A transformation (like rotating or scaling data)
- A weight table in machine learning models

2.1.3 Common Operations Used in Data Science

Vector Addition and Subtraction

Add vectors element by element:

Example:

$$\begin{bmatrix} 2 \\ 8 \end{bmatrix} + \begin{bmatrix} 4 \\ 6 \end{bmatrix} = \begin{bmatrix} 6 \\ 14 \end{bmatrix}$$

Used in:

- Gradient updates in machine learning
- Combining feature vectors

Scalar Multiplication

Multiply each element of a vector or matrix by a single number (scalar):

Example:

$$5 \times \begin{bmatrix} 4 \\ 6 \end{bmatrix} = \begin{bmatrix} 20 \\ 30 \end{bmatrix}$$

Used in:

- Normalizing data
- Rescaling features

Matrix Multiplication

Multiply matrices to **transform data**, especially in deep learning (e.g., linear layers).

$$\text{If } A = (m \times n) \text{ and } B = (n \times p), \text{ their product } AB = (m \times p).$$

Example:

$$\begin{bmatrix} 1 & 3 \end{bmatrix} \times \begin{bmatrix} 4 \\ 6 \end{bmatrix} = 1 \times 3 + 2 \times 4 = 11$$

Used in:

- Neural networks
- Linear regression ($X\beta = y$)
- Dimensionality reduction (PCA)

Transpose of a Matrix

Flip a matrix over its diagonal where rows become columns.

Example:

$$A = \begin{bmatrix} 1 & 3 \\ 5 & 6 \end{bmatrix} \Rightarrow A^T = \begin{bmatrix} 1 & 5 \\ 3 & 6 \end{bmatrix}$$

Used in:

- Dot product
- Vector projections
- Correlation matrices

Dot Product (Inner Product)

Multiply corresponding elements of two vectors and add them.

Example:

$$\begin{bmatrix} 1 & 2 & 3 \end{bmatrix} \cdot \begin{bmatrix} 4 & 5 & 6 \end{bmatrix} = 1 \times 4 + 2 \times 5 + 3 \times 6 = 32$$

Used in:

- Measuring similarity (like in NLP)
- Building recommendation systems

How are Vectors and Matrices Used in Data Science?

Concept	Vector/Matrices Used	Example
Machine Learning	Feature vectors, weight matrices	Logistic regression, Neural Networks
Data Storage	Matrix = dataset	Rows = data points
NLP (Natural Language Processing)	Word embeddings = vectors	Word2Vec, BERT
Image Processing	Images = 2D or 3D matrices	Convolutional Neural Networks
Linear Regression	$y = x\beta$ (Matrix equation)	Predictions via dot product
PCA (Dimensionality Reduction)	Eigenvectors and matrices	Transform high-dimensional data

Problem

You are a data scientist. You want to predict a student's final exam score based on:

1. Hours Studied
2. Assignments Completed

We'll use linear regression to model the relationship.

Solution:

Step 1: Create a Small Dataset

Student	Hours Studied (x_1)	Assignments Completed (x_2)	Final Score (y)
1	2	1	65
2	4	2	70
3	6	3	75
4	8	4	80

Step 2: Represent as Matrices

Let:
- X be the feature matrix (with a bias column of 1)
- y be the target vector

Feature Matrix X:

$$X = \begin{bmatrix} 1 & 2 & 1 \\ 1 & 4 & 2 \\ 1 & 6 & 3 \\ 1 & 8 & 4 \end{bmatrix} \text{(Add 1}^{\text{st}}\text{ column for intercept)}$$

Target Vector y:

$$y = \begin{bmatrix} 65 \\ 70 \\ 75 \\ 80 \end{bmatrix}$$

Step 3: Apply Linear Regression Using Matrix Formula

Formula:

$$\beta = \left(X^T X \right)^{-1} X^T y$$

Where:

- β is the vector of coefficients (intercept + weights)
- X^T is the transpose of X
- $X^T X$ is the dot product of X transpose and X
- $(X^T X)^{-1}$ is the inverse matrix
- $X^T y$ is the dot product of X transpose and y

Output:

$$\beta = \begin{bmatrix} 60 \\ 2.5 \\ 2.5 \end{bmatrix}$$

Step 4: Build the Model

Linear Equation:

Score = 60 + 2.5 × (Hours Studied) + 2.5 × (Assignments Completed)

Step 5: Predict New Student's Score

Suppose a student studies **5 hours** and completes **2 assignments**.
Predicted Score = 60 + 2.5(5) + 2.5(2) = 60 + 12.5 + 5 = 77.5
So, the predicted score is 77.5.

System of Linear Equations

What is a system of linear equations?

A system of linear equations is a collection of one or more linear equations involving the same set of variables.

General form:

For **two variables** (x and y), the system may look like:

$$a_{11}x + a_{12}y = b_1$$
$$a_{21}x + a_{22}y = b_2$$

For n variables, a system with m equations is:

$$a_{11}x_1 + a_{12}x_2 + \ldots + a_{1n}x_n = b_1$$
$$a_{21}x_1 + a_{22}x_2 + \ldots + a_{2n}x_n = b_2$$
$$\ldots\ldots\ldots\ldots\ldots\ldots\ldots\ldots\ldots\ldots\ldots\ldots$$
$$a_{m1}x_1 + a_{m2}x_2 + \ldots + a_{mn}x_n = b_m$$

Types of Solutions

A system of equations can have:

Unique solution: The lines or planes intersect at one point.

Infinite solutions: The lines or planes are coincident (same line or plane).

No solution: The lines or planes are parallel and never intersect (inconsistent system).

Solution Methods (with Examples):

Let's use the system:

$$2x + y = 5 \qquad (1)$$
$$4x - 3y = 1 \qquad (2)$$

A. Graphical Method

Plot both equations on a graph.
Intersection point is the solution.

Drawback: Inaccurate for large systems or when solutions are not integers.

B. Substitution Method

Let's use the system:
$$2x + y = 5 \qquad (1)$$
$$4x - 3y = 1 \qquad (2)$$

Step 1: Solve one equation for one variable.
From (1):

$$y = 5 - 2x$$

Step 2: Substitute in the second equation:

$$4x - 3y = 1$$
$$4x - 3(5 - 2x) = 1$$
$$10x = 16$$
$$\Rightarrow x = \frac{16}{10} = \frac{8}{5}$$

Step 3: Plug back to find y:

$$y = 5 - 2x = 5 - 2\left(\frac{8}{5}\right) = \frac{9}{5}$$

Solution: $\Rightarrow x = \frac{8}{5}; \, y = \frac{9}{5}$

C. Elimination Method

Let's use the system:

$$2x + y = 5 \tag{1}$$
$$4x - 3y = 1 \tag{2}$$

Step 1: Equation (1) is multiplied by 3 and equation (2) is multiplied by 1 to make coefficients of one variable equal.

$$6x + 3y = 15 \tag{3}$$
$$4x - 3y = 1 \tag{4}$$

Step 2: Add eqn. (3) and eqn. (4):

$$6x + 3y + \left(4x - 3y\right) = 15 + 1$$
$$10x = 16$$
$$x = \frac{8}{5}$$

Step 3: Plug back equation (1) to find y:

$$2 \cdot \left(\frac{8}{5}\right) + y = 5 \Rightarrow y = \frac{9}{5}$$

Solution: $\Rightarrow x = \frac{8}{5}; \, y = \frac{9}{5}$

D. Matrix Method (Gaussian Elimination)

Let's use the system:

$$6x + 3y = 15 \tag{1}$$
$$4x - 3y = 1 \tag{2}$$

The system of equations can be written as in matrix form:

$$\begin{bmatrix} 2 & 1 \\ 4 & -3 \end{bmatrix}\begin{bmatrix} x \\ y \end{bmatrix} = \begin{bmatrix} 5 \\ 1 \end{bmatrix}$$

We write the system as an augmented matrix:

$$\left[\begin{array}{cc|c} 2 & 1 & 5 \\ 4 & -3 & 1 \end{array}\right]$$

Step 1: Make pivot in row 1 to be 1. (Divide R_1 by 2):

$$\left[\begin{array}{cc|c} 1 & 0.5 & 2.5 \\ 4 & -3 & 1 \end{array}\right]$$

Step 2: Eliminate first column of row 2:

$$\left[\begin{array}{cc|c} 1 & 0.5 & 2.5 \\ 0 & -5 & -9 \end{array}\right]$$

Step 3: Make pivot in $R_2 = 1$: $R_2' = \dfrac{R_2}{-5}$

$$\left[\begin{array}{cc|c} 1 & 0.5 & 2.5 \\ 0 & 1 & 1.8 \end{array}\right]$$

Step 4: Eliminate second column of R_1: $R_1' = R_1 - 0.5R_2$

$$\left[\begin{array}{cc|c} 1 & 0 & 1.6 \\ 0 & 1 & 1.8 \end{array}\right]$$

Solution: $\Rightarrow x = 1.6$; $y = 1.8$

E. Cramer's Rule (For 2 or 3 variable systems)

Given:
$$a_{11}x + a_{12}y = b_1$$
$$a_{21}x + a_{22}y = b_2$$

Let,
$$D = \begin{vmatrix} a_{11} & a_{12} \\ a_{21} & a_{22} \end{vmatrix}, \quad D_1 = \begin{vmatrix} b_1 & a_{12} \\ b_2 & a_{22} \end{vmatrix} \quad D_2 = \begin{vmatrix} a_{11} & b_1 \\ a_{21} & b_2 \end{vmatrix}$$

Then,
$$x = \frac{D_1}{D} ; y = \frac{D_2}{D}$$

Let's use the system:

$$6x + 3y = 15 \tag{1}$$

$$4x - 3y = 1 \tag{2}$$

Let,
$$D = \begin{vmatrix} 6 & 3 \\ 4 & -3 \end{vmatrix} = -18 - 12 = -30$$

$$D_1 = \begin{vmatrix} 15 & 3 \\ 1 & -3 \end{vmatrix} = 45 - 3 = -48$$

$$D_2 = \begin{vmatrix} 6 & 15 \\ 4 & 1 \end{vmatrix} = 6 - 60 = -54$$

Then,
$$x = \frac{D_1}{D} = \frac{-48}{-30} = \frac{8}{5} ; y = \frac{-54}{-30} = \frac{9}{5}$$

Applications

Systems of linear equations appear in:

- **Economics:** Market equilibrium models.
- **Engineering:** Circuit analysis (Kirchhoff's Laws).
- **Computer Science:** Linear programming.
- **Statistics:** Regression analysis (normal equations).
- **Physics:** Solving simultaneous forces or motion equations.

2.2 BASIC PROBABILITY CONCEPTS

The theory of probability has its origin in the games of chance related to gambling such as tossing of a coin, throwing of a die, drawing cards from a pack of cards, etc. Jerame Cardon, an Italian mathematician wrote 'A book on games of chance' which was published on 1663.

Probability theory is being applied in the solution of social, economic, business problems. Today the concept of probability has assumed greater importance and the mathematical theory of probability has become the basis for statistical applications in both social and decision-making research.

Random experiment: Random experiment is one whose results depend on chance, that is the result cannot be predicted. Tossing of coins, throwing of dice are some examples of random experiments.

Trial: Performing a random experiment is called a trial.

Outcomes: The results of a random experiment are called its outcomes. When two coins are tossed the possible outcomes are HH, HT, TH, TT.

Definition of Probability

Probability is a branch of mathematics that deals with the study of uncertain events. It provides a measure of the likelihood that a particular event will occur.

Classical Definition: If an experiment has n equally likely outcomes and m of them are favourable to an event A, then

$$P(A) = \frac{m}{n}$$

Experimental Definition: Probability is estimated based on the outcomes of actual experiments (also called empirical probability).

$$P(A) = \frac{\text{Number of times event } A \text{ occurs}}{\text{Total number of trials}}$$

Axiomatic Definition (Kolmogorov's Axioms): For a sample space S, and any event $A \subseteq S$:

- $P(A) \geq 0$
- $P(S) = 1$
- If $A_1, A_2, \ldots, A_n$ are mutually exclusive events, then $P\left(\bigcup_i A_i\right) = \sum_i P(A_i)$

2.2.1 Sample Spaces and Events

Event: An outcome or a combination of outcomes of a random experiment is called an event.

For example, tossing of a coin is a random experiment and getting a head or tail is an event.

Sample Space: Each conceivable outcome of an experiment is called a sample point. The totality of all sample points is called a sample space and is denoted by S.

For example, when a coin is tossed, the sample space is $S = \{H, T\}$. H and T are the sample points of the sample space S.

Types of Events

Simple Event: Contains only one outcome.

Compound Event: Contains more than one outcome.

Equally likely events: Two or more events are said to be equally likely if each one of them has an equal chance of occurring. For example, in tossing of a coin, the event of getting a head and the event of getting a tail are equally likely events.

Mutually exclusive events: Two or more events are said to be mutually exclusive, when the occurrence of any one event excludes the occurrence of the other event. Mutually exclusive events cannot occur simultaneously.

For example, when a coin is tossed, either the head or the tail will come up. Therefore, the occurrence of the head completely excludes the occurrence of the tail. Thus, getting head or tail in tossing of a coin is a mutually exclusive event.

Exhaustive events: Events are said to be exhaustive when their totality includes all the possible outcomes of a random experiment. For example, while throwing a die, the possible outcomes are {1, 2, 3, 4, 5, 6} and hence the number of cases is 6.

Compound events: The joint occurrence of two or more events is called compound events. Thus compound events imply the simultaneous occurrence of two or more simple events.

The compound events may be further classified as

(1) Independent event
(2) Dependent event

Independent events: If two or more events occur in such a way that the occurrence of one does not affect the occurrence of another, they are said to be independent events.

Dependent events: If the occurrence of one event influences the occurrence of the other, then the second event is said to be dependent on the first.

Example: A dice is rolled. What is the probability of getting a number less than 4?

Solution: Sample Space $(S) = \{1, 2, 3, 4, 5, 6\}; n(S) = 6$

Favourable Outcomes $= A = \{1, 2, 3\}; n(A) = 3$

$$P(\text{Number} < 4) = \frac{\text{Number of favorable outcomes}}{\text{Total outcomes}} = \frac{n(A)}{n(S)} = \frac{3}{6} = 0.5$$

Example: A bag contains 5 red balls and 3 blue balls. One ball is picked at random. What is the probability it is red?

Solution: Total balls = 5 + 3 = 8

Favourable outcomes (red) = 5

$$P(\text{Red ball}) = \frac{\text{Number of favorable outcomes}}{\text{Total outcomes}} = \frac{5}{8}$$

Example: A number is chosen at random from 1 to 20. What is the probability that it is a multiple of 3?

Solution: Multiples of 3 between 1 and 20: $A = \{3, 6, 9, 12, 15, 18\}$, $n(A) = 6$ numbers.

Total outcomes $= 20 = n(S)$

$$P(\text{Mutiple of 3}) = \frac{\text{Number of favorable outcomes}}{\text{Total outcomes}} = \frac{n(A)}{n(S)} = \frac{6}{20} = \frac{3}{10}$$

Example: Two coins are tossed together. What is the sample space? What is the event of getting exactly one head?

Solution: Sample Space (S) = {*HH, HT, TH, TT*}; $n(S) = 4$

Event A: Getting exactly one head = {*HT, TH*}; $n(A) = 2$

So,
$$P(A) = \frac{n(A)}{n(S)} = \frac{2}{4} = 0.5.$$

Example: A coin is tossed three times. What is the sample space? What is the probability of getting exactly two heads?

Solution: Sample Space (S) = {*HHH, HHT, HTH, HTT, THH, THT, TTH, TTT*}, $n(S) = 8$ outcomes

Event A = exactly 2 heads = {*HHT, HTH, THH*}, $n(A) = 3$ outcomes

$$P(A) = \frac{n(A)}{n(S)} = \frac{3}{8}$$

Example: A die is rolled. Define the event B = getting an even number.

Sample Space = {1, 2, 3, 4, 5, 6}

Event B = {2, 4, 6}

$$P(B) = \frac{3}{6} = \frac{1}{2}.$$

2.2.2 Conditional Probability and Independence

Conditional Probability

The probability of event A occurring given that event B has already occurred is:

$$P(A|B) = \frac{P(A \cap B)}{P(B)} \quad (\text{provided } P(B) > 0)$$

Example: A card is drawn from a deck of 52 cards. What is the probability that it is a king **given that** it is a face card?

- Face cards = Jack, Queen, King (3 per suit) → Total face cards = 12
- Number of Kings = 4
- Kings among face cards = 4 (because all Kings are face cards)

$$P(\text{King}|\text{Face card}) = \frac{\text{No of Kings}}{\text{No of face cards}} = \frac{4}{12} = \frac{1}{3}$$

Independence of Events:

Two events A and B are independent if:

$$P(A \cap B) = P(A) \cdot P(B)$$

Which implies:

$$P(A|B) = P(A), P(B|A) = P(B)$$

Example: Tossing two coins:

Let, A = getting Head on coin 1

B = getting Head on coin 2

Each coin is independent, so:

$$P(A) = P(B) = \frac{1}{2}; P(A \cap B) = \frac{1}{4}$$

Now, check:

$$P(A) \cdot P(B) = \frac{1}{2} \cdot \frac{1}{2} = \frac{1}{4} = P(A \cap B)$$

Hence, A and B are **independent**.

2.2.3 Law of Total Probability and Bayes' Theorem

Law of Total Probability: Let $B_1, B_2, ..., B_n$ be mutually exclusive and exhaustive events, and let A be any event. Then:

$$P(A) = \sum_{j=1}^{n} P(B_i) \cdot P(A|B_i)$$

Example: A factory has 3 machines. M_1 produces 30% of items, defect rate = 2%. M_2 produces 50% of items, defect rate = 3%. M_3 produces 20% of items, defect rate = 5%. One machine is chosen at random and selecting one item which is defective. What is the probability that a randomly chosen item is defective?

Solution: Let D be the event of defective item.

$$P(M_1) = 0.3, P(M_2) = 0.5, P(M_3)0.2$$
$$P(D|M_1) = 0.02, P(D|M_2) = 0.03, P(D|M_3) = 0.05$$
$$P(D) = P(M_1)P(D|M_1) + P(M_2)P(D|M_2) + P(M_3)P(D|M_3)$$
$$= (0.3)(0.2) + (0.5)(0.3) + (0.2)(0.05) = 0.031$$

So, $\qquad P(D = \text{Defective item}) = 3.1\%$

Bayes' Theorem: It relates conditional probabilities in reverse:

$$P(B_i|A) = \frac{P(B_i) \cdot P(A|B_i)}{\sum_{j=}^{n} P(B_i) \cdot P(A|B_i)}$$

Use case: Updating the probability of a hypothesis (event B_i) based on new evidence (event A).

Example: A factory has 3 machines. M_1 produces 30% of items, defect rate = 2%. M_2 produces 50% of items, defect rate = 3%. M_3 produces 20% of items, defect rate = 5%. One machine is chosen at random and selecting one item which is defective. What is the probability that a defective item came from M_3?

Solution: Let D be the event of defective item.

$$P(M_1) = 0.3, P(M_2) = 0.5, P(M_3)\,0.2,$$

$$P(D|M_1) = 0.02, P(D|M_2) = 0.03, P(D|M_3) = 0.05$$

Using Baye's theorem,

$$P(M_3|D) = \frac{P(M_3)P(D|M_3)}{P(M_1)P(D|M_1) + P(M_2)P(D|M_2) + P(M_3)P(D|M_3)}$$

$$= \frac{(0.2)(0.05)}{(0.3)(0.02) + (0.5)(0.03) + (0.2)(0.05)} = \frac{0.01}{0.031} = 0.3226$$

So,
$$P(\text{Item came from } M_3|D) = 32.26\%$$

Example: Bag I contains 4 red and 3 black balls while another bag II contains 6 red and 5 black balls. One of the bags is selected at random and a ball is drawn from it. Find the probability that the ball is drawn from Bag II, if it is known that the ball drawn is red.

Solution: Let E_1 and E_2 be the events of selecting Bag I and Bag II, respectively and A be the event of selecting a red ball.

$$P(E_1) = \frac{1}{2}, \quad P(E_2) = \frac{1}{2},$$

P(drawing a red ball from Bag I) = $P(A|E_1)$ = 0.02,

P(drawing a red ball from Bag II) = $P(A|E_2)$ = 0.03,

Using Baye's theorem,

$$P(E_2|A) = \frac{P(E_2)P(A|E_2)}{P(E_1)P(A|E_1) + P(M_2)P(A|E_2)}$$

$$= \frac{\left(\dfrac{1}{2}\right)\left(\dfrac{6}{11}\right)}{\left(\dfrac{1}{2}\right)\left(\dfrac{4}{7}\right) + \left(\dfrac{1}{2}\right)\left(\dfrac{6}{11}\right)} = \frac{22}{43}$$

2.3 RANDOM VARIABLE AND ITS TYPES

A random variable is a function that assigns a real number to each outcome in the sample space of a random experiment.

A discrete random variable is a random variable with a finite (or countably infinite) range.

A continuous random variable is a random variable with an interval (either finite or infinite) of real numbers for its range.

A random variable is denoted by an uppercase letter such as X and Y. After experiment is conducted, the measured value of the random variable is denoted by a lowercase letter such as x and y.

2.3.1 Expectation, Variance, and Higher-order Moments for Discrete Random Variable

Expectation (Mean)

The expectation or expected value of a discrete random variable X, denoted by $E[X]$ gives a measure of the central tendency (average) of the distribution.

Formula: $E[X] = \sum_{x} x \cdot P(X = x) = \mu$

Where, x: possible values of the random variable
$P(X = x)$: probability that $X = x$.

Variance

The **variance** measures the **spread** or **dispersion** of the distribution from the mean.

Formula: $\mathrm{Var}(X) = E\left[(X - \mu)^2\right] = \sum_{x}(x - \mu)^2 \cdot P(X = x)$

Or alternatively, $\mathrm{Var}(X) = E\left[X^2\right] - \left(E[X]\right)^2$, where $E[X] = \mu$.

Higher-Order Moments

These give more detailed information about the **shape** of the distribution.

n^{th} **Moment about Origin (Raw Moment):** $\mu'_n = E\left[X^n\right] = \sum_{x} x^n \cdot P(X = x)$

n^{th} **Central Moment:** $\mu_n = E\left[(X - \mu)^n\right] = \sum_{x}(x - \mu)^n \cdot P(X = x)$

Common Moments:

1st moment: $\mu'_1 = E(X)$

2nd central moment: $\mu_2 \mathrm{Var}(X)$

3rd central moment μ_3**:** Measures **skewness** (asymmetry)

4th central moment μ_4**:** Measures **kurtosis** (peakedness)

Skewness and Kurtosis:

$$\text{Skewness} = \frac{\mu_3}{\sigma^3}$$

$$\text{Kurtosis} = \frac{\mu_4}{\sigma^4} \quad \textbf{where} \quad \sigma = \sqrt{\text{Var}(X)}$$

If Kurtosis > 3: **Leptokurtic** (peaked)

If Kurtosis = 3: **Mesokurtic** (normal-like)

If Kurtosis < 3: **Platykurtic** (flat)

Example: If X has the following distribution:

$X = x$	1	2	3	4
$P(X = x)$	0.2	0.3	0.4	0.2

We'll calculate the following: (i) Expectation, (ii) Variance, (iii) Third central moment, (iv) Fourth central moment, (v) Skewness, (vi) Kurtosis.

Solution:

Step 1: Expectation $E[X]$

$$\text{E}[X] = \sum_x x \cdot P(X = x) = 1(0.2) + 2(0.3) + 3(0.4) + 4(0.2) = 2.7 = \mu$$

Step 2: Find $\text{E}\left[X^2\right]$

$$\text{E}\left[X^2\right] = \sum_x x^2 \cdot P(X = x) = 1^2(0.2) + 2^2(0.3) + 3^2(0.4) + 4^2(0.2) = 8.1$$

Step 3: Variance

$$\text{Var}(X) = \text{E}\left[X^2\right] - \left(\text{E}[X]\right)^2 = 8.1 - (2.7)^2 = 8.1 - 7.29 = 0.81$$

Step 4: Standard Deviation

$$\sigma = \sqrt{\text{Var}(X)} = \sqrt{0.81} = 0.9$$

Step 5: Third Central Moment μ_3

$$\mu_3 = \text{E}\left[(X - \mu)^3\right] = \sum_x (x - \mu)^3 \cdot P(X = x); \text{ using } \mu = 2.7$$

$$= (1 - 2.7)^3(0.1) + (2 - 2.7)^3(0.3) + (3 - 2.7)^3(0.4) + (4 - 2.7)^3(0.2)$$

$$= (-1.7)^3(0.1) + (-0.7)^3(0.3) + (0.3)^3(0.4) + (1.3)^3(0.2) = -0.144$$

Step 6: Fourth Central Moment μ_4

$$\mu_4 = \mathrm{E}\left[(X-\mu)^4\right] = \sum_x (x-\mu)^4 \cdot P(X=x); \quad \text{using } \mu = 2.7$$

$$= (1-2.7)^4 (0.1) + (2-2.7)^4 (0.3) + (3-2.7)^4 (0.4) + (4-2.7)^4 (0.2)$$

$$= (-1.7)^4 (0.1) + (-0.7)^4 (0.3) + (0.3)^4 (0.4) + (1.3)^4 (0.2) = 1.4816$$

Step 7: Skewness

Skewness $= \dfrac{\mu_3}{\sigma^3} = \dfrac{-0.144}{(0.9)^3} = -0.1975$, using $\sigma = 0.9$

Interpretation: Slightly left-skewed (negative skew)

Step 8: Kurtosis

Kurtosis $= \dfrac{\mu_4}{\sigma^4} = \dfrac{1.4816}{(0.9)^4} = 2.26$ using $\sigma = 0.9$

Interpretation: Platykurtic (flatter than normal distribution).

2.3.2 Expectation, Variance, and Higher-order Moments for Continuous Random Variable

Expectation (Mean)

For a continuous random variable X with probability density function (PDF) $f(x)$:

Formula: $\mathrm{E}[X] = \mu = \int_{-\infty}^{\infty} x f(x)\, dx$

Variance

Variance measures the spread of the distribution around the mean μ

Formula: $\mathrm{Var}(X) = \mathrm{E}\left[(X-\mu)^2\right] = \int_{-\infty}^{\infty} (x-\mu)^2 f(x)\, dx$

Or alternatively: $\mathrm{Var}(X) = \mathrm{E}\left[X^2\right] - \left(\mathrm{E}[X]\right)^2$, where $\mathrm{E}[X] = \mu$.

Higher-Order Moments

Higher-order moments describe additional characteristics of the distribution's shape.

n^{th} **Moment about Origin (Raw Moment):** $\mu_n' = \mathrm{E}[X^n] = \int_{-\infty}^{\infty} x^n f(x)\, dx$

n^{th} **Central Moment:** $\mu_n = \mathrm{E}\left[(X-\mu)^n\right] = \int_{-\infty}^{\infty} (x-\mu)^n f(x)\, dx$

Common Moments:

1st moment: $\mu_1' = E(X)$

2nd central moment: $\mu_2 = \mathrm{Var}(X)$

3rd central moment μ_3: Measures **skewness** (asymmetry)

4th central moment μ_4: Measures **kurtosis** (peakedness)

Skewness and Kurtosis

Skewness $= \dfrac{\mu_3}{\sigma^3}$

Kurtosis $= \dfrac{\mu_4}{\sigma^4}$ **where** $\sigma = \sqrt{\operatorname{Var}(X)}$

If Kurtosis > 3: **Leptokurtic** (peaked)

If Kurtosis = 3: **Mesokurtic** (normal-like)

If Kurtosis < 3: **Platykurtic** (flat)

Example: If X be a continuous random variable with the following probability density function (PDF):

$$f(x) = \begin{cases} 2x & 0 \le x \le 1 \\ 0 & \text{otherwise} \end{cases}$$

Calculate the following: (i) Expectation, (ii) Variance, (iii) Third central moment, (iv) Fourth central moment, (v) Skewness, (vi) Kurtosis.

Solution:

Step 1: Expectation $\mathrm{E}[X]$

$$\mathrm{E}[X] = \mu = \int_{-\infty}^{\infty} x f(x)\,dx = \int_0^1 x.2x\,dx = \int_0^1 2x^2\,dx = \left[\frac{2x^3}{3}\right]_0^1 = \frac{2}{3}$$

Step 2: Find $\mathrm{E}\left[X^2\right]$

$$\mathrm{E}\left[X^2\right] = \int_{-\infty}^{\infty} x^2 f(x)\,dx = \int_0^1 x^2.2x\,dx = \int_0^1 2x^3\,dx = \left[\frac{2x^4}{4}\right]_0^1 = \frac{2}{4} = \frac{1}{2}$$

Step 3: Variance

$$\operatorname{Var}(X) = \mathrm{E}\left[X^2\right] - \left(\mathrm{E}[X]\right)^2 = \frac{1}{2} - \left(\frac{2}{3}\right)^2 = \frac{9-8}{18} = \frac{1}{18}$$

Step 4: Standard Deviation

$$\sigma = \sqrt{\operatorname{Var}(X)} = \sqrt{\frac{1}{18}} \approx 0.2357$$

Step 5: Third Central Moment μ_3

$$\mu_3 = \mathrm{E}\left[(X-\mu)^3\right] = \int_{-\infty}^{\infty} (x-\mu)^3 f(x)\,dx \, ; \text{ where } \mu = \frac{2}{3}$$

Instead, we simplify using identity:

$$\mu_3 = \mathrm{E}\left[X^3\right] - 3\mu\mathrm{E}\left[X^2\right] + 3\mu^2\mathrm{E}[X] - \mu^3$$

We need $\mathrm{E}\left[X^3\right]$

$$\mathrm{E}\left[X^3\right] = \int_{-\infty}^{\infty} x^3 f(x)\,dx = \int_0^1 x^3 . 2x\,dx = \int_0^1 2x^4\,dx = \left[\frac{2x^5}{5}\right]_0^1 = \frac{2}{5}$$

$$\therefore \qquad \mu_3 = \mathrm{E}\left[X^3\right] - 3\mu\mathrm{E}\left[X^2\right] + 3\mu^2\mathrm{E}[X] - \mu^3$$

$$= \frac{2}{5} - 3\left(\frac{2}{3}\right)\left(\frac{1}{2}\right) + 3\left(\frac{2}{3}\right)^2\left(\frac{2}{3}\right) - \left(\frac{2}{3}\right)^3$$

$$= \frac{2}{5} - 1 + \left(\frac{8}{9}\right) - \left(\frac{8}{27}\right) = -\frac{1}{135} \approx -0.0074$$

Step 6: Fourth Central Moment μ_4

$$\mu_4 = \mathrm{E}\left[(X-\mu)^4\right] = \int_{-\infty}^{\infty} (x-\mu)^4 f(x)\,dx ; \text{ where } \mu = \frac{2}{3}$$

Instead, we simplify using identity:

$$\mu_4 = \mathrm{E}\left[X^4\right] - 4\mu\mathrm{E}\left[X^3\right] + 6\mu^2\mathrm{E}\left[X^2\right] - 4\mu^3\mathrm{E}[X] + \mu^4$$

We need $\mathrm{E}\left[X^4\right]$

$$\mathrm{E}\left[X^4\right] = \int_{-\infty}^{\infty} x^4 f(x)\,dx = \int_0^1 x^4 . 2x\,dx = \int_0^1 2x^5\,dx = \left[\frac{2x^6}{6}\right]_0^1 = \frac{1}{3}$$

$$\therefore \qquad \mu_4 = \mathrm{E}\left[X^4\right] - 4\mu\mathrm{E}\left[X^3\right] + 6\mu^2\mathrm{E}\left[X^2\right] - 4\mu^3\mathrm{E}[X] + \mu^4$$

$$= \frac{1}{3} - 4\left(\frac{2}{3}\right)\left(\frac{2}{5}\right) + 6\left(\frac{2}{3}\right)^2\left(\frac{1}{2}\right) - 4\left(\frac{2}{3}\right)^3\left(\frac{2}{3}\right) + \left(\frac{2}{3}\right)^4 = \frac{543}{405} = 1.34$$

Step 7: Skewness

$$\textbf{Skewness } = \frac{\mu_3}{\sigma^3} = \frac{-\dfrac{1}{135}}{\left(\sqrt{\dfrac{1}{18}}\right)^3} = -0.566 ,$$

Interpretation: Slightly left-skewed (negative skew)

Step 8: Kurtosis

$$\textbf{Kurtosis } = \frac{\mu_4}{\sigma^4} = \frac{1.35}{\left(\sqrt{\dfrac{1}{18}}\right)^4} = 434.16$$

Interpretation: Very leptokurtic

2.4 CONDITIONAL EXPECTATION

Conditional expectation is the expected value (mean) of a random variable given that another event or random variable has occurred (or taken a particular value).

It is denoted as $\mathrm{E}[X|A]$ or $\mathrm{E}[X|Y]$.

Conditional expectation is used in:

1. Probability updates (Bayesian inference)
2. Decision theory
3. Time series (forecasting)
4. Machine learning (e.g., expectation in EM algorithm)

Type 1: Discrete Case

Let X and Y be discrete random variables.

Formula: $\mathrm{E}[X|Y=y]=\sum_{x} x \cdot P(X=x|Y=y)$

This gives the average value of X when we know $X = y$.

Example: Find $\mathrm{E}[X|Y=2]$ where the joint probability table is

$X\backslash Y$	1	2
1	0.1	0.2
2	0.2	0.5

Solution:

Step 1: Find the conditional distribution $P(X=x|Y=2)$

Marginal $P(Y=2)=0.2+0.5=0.7$

$$P(X=0|Y=2)=\frac{0.2}{0.7}; \quad P(X=1|Y=2)=\frac{0.5}{0.7}$$

Step 2: compute conditional expectation

$$P(X=x|Y=2)=0.\left(\frac{0.2}{0.7}\right)+1\left(\frac{0.5}{0.7}\right)=\frac{0.5}{0.7}=\frac{5}{7}.$$

Type 2: Continuous Case

Let X and Y be continuous random variables with the joint PDF $f_{X,Y}(x,y)$

Formula: $\mathrm{E}[X|Y=y]=\displaystyle\int_{-\infty}^{\infty} x f_{X|Y}(x|y)\,dx$

where $f_{X|Y}(x|y)=\dfrac{f_{X,Y}(x,y)}{f_{Y}(y)}$

Example: Find $\mathrm{E}\left[X|Y=y\right]$ where the joint PDF is

$$f_{X,Y}(x,y) = \begin{cases} 4xy & 0 \le x \le 1, 0 \le y \le 1 \\ 0 & \text{otherwise} \end{cases}$$

Solution:

Step 1: Marginal PDF of Y

$$f_Y(y) = \int_{-\infty}^{\infty} f_{X,Y}(x,y)\,dx = \int_0^1 4xy\,dx = 4y\int_0^1 x\,dx = 4y\left[\frac{x^2}{2}\right]_0^1 = 2y$$

Step 2: Conditional PDF $f_{X|Y}(x|y)$

$$f_{X|Y}(x|y) = \frac{f_{X,Y}(x,y)}{f_Y(y)} = \frac{4xy}{2y} = 2x \quad \text{valid for } 0 \le x \le 1.$$

Step 3: Conditional Expectation

$$\mathrm{E}\left[X|Y=y\right] = \int_{-\infty}^{\infty} x f_{X|Y}(x|y)\,dx = \int_0^1 x.2x\,dx = \int_0^1 2x^2\,dx = 2\left[\frac{x^3}{3}\right]_0^1 = \frac{2}{3}$$

2.5 PROBABILITY DISTRIBUTIONS

A probability distribution is a mathematical function or table that describes the likelihood of all possible outcomes for a random variable in a given experiment. They are fundamental in statistics for modeling uncertainty, analyzing data patterns, and making predictions across various fields like science, engineering, finance, and machine learning.

2.6 COMMON DISCRETE DISTRIBUTIONS

2.6.1 Discrete Probability Distributions

Discrete distributions describe the probability of individual, countable outcomes—like the number of clicks on a website, or how many defective items are in a batch.

Bernoulli Distribution

The Bernoulli distribution is a discrete probability distribution that models a single random experiment (called a Bernoulli trial) with exactly two possible outcomes: "success" (usually represented as 1) and "failure" (usually represented as 0)

Examples:

Coin flip (Head = 1, Tail = 0)
Click or no click on an ad

Characteristics:

- **Parameter:** p = probability of success
- **Outcomes:** $\{0, 1\}$

Probability Mass Function (PMF):

$$P(X = x) = p^x (1-p)^{1-x}, x \in \{0,1\}$$

Use in Data Science:

- Binary classification (e.g., logistic regression target)
- Feature occurrence (e.g., did user buy = 1/0)

Example: Suppose the probability that a user clicks on an ad is $p = 0.3$. We model this with a Bernoulli distribution.

Question: What is the probability that a user clicks on the ad ($X = 1$)?

Solution:

$$P(X = 1) = p = 0.3$$
$$P(X = 0) = 1 - p = 0.7$$

So,

- **Click (Success)** $\rightarrow$ 30%
- **No Click (Failure)** $\rightarrow$ 70%

This is used in **binary classification** tasks in machine learning.

2.6.2 Discrete Uniform Distribution

Definition: The Discrete Uniform Distribution is a type of probability distribution where a finite number of outcomes are all equally likely to occur. Every possible value within its defined range has the exact same probability, meaning there is no bias toward any single outcome Example: Rolling a fair die (1 to 6).

Characteristics:

- **Parameter:** n = number of outcomes
- **Outcomes:** $\{1, 2, ..., n\}$

Probability Mass Function (PMF):

$$P(X = x) = \frac{1}{n}, x = 1, 2, 3, 4, ..., n$$

Use in Data Science:

- Simulating random choices
- Modeling equal-likelihood events (e.g., A/B testing)

Example: A user selects a random day to log in during a 5-day workweek. Each day is equally likely.

Question: What is the probability the user logs in on a Wednesday?

Solution: Total outcomes = 5 (Mon to Fri)

$$P(X = Wednesday) = \frac{1}{5} = 0.2$$

This is useful when **all events are equally likely**, like A/B/C testing.

2.6.3 Binomial Distribution

Definition: The Binomial Distribution is a discrete probability distribution that models the number of successes in a fixed number of independent Bernoulli trials. It is one of the most widely used distributions in statistics for analyzing experiments with binary outcomes. Example: Number of successful email deliveries in 10 attempts.

Characteristics:

- **Parameters:** n = number of trials, p = success probability
- **Outcomes:** $\{0, 1, ..., n\}$

Probability Mass Function (PMF):

$$P(X = x) = \binom{n}{x} p^x (1-p)^{n-x}, x = 0,1,2,3,4,...,n$$

Use in Data Science:

- Predicting user conversion over multiple trials
- Feature engineering (e.g., success count from historical data)

Example: Suppose there's a 0.6 probability that a user will make a purchase during a visit. What's the probability that **exactly 2 users** out of 3 make a purchase?

Let:

    $n = 3$ (number of users)
    $p = 0.6$ (purchase probability)
    $X = 2$

Solution:

$$P(X = 2) = \binom{3}{2}(0.6)^2 (1-0.6)^{3-2} = 0.432$$

So, **43.2%** chance exactly 2 of 3 users buy something.

2.6.4 Poisson Distribution

Definition: The Poisson distribution is a discrete probability distribution that expresses the probability of a given number of events occurring within a fixed interval of time or space if these events happen with a known constant mean rate and independently of the time since the last event. Example: Number of customer service calls per hour.

Characteristics:

- **Parameter:** λ (lambda) = expected number of events per interval
- **Outcomes:** $\{0, 1, 2, ...\}$

Probability Mass Function (PMF):

$$P(X = i) = \frac{e^{-\lambda}\lambda^i}{i!}, i = 0, 1, 2, 3, 4, ...\infty$$

Use in Data Science:

- Modeling arrival rates (e.g., web traffic)
- Anomaly detection (e.g., sudden spike in logins)

Example: Suppose a server receives an average of 4 login attempts per minute ($\lambda = 4$). What's the probability there are exactly 2 login attempts in a minute?

Solution:

Let $i = 2$, $\lambda = 4$

$$P(X = 2) = \frac{e^{-4}4^2}{2!} = 0.1464$$

So, the probability there are exactly 2 login attempts in a minute is 0.1464.

Useful in **event count modeling,** e.g., number of hits on a website per minute.

2.6.5 Geometric Distribution

Definition: The Geometric Distribution is a discrete probability distribution that models the number of trials required to achieve the first success in a series of independent and identical Bernoulli trials. The key difference from the Binomial distribution is that the number of trials (n) is not fixed in advance; the process stops as soon as the first success occurs. Example: Number of times a user sees an ad before clicking.

Characteristics:

- **Parameter:** p = success probability
- **Outcomes:** $\{1, 2, 3, ...\}$

Probability Mass Function (PMF):

$$P(X = x) = (1 - p)^{x-1} p$$

Use in Data Science:

- Modeling user behaviour (first success)
- Estimating retry or failure attempts

Example: A user has a 0.25 probability of clicking on a recommendation. What's the probability they **click for the first time on the 3rd attempt?**

Let $p = 0.25$, $X = 3$

Solution:

$$P(X=3)=(1-p)^{3-1}\,p=(1-0.25)^{3-1}(0.25)=0.1406$$

So, **14.06%** chance of first click on the 3rd try.

Helpful in modeling retry behaviour or engagement timing.

2.7 COMMON CONTINUOUS DISTRIBUTIONS

2.7.1 Rectangular Distribution (Continuous Uniform Distribution)

The Rectangular distribution, also known as the Continuous Uniform distribution, describes a scenario where all outcomes within a specific interval are equally likely. The PDF is a constant function over this interval, forming a rectangle when graphed.

Characteristics: Constant probability density across the range.

The total area under the PDF curve is always 1.

Probability Density Function (PDF):

$$f(x)=\begin{cases}\dfrac{1}{b-a} & a \le x \le b \\ 0 & \text{otherwise}\end{cases}$$

Parameters: Minimum value (a) and maximum value (b), where $a \le b$.

Properties:

Mean: $E(X)=\dfrac{a+b}{2}$

Variance: $\text{Var}(X)=\dfrac{(a-b)^2}{12}$

Symmetric about the mean:
Each value between a and b has the same chance.

Example: A train arrives every 20 minutes. The waiting time for a person arriving at a random time follows a uniform distribution over the interval [0, 20] minutes, but you have no idea when the last train left. Find probability you wait **less than 5 minutes.**

Solution: Let X be the random variable for waiting time which follows a uniform distribution over the interval [0, 20] minutes. The PDF of the uniform Distribution is:

$$f(x) = \begin{cases} \dfrac{1}{20-0} & 0 \le x \le 20 \\ 0 & \text{otherwise} \end{cases}$$

Then, $P(\text{waiting less than 5 minutes}) = P(X < 5) = P(-\infty < X < 5)$

$$= \int_0^5 f(x)\,dx = \int_0^5 \frac{1}{20}\,dx = \frac{5-0}{20} = \frac{1}{4}.$$

2.7.2 Normal Distribution (Gaussian Distribution, Bell Curve)

The Normal distribution is arguably the most important and widely used probability distribution, commonly occurring in many natural phenomena due to the Central Limit Theorem. It is a symmetric, bell-shaped distribution centered around its mean.

Characteristics: Symmetric about the mean (μ), where the mean, median, and mode are all equal. The curve is bell-shaped, with higher density near the mean and lower density further away. Approximately 68% of data falls within 1 standard deviation of the mean.

Probability Density Function (PDF):

$$f(x) = \frac{1}{\sigma\sqrt{2\pi}}\, e^{-\frac{(x-\mu)^2}{2\sigma^2}}, \quad -\infty < x < \infty$$

Parameters: Minimum Mean (μ) and standard deviation (σ).

Properties: Mean = Median = Mode = μ

Variance = σ^2

Example: A random variable X follows Normal distribution with mean 50 and standard deviation 10. Find $P(60 \le X \le 70)$,

Given that $\dfrac{1}{\sqrt{2\pi}} \displaystyle\int_0^2 e^{-\frac{z^2}{2}}\,dz = 0.4772$ and $\dfrac{1}{\sqrt{2\pi}} \displaystyle\int_0^1 e^{-\frac{z^2}{2}}\,dz = 0.3413$

Solution: Here X follows Normal distribution with mean $\mu = 50$ and standard deviation $\sigma = 10$.

$$P(60 \le X \le 70) = P\left(\frac{60-m}{\sigma} \le \frac{X-m}{\sigma} \le \frac{70-m}{\sigma}\right) = P\left(\frac{60-50}{10} \le \frac{X-m}{\sigma} \le \frac{70-50}{10}\right)$$

$$= P(1 \le Z \le 2)$$

$$= P(0 \le Z \le 2) - P(0 \le Z \le 1) = 0.4772 - 0.3413 = 0.1359$$

Example: A random variable X follows Normal distribution with mean 68 and standard deviation 3. Find $P(65 \leq X \leq 71)$,

Given that $\dfrac{1}{\sqrt{2\pi}} \displaystyle\int_{-\infty}^{1} e^{-\frac{z^2}{2}} dz = 0.8413$.

Solution: Here X follows Normal distribution with mean $\mu = 68$ and standard deviation $\sigma = 3$.

$$
\begin{aligned}
P(65 \leq X \leq 71) &= P\left(\frac{65-m}{\sigma} \leq \frac{X-m}{\sigma} \leq \frac{71-m}{\sigma} \right) \\
&= P\left(\frac{65-68}{3} \leq \frac{X-m}{\sigma} \leq \frac{71-68}{3} \right) \\
&= P(-1 \leq Z \leq 1) \\
&= P(-\infty < Z \leq 1) - P(-\infty < Z \leq -1) \\
&= 0.8413 - P(1 \leq Z < \infty) \text{ by symmetry} \\
&= 0.8413 - \left(1 - P(-\infty < Z \leq 1)\right) \\
&= 0.8413 - (1 - 0.8413) = 0.6826
\end{aligned}
$$

2.7.3 Exponential Distribution

The Exponential distribution is a continuous distribution used to model the time elapsed between events in a Poisson process (events occurring continuously and independently at a constant average rate).

Characteristics: Right-skewed distribution, with the highest density at time zero.

Possesses the memoryless property: The probability of an event occurring in the future is independent of how much time has already passed.

Probability Density Function (PDF):

$$
f(x) = \begin{cases} \lambda e^{-\lambda x} & x \geq 0 \\ 0 & \text{otherwise} \end{cases}
$$

Parameters: Rate parameter $(\lambda > 0)$. The mean time between events is $\dfrac{1}{\lambda}$.

Properties:

Mean: $E(X) = \dfrac{1}{\lambda}$

Variance: $\mathrm{Var}(X) = \dfrac{1}{\lambda^2}$

Example: The average time between two incoming phone calls is 4 minutes. Find the probability that next call arrives within 3 minutes.

Solution: Let X be the random variable incoming phone call. The average time between two incoming phone calls is 4 minutes.

$$E(X) = \frac{1}{\lambda} = \frac{1}{4} = 0.25$$

$$P(X \leq 3) = P(-\infty < X \leq 3) = P(-\infty < X < 0) + P(0 \leq X \leq 3)$$

$$= 0 + (1 - e^{-0.25 \times 3})$$

2.7.4 Beta Distribution

The Beta distribution is a highly flexible continuous distribution that models random variables constrained to a finite interval, typically $[0,1]$. Its shape can vary significantly based on its parameters, allowing it to fit various data patterns including uniform, U-shaped, J-shaped, or bell-shaped curves.

Characteristics: Defined within a closed interval (usually 0 to 1).

Versatile in shape depending on α and β. If $\alpha = 1$ and $\beta = 1$, it becomes a uniform distribution.

Probability Density Function (PDF):

$$f(x;\alpha,\beta) = \frac{1}{B(\alpha,\beta)} x^{\alpha-1} (1-x)^{\beta-1}, 0 \leq x \leq 1,$$

where $B(\alpha,\beta)$ is the Beta function, a normalization constant to ensure the total area is 1.

Properties:

Mean: $E(X) = \dfrac{\alpha}{\alpha+\beta}$, Variance: $Var(X) = \dfrac{\alpha\beta}{(\alpha+\beta)^2 (\alpha+\beta+1)}$

Shape varies:

Symmetric if $\alpha = \beta$

Skewed if $\alpha \neq \beta$

2.8 RANDOM VECTORS AND JOINT DISTRIBUTIONS

2.8.1 Random Vector

A **random vector** is a collection (or tuple) of **multiple random variables** that are considered together. These variables can be dependent or independent, and they are usually defined on the **same probability space**.

Formally: If $X_1, X_2, X_3, ..., X_n$ are random variables defined on the same probability space (Ω, F, P), then the vector.

$X = (X_1, X_2, X_3, ..., X)$ is called a **random vector** of dimension n.

Notation and Types

1. **Notation:** $X = (X_1, X_2, X_3, ..., X_n)^T$

2. **Dimension:** If it contains n random variables, it is an n-dimensional random vector.

Types:

Discrete Random Vector: Each X_i is a discrete random variable.

Continuous Random Vector: Each X_i is continuous.

Mixed: Contains both discrete and continuous components.

Example 1: Discrete Random Vector

Suppose we toss a fair die and flip a coin:

Let X = result of the die roll (values: 1 to 6)

Let Y = result of the coin flip (0 for Heads, 1 for Tails)

Then the random vector is: $Z = (X, Y)^T$

This vector has values like (2, 0), (5, 1), (6, 1), etc.

Example 2: Continuous Random Vector

Let X be the height of a student (in cm) and Y be the weight (in kg).

$$X = (X, Y)^T$$

If we randomly select a student from a population, then (X, Y) becomes a continuous random vector, as both height and weight can take a continuum of values.

Joint Distribution of a Random Vector

For a random vector $X = (X_1, X_2)$, we often talk about its joint distribution.

Joint PDF (continuous case):

$f_{X_1, X_2}(x_1, x_2) =$ Probability density function of (X_1, X_2)

Joint PMF (discrete case):

$$P(X_1 = x_1, X_2 = x_2)$$

Important Concepts Related to Random Vectors

Concept	Meaning
Marginal distribution	Distribution of individual components (e.g., X_1 or X_2)
Covariance matrix	Matrix of pairwise covariances between the components of the vector
Expectation vector	Vector of expected values: $$E[X] = \left(E[X_1], E[X_2], ..., E[X_n] \right)^T$$
Independence	Components are independent if joint PDF = product of marginals

Example 3: Random Vector in Statistics

Suppose you collect data on:

X_1 = Math score

X_2 = Science score

X_3 = English score

Then $X = \left(X_1, X_2, X_3 \right)^T$ is a **3-dimensional random vector** representing the academic profile of a student.

2.8.2   Joint, Marginal, and Conditional Distributions

The **joint distribution** describes the probability of two (or more) random variables occurring **simultaneously**.

For discrete variables X and Y: $P(X = x, Y = y) =$ Joint probability

For continuous variables:

The joint probability density function (PDF) is $f_{X,Y}(x, y)$

$$P(a \leq X \leq b, \, c \leq Y \leq d) = \int_c^d \int_a^b f_{X,Y}(x, y) \, dxdy$$

Marginal Distribution

The **marginal distribution** is the probability distribution of one variable **irrespective of the other**.

For discrete variables:

$$P(X = x) = \sum_y P(X = x, Y = y)$$

$$P(Y = y) = \sum_x P(X = x, Y = y)$$

Conditional Distribution

The conditional distribution of Y given $X = x$ is:

$$P\left(Y = y \mid X = x\right) = \frac{P\left(X = x, Y = y\right)}{P\left(X = x\right)}$$

Distributions of Functions of Random Variables

When you apply a **function** to a random variable, the distribution changes. We often need to find the distribution of:

$$Z = X + Y$$
$$W = g\left(X\right), \text{ etc.}$$

(A) For Discrete Random Variables:

Let
$$Z = X + Y.$$
Use **convolution** (sum over all combinations):

$$P\left(Z = z\right) = \sum_{y} P\left(X = x, Y = z - x\right)$$

(B) For Continuous Random Variables:

If $Z = X + Y$, then:

$$f_Z\left(z\right) = \int_{-\infty}^{\infty} f_X\left(x\right) f_Y\left(z - x\right) dx$$

(again, convolution formula)

Wrap-up

Probability and linear algebra form the backbone of modern data science. This chapter introduced the essential mathematical foundations—vectors, matrices, and their operations—that enable structured representation and manipulation of data. These tools establish a rigorous foundation for analyzing complex data, ensuring that subsequent methods in statistics and machine learning rest on solid mathematical and probabilistic principles.

QUESTIONS FOR PRACTICE

1. Define probability and explain the concept of sample space with examples.
   Anna University, 2021

2. Explain conditional probability and independence with suitable examples.
   IIT Bombay, 2022

3. State and explain the Law of Total Probability and Bayes' Theorem with an example. *Vellore Institute of Technology, 2021*

4. What is the role of expectation and variance in analyzing data?

5. When would you use a Binomial distribution in a real-world data science problem?

6. Distinguish between discrete and continuous probability distributions with examples.

7. Explain random variables and probability mass function (PMF) with suitable illustrations.

8. State and explain the properties of expectation and variance with examples.

9. Illustrate the concept of joint probability distribution and marginal probability with examples.

10. Explain the Central Limit Theorem and its significance in data science applications.

3

Essential Mathematics for Data Science: II Statistics

3.1 DESCRIPTIVE STATISTICS

Descriptive statistics is a term given to the analysis of data that helps to describe, show and summarize data in a meaningful way. It is a simple way to describe our data. Descriptive statistics is very important to present our raw data ineffective/meaningful way using numerical calculations or graphs or tables. Without descriptive statistics it would be hard for us to visualize the data, especially in cases which involves a large quantity of data.

Descriptive statistics therefore enables us to present the data in a more meaningful way, which allows simpler interpretation of the data. However, it is important to note that this type of statistics is applied on already known data Descriptive statistics describes the important characteristics/properties of the data using the measures the central tendency like mean/median/mode and the measures of dispersion like range, standard deviation, variance, etc. subsequently, data can be summarized and represented in an accurate way using charts, tables and graphs.

3.2 MEASURES OF CENTRAL TENDENCY

3.2.1 Mean (Arithmetic Average)

Arithmetic mean or simply the mean of a variable is defined as the sum of the observations divided by the number of observations.

A. **Individual Data (Ungrouped and No Frequency)**

Example: Find mean of 5, 7, 3, 9, 6

Solution:

$$\text{Mean} = \frac{\sum x}{n} = \frac{5+7+3+9+6}{5} = 6$$

Short-cut method: Under this method an assumed or an arbitrary average (indicated by A) is used as the basis of calculation of deviations from individual values. The formula is:

$$\bar{x} = A + \frac{\sum d}{n}$$

where,

A = the assumed mean or any value in x

d = the deviation of each value from the assumed mean

Example: A student' s marks in 5 subjects are 75, 68, 80, 92, 56. Find his average mark.

Solution:

x	$d = x - A$
75	7
68 = A	0
80	12
92	24
56	–12
Total	31

$$\bar{x} = A + \frac{\sum d}{n} = 68 + \frac{31}{5} = 74.2$$

B. Individual Data with Frequency

Example: Find mean of

x	2	4	5	6
f	3	2	1	4

Solution:

$$\text{Mean} = \frac{\sum fx}{\sum f} = \frac{(2\times3)+(4\times2)+(5\times1)+(6\times4)}{3+2+1+4} = 4.3$$

Short-cut method:

$$\bar{x} = A + \frac{\sum fd}{N}$$

A = any value in x

N = total frequency

$d = x - A$

Example: Find mean of

x	64	63	62	61	60	59
f	8	18	12	9	7	6

Solution:

x	f	$d = x - A$	fd
64	8	2	16
63	18	1	18
62 = A	12	0	0
61	9	−1	−9
60	7	−2	−14
59	6	−3	18
$\sum f = N = 60$			$\sum fd = -7$

$$\text{Mean} = \overline{x} = A + \frac{\sum fd}{N} = 62 + \frac{7}{60} = 61.88$$

C. Grouped Data with Frequency (Class Intervals)

Example: Find mean of

Class interval	0–10	10–20	20–30	30–40	40–50
f	4	6	10	5	5

Solution: Mean:

Class	f	Midpoint (x)	fx
0–10	4	5	20
10–20	6	15	90
20–30	10	25	250
30–40	5	35	175
40–50	5	45	225

$$\text{Mean} = \frac{\sum fx}{\sum f} = \frac{760}{30} = 25.33$$

3.2.2 Median

The median is that value of the variate which divides the group into two equal parts, one part comprising all values greater, and the other, all values less than median. If the number of data points is **odd**, it's the middle number. If **even**, it's the average of the two middle numbers.

A. **Individual Data (Ungrouped and No Frequency)**

Example: Find median of 5, 7, 3, 9, 6

Solution: Arrange in ascending order: 3, 5, 6, 7, 9

Here $n = 5$(odd)

$$\text{Median} = \left(\frac{n+1}{2}\right)\text{th term} = \left(\frac{5+1}{2}\right)\text{th} = 3\text{rd term} = 6$$

Example: Find median of 5, 7, 3, 9, 6, 12

Solution: Arrange in ascending order: 3, 5, 6, 7, 9, 12

Here $n = 6$ (even)

$$\text{Median} = \text{average of } \left\{\left(\frac{n}{2}\right)\text{th term and } \left(\frac{n}{2}+1\right)\text{th tern}\right\}\text{s}$$

$$= \left\{\frac{\left(\frac{n}{2}\right)\text{th} + \left(\frac{n}{2}+1\right)\text{th}}{2}\right\} = \left\{\frac{6+7}{2}\right\} = \frac{13}{2} = 6.5 \cdot$$

B. Individual Data with Frequency

Step 1: Find cumulative frequencies.

Step 2: Find $\left(\frac{N+1}{2}\right)$ where $N = \sum f$,

Step 3: See in the cumulative frequencies the value just greater than $\left(\frac{N+1}{2}\right)$

Step 4: Then the corresponding value of x is median.

Example: Find median of

x	2	4	5	6
f	3	2	1	4

Solution: Arrange data in order with cumulative frequencies:

x	f	Cumulative f
2	3	3
4	2	5
5	1	6
6	4	10

Total frequency $= N = \sum f = 10$

$$\left(\frac{N+1}{2}\right) = \frac{10+1}{2} = 5.5$$

Here, the cumulative frequencies the value just greater than $\left(\frac{N+1}{2}\right)$ is 6 and the corresponding value of x is 5

Median = 5.

C. Grouped Data with Frequency (Class Intervals)

The steps given below are followed for the calculation of median in continuous series.

Step 1: Find cumulative frequencies.

Step 2: Find $\left(\dfrac{N}{2}\right)$

Step 3: See in the cumulative frequency the value first greater than, $\left(\dfrac{N}{2}\right)$

Then the corresponding class interval is called the Median class. Then apply the formula

$$\text{Median} = L + \left(\dfrac{\dfrac{N}{2} - m}{f}\right) \times h$$

Where

L = Lower limit of the median class

m = cumulative frequency preceding the median

h = width of the median class

f = frequency in the median class

N = Total frequency

Example: Find median of

Class interval	0–10	10–20	20–30	30–40	40–50
f	4	6	10	5	5

Solution:

Total $f = 30 \rightarrow$ Median class = 20–30 ($\dfrac{N}{2} = 15$th value lies here)

Use formula:

$$\text{Median} = L + \left(\dfrac{\dfrac{n}{2} - m}{f}\right) \times h$$

Where:

$L = 20$

$N = 30$

$m = 10$ (cumulative frequency before median class)

$f = 10$

$h = 10$

$$\text{Median} = L + \left(\dfrac{\dfrac{n}{2} - m}{f}\right) \times h = 20 + \dfrac{(15 - 10)}{10} \times 10 = 20 + 5 = 25$$

3.2.3 Mode

The **mode** is the value (*s*) that occurs most frequently.

A. **Individual Data (Ungrouped and No Frequency)**

Example: Find mode of 5, 7, 3, 9, 6

Solution: The given data set is of 5, 7, 3, 9, 6

No repetition → **No mode**

Example: Find mode of 4, 6, 2, 9, 6, 11

Solution: The given data set is 4, 6, 2, 9, 6, 11

Here 6 repeats two times (highest number), mode is 6.

B. **Individual Data with Frequency**

Example: Find mode of

x	2	4	5	6
f	3	2	1	4

Solution:

The given table is

x	2	4	5	6
f	3	2	1	4

Mode: Value with highest frequency = **6** (frequency 4) → **Mode = 6**

C. **Grouped Data with Frequency (Class Intervals)**

$$\text{Mode} = L + \left(\frac{f_1 - f_0}{2f_1 - f_0 - f_2} \right) \times h$$

f_1 = frequency of the modal class
f_0 = frequency of the class preceding the modal class
f_2 = frequency of the class succeeding the modal class
h = width of the modal class

Example: Find mode of

Class interval	0–10	10–20	20–30	30–40	40–50
f	4	6	10	5	5

Solution: Use modal class = class with highest frequency → 20–30 ($f = 10$)

$$\text{Mode} = L + \left(\frac{f_1 - f_0}{2f_1 - f_0 - f_2} \right) \times h$$

Where:

$L = 20$

$f_1 = 10$ (modal class frequency)

$f_0 = 6$ (previous class frequency)

$f_2 = 5$ (next class frequency)

$h = 10$

$$\text{Mode} = 20 + \left(\frac{10 - 6}{2 \times 10 - 6 - 5} \right) \times 10 = 24.44$$

3.3 MEASURES OF DISPERSION

3.3.1 Variance

Variance measures the **average squared deviation** of each data point from the mean. It tells us **how spread out** the data values are.

Formula (for population):

$$\sigma^2 = \frac{\sum (x - \bar{x})^2}{n}$$

Formula (for sample):

$$s^2 = \frac{\sum (x - \bar{x})^2}{n - 1}$$

Key Points:
- The unit of variance is the **square of the original unit.**
- A higher variance means more spread in the data.

3.3.2 Standard Deviation

Definition: Standard deviation is the **square root of the variance**. It shows the **average distance** of data points from the mean in the **same unit** as the data.

Formula (population):

$$\sigma = \sqrt{\sigma^2}$$

Formula (sample):

$$s = \sqrt{s^2}$$

Key Points:
- Most commonly used measure of dispersion.
- Helps to understand consistency or variability in data.

3.3.3 Interquartile Range (IQR)

Definition: IQR measures the spread of the middle 50% of the data. It is the difference between the third quartile (Q_3) and the first quartile (Q_1).

$$\text{IQR} = Q_3 - Q_1$$

Key Points:
- Not affected by extreme values or outliers.
- Useful for **skewed distributions**.

A. Individual Data (Ungrouped, No Frequency)

Example: Find variance, standard deviation and interquartile range of 5, 7, 3, 9, 6

Solution:

$$\text{Mean} = \bar{x} = \frac{5+7+3+9+6}{5} = 6$$

Variance:

$$\sigma^2 = \frac{\sum(x-\bar{x})^2}{n} = \frac{(5-6)^2+(7-6)^2+(3-6)^2+(9-6)^2+(6-6)^2}{5} = 4$$

Standard Deviation: $\sigma = \sqrt{\sigma^2} = \sqrt{4} = 2$

Interquartile Range (IQR): Arrange: 3, 5, 6, 7, 9

- Q_1 (**1st Quartile**) = median of lower half = (3, 5) $\rightarrow$ $Q_1 = 4$
- Q_3 (**3rd Quartile**) = median of upper half = (7, 9) $\rightarrow$ $Q_3 = 8$

IQR = $Q_3 - Q_1$ = 8 − 4 = 4

B. Individual Data with Frequency

Example: Find variance, standard deviation and interquartile range of

x	2	4	6
f	2	3	5

Solution:

$$\text{Mean} = \bar{x} = \frac{\sum fx}{\sum f} = \frac{(2\times2)+(4\times3)+(6\times5)}{2+3+5} = 4.6$$

x	f	$(x-\bar{x})$	$(x-\bar{x})^2$	$f(x-\bar{x})^2$
2	2	−2.6	6.76	13.52
4	3	−0.6	0.36	1.08
6	5	1.4	1.96	9.80

$$\text{Variance} = \sigma^2 = \frac{\sum f(x-\bar{x})^2}{\sum f} = \frac{13.52+1.08+9.80}{10} = 2.44$$

$$\text{Standard Deviation} = \sigma = \sqrt{\sigma^2} = \sqrt{2.44} = 1.56$$

Interquartile Range (IQR)

x	f	Cumulative f
2	2	2
4	3	5
6	5	10

Total $f = 10$

- Q_1 = value at 2.5th position = **4**
- Q_3 = value at 7.5th position = **6**

IQR = $Q_3 - Q_1 = 6 - 4 = 2$.

C. Grouped Data with Frequency (Class Intervals)

Example: Find variance, standard deviation and interquartile range of

Class interval	0–10	10–20	20–30	30–40
f	3	5	7	5

Solution:

Class	f	Midpoint (x)	fx
0–10	3	5	15
10–20	5	15	75
20–30	7	25	175
30–40	5	35	175

$$\text{Mean} = \overline{x} = \frac{\sum fx}{\sum f} = \frac{440}{20} = 22$$

Variance:

x	f	$(x - \overline{x})$	$(x - \overline{x})^2$	$f(x - \overline{x})^2$
5	3	–17	289	867
15	5	–7	49	245
25	7	3	9	63
35	5	13	169	845

$$\text{Variance} = \sigma^2 = \frac{\sum f(x - \overline{x})^2}{\sum f} = \frac{2020}{20} = 101$$

$$\text{Standard Deviation} = \sigma = \sqrt{\sigma^2} = \sqrt{101} = 10.05$$

Interquartile Range (IQR):

Total frequency = 20

- Q_1 position = 5th value → lies in 10 – 20
- Q_3 position = 15th value → lies in 30 – 40

Use interpolation:

$$Q_1 \text{ formula } = L + \left(\frac{\frac{n}{4} - F}{f} \right) \times h$$

Where:

- $L = 10$, $F = 3$, $f = 5$, $h = 10$

$$Q_1 = 10 + \frac{(5-3)}{5} \times 10 = 14$$

$$Q_3 \text{ formula } = L + \left(\frac{\frac{3n}{4} - F}{f} \right) \times h$$

Where:

- $L = 30$, $F = 15$, $f = 5$, $h = 10$

$$Q_3 = 30 + \frac{(15-15)}{5} \times 10 = 30$$

Interquartile Range (IQR): $Q_3 - Q_1 = 30 - 14 = 16$

3.4 DATA VISUALIZATION TECHNIQUES

3.4.1 Histogram

Purpose: Used to show the distribution of a **single continuous variable** by dividing the data into intervals (called bins or classes) and plotting the frequency of data points in each interval.

Features:

- **X-axis:** Represents the data intervals (bins)
- **Y-axis:** Represents frequency or count of observations in each bin
- Bars are **adjacent (no gaps)** since the data is continuous

Example: Suppose you have the marks of 50 students in a mathematics exam. A histogram can show how many students scored:

- 0–10
- 11–20
- 21–30, etc.

This helps you quickly see if the scores are normally distributed, skewed, or bimodal.

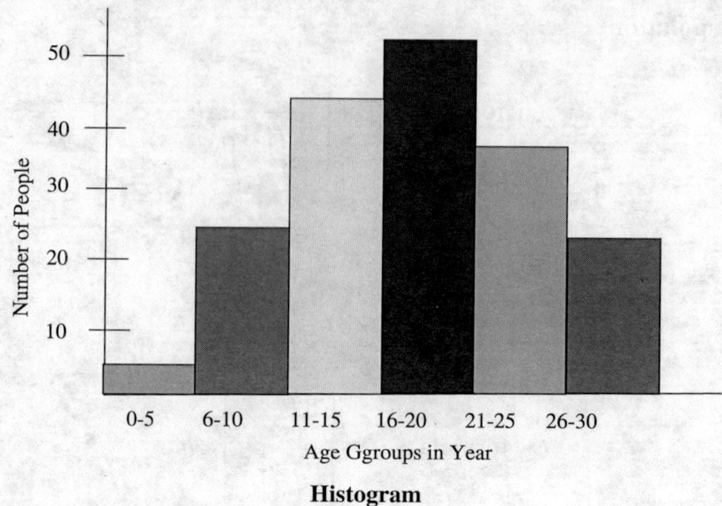

Histogram

3.4.2　Box Plot (Box-and-Whisker Plot)

Purpose: Used to **summarize the distribution** of a dataset based on five summary statistics:

- Minimum
- First quartile (Q_1)
- Median (Q_2)
- Third quartile (Q_3)
- Maximum

Features:

- Shows **spread** and **center**
- Identifies **outliers**
- **Box** shows the Interquartile range (IQR = $Q_3 - Q_1$)
- **Line** inside the box represents the median
- **Whiskers** extend to the smallest and largest values within 1.5 × IQR
- **Dots** beyond the whiskers represent **outliers**

Example: If you're comparing the salaries of employees in three different departments, box plots can show which department has a higher median salary or more variability.

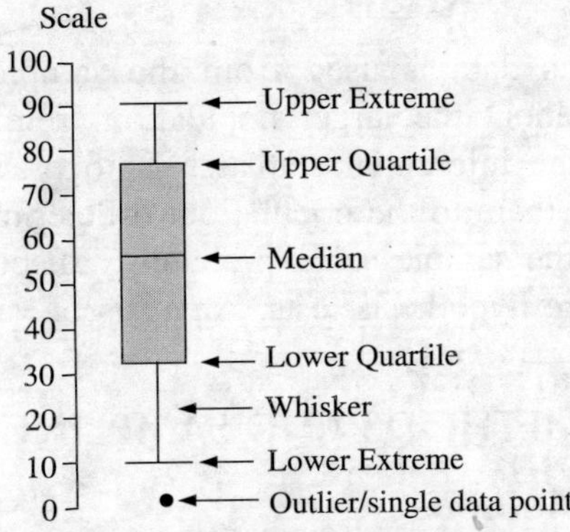

Box Plot (Box-and-Whisker Plot)

3.4.3 Scatter Plot

Purpose: Used to show the **relationship between two continuous variables**. It helps to identify **correlation** and **trends**.

Features:

- **X-axis:** One variable
- **Y-axis:** Another variable
- Each point represents an observation
- Pattern may indicate:
  - ♦ **Positive correlation** (rises upward)
  - ♦ **Negative correlation** (falls downward)
  - ♦ **No correlation** (random spread)

Example: If you plot the number of hours studied vs. exam scores of students, a scatter plot can show whether more study hours are associated with higher scores.

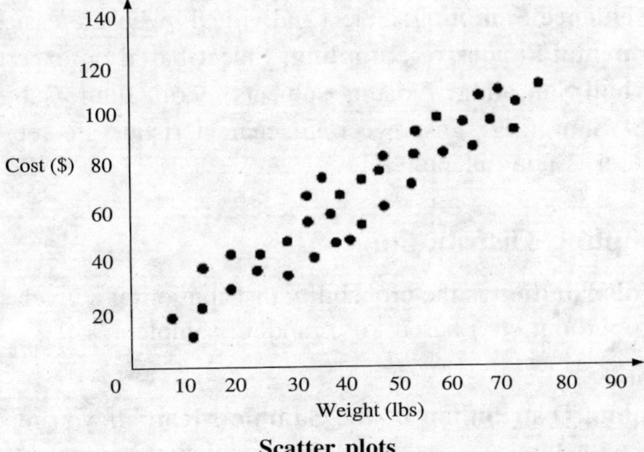

Scatter plots

3.5   INFERENTIAL STATISTICS

In inferential statistics data is used from the sample and conclusions or inferences are made about the larger population from which the sample is drawn. The goal of the inferential statistics is to draw conclusions from a sample and generalize them to the population. It determines the probability of the characteristics of the sample using probability theory. The most common methodologies used are hypothesis tests, Analysis of variance, etc.

3.6   SAMPLING METHODS AND SAMPLING DISTRIBUTIONS

3.6.1   Sampling Methods

Sampling is the process of selecting a subset (sample) from a larger group (population) to make inferences about that population. Common sampling methods include:

A. Probability Sampling

Each member of the population has a known, non-zero chance of being selected.

- **Simple Random Sampling:** Every member has an equal chance of being selected.
- **Systematic Sampling:** Select every kth element from a list (e.g., every 10th person).
- **Stratified Sampling:** Divide the population into subgroups (strata) and randomly sample from each group.
- **Cluster Sampling:** Divide population into clusters (often geographically), randomly select some clusters, and sample all or some members within them.

B. Non-Probability Sampling

Not all members have a known or equal chance of being selected.

- **Convenience Sampling:** Select individuals who are easiest to reach.
- **Judgmental/Purposive Sampling:** Select based on expert judgment.
- **Snowball Sampling:** Existing subjects recruit future subjects.
- **Quota Sampling:** Ensure certain characteristics are represented, but selection is non-random.

3.6.2   Sampling Distributions

A **sampling distribution** is the probability distribution of a given statistic (like the mean, proportion, etc.) based on a random sample.

Key Concepts:
- **Sampling Distribution of the Sample Mean:** If you repeatedly take samples of the same size n from a population and calculate the mean

of each sample, those means form the sampling distribution of the sample mean.

- **Central Limit Theorem (CLT):** Regardless of the population's distribution, the sampling distribution of the sample mean will approach a normal distribution as sample size n increases (typically $n \geq 30$).
- **Standard Error (SE):** The standard deviation of a sampling distribution. For the mean:

$$SE = \frac{\sigma}{\sqrt{n}}$$

whereis σ the population standard deviation, and n is the sample size.

Why Sampling Distributions Matter:

- Help estimate population parameters.
- Allow calculation of confidence intervals.
- Form the basis for hypothesis testing.

3.6.3 Confidence Intervals

A **confidence interval** gives a **range of values** that is likely to contain the true population parameter (like a mean or proportion) with a certain level of confidence (commonly 90%, 95%, or 99%).

Point Estimate

This is the single best estimate of a population parameter, like a sample mean $(\bar{x})$ or sample proportion $(\hat{p})$.

Margin of Error (ME)

This accounts for sampling variability. It's based on the **standard error** and how confident you want to be.

$$ME = Z \times SE$$

Confidence Interval Formula

For a **population mean**, when population standard deviation σ is unknown and sample size is large $(n \geq 30)$:

$$CI = \bar{x} \pm Z \times \frac{s}{\sqrt{n}}$$

where:
    $\bar{x} = 42 =$ sample mean
    $s = 4 =$ sample standard deviation
    $n =$ sample size
    $Z = $ Z-score for the desired confidence level (e.g., 1.96 for 95%)

Example: Let's say a company wants to estimate the average number of hours their employees work per week.

They survey a **random sample of 64 employees**, and find:

Sample mean $\bar{x} = 42$ hours
Sample standard deviation $s = 4$ hours
Confidence level: 95%

Step 1: Find Standard Error (SE)

$$SE = \frac{s}{\sqrt{n}} = \frac{4}{\sqrt{64}} = \frac{4}{8} = 0.5$$

Step 2: Find Critical Value (Z)

$$\text{For 95\% confidence,} \quad = 1.96$$

Step 3: Compute Margin of Error

$$ME = Z \times SE = 1.96 \times 0.5 = 0.98$$

Step 4: Confidence Interval

$$CI = 42 \pm 0.98 = \left(41.02, 42.98\right)$$

Interpretation: "We are 95% confident that the true average number of hours all employees work per week is between **41.02 and 42.98** hours."

Confidence Interval for a Proportion

If you're estimating a **proportion**, like the percentage of customers who are satisfied:

$$CI = \hat{p} \pm Z \times \sqrt{\frac{\hat{p}(1 - \hat{p})}{n}}$$

where: $\hat{p}$ = sample proportion; n = sample size; Z = Z-score (e.g., 1.96 for 95%)

Example: Estimating Average Daily Coffee Consumption

Suppose a university wants to estimate how much coffee its students drink daily, but surveying all 10,000 students is impractical. Instead, they decide to sample.

Step 1: Sampling Method

Let's say they use Stratified Random Sampling:

- They divide students into 3 groups (strata)—undergraduates, master's, and PhD students.
- Then they randomly sample 100 students from each group.

*This ensures all student levels are represented.

Step 2: Collect Data from Samples

Each sampled student reports their daily coffee intake (in cups).
You now have 300 sample data points.
Let's say the sample mean = 2.5 cups/day, and the sample standard deviation = 1.2 cups.

Step 3: Sampling Distribution of the Mean

Imagine you repeat this process (sampling 300 students) 1,000 times.

You'd get 1,000 sample means.

Now plot those 1,000 samples means in a histogram—this forms the sampling distribution of the mean.

Here's what you'd notice:

The histogram looks roughly normal (bell-shaped) thanks to the Central Limit Theorem.

The mean of the sampling distribution will be close to the true population mean.

The spread (how much those sample means vary) is called the standard error:

Step 4: Confidence Interval

Now you can estimate the population mean with a 95% confidence interval:

$$CI = \overline{x} \pm Z \times SE$$

Where $\overline{x} = 2.5$; $Z = 1.96$ for 95% confidence; $SE \approx 0.069$

$$\therefore \qquad CI = 2.5 \pm 1.96 \times 0.069 = 2.5 \pm 0.135$$

So, you're 95% confident that students drink between 2.365 and 2.635 cups/ day on average.

3.7 HYPOTHESIS TESTING

3.7.1 Null and Alternative Hypotheses

Null Hypothesis (H_0):

- A statement of no effect or no difference.
- It's the hypothesis you test **against**.
- **Example:** $H_0 : \mu = 100$ (The population mean is 100)

Alternative Hypothesis (H_1 or H_a):

- A statement that indicates the presence of an effect or difference.
- It's what you want to provide evidence for.
- Example: $H_1 : \mu \neq 100$ (The population mean is not 100)

Depending on the direction of interest:

- **Two-tailed test:** $H_1 : \mu \neq 100$
- **Left-tailed test:** $H_1 : \mu < 100$
- **Right-tailed test:** $H_1 : \mu > 100$

3.7.2 P-value

The **p-value** is the probability of observing a test statistic as extreme as, or more extreme than, the one obtained—assuming the null hypothesis is true.

Decision Rule:

- If **p-value** $\leq$ α **(significance level, often 0.05):** reject H_0
- If **p-value** $>$: α fail to reject H_0

Example:

- **You test** H_0: $\mu = 100$
- Your test results in a p-value of 0.03
- If $\alpha = 0.05$, then $0.03 < 0.05 \rightarrow$ reject H_0

3.7.3 Errors in Hypothesis Testing

Error Type	Description	Consequence
Type I Error (α)	Rejecting H_0 when it's actually true	False positive – finding an effect that's not real
Type II Error (β)	Failing to reject H_0 when H_1 is actually true	False negative – missing a real effect

- α **(alpha):** Significance level = Probability of Type I error
- β **(beta):** Probability of Type II error
- **Power of a test** $=$ $1- \beta$ = Probability of correctly rejecting H_0 when H_1 is true

Example: Is a New Diet Effective?

A nutritionist wants to test if a new diet leads to weight loss. On average, people lose 5 kg on the standard diet. The claim is that the **new diet results in more weight loss**.

Solution:

Step 1: Define Hypotheses

Let μ be the **mean weight loss** on the new diet.

Null hypothesis $H_0 : \mu = 5$ kg (no improvement)

Alternative hypothesis $H_1 : \mu > 5$ kg (more effective right -tailed test)

Step 2: Collect Sample Data

Suppose we collect a random sample of **30 individuals** using the new diet. The data:

Sample mean ($\bar{x}$): 6 kg
Sample standard deviation (s): 2 kg
Sample size (n): 30
Significance level (α): 0.05

Step 3: Compute the Test Statistic

We use a **one-sample t-test** because the population standard deviation is unknown.

$$t = \frac{\bar{x} - \mu_0}{\frac{s}{\sqrt{n}}} = \frac{6-5}{\frac{2}{\sqrt{30}}} \approx \frac{1}{0.365} \approx 2.74$$

Step 4: Find the P-value

Degrees of freedom (*df*): $30 - 1 = 29$

For $t = 2.74$ and $df = 29$, the **right-tailed p-value $\approx$ 0.005** (from a t-distribution table or software)

Step 5: Make a Decision

p-value $= 0.005 < \alpha = 0.05$

Reject H_0

Conclusion: There is statistically significant evidence at the 5% level to suggest that the new diet results in **greater weight loss** than the standard diet.

Error Risk

Type I Error risk (α = 0.05): There's a 5% chance we incorrectly conclude the diet is better when it's not.

Type II Error (β): Not calculable here without more data, but it would be the chance of missing a truly effective diet.

3.7.4   Small Sample Tests (t-tests, chi-square, F-tests)

t-Test (Student's t-Test)

Used When:

- Sample size is small ($n < 30$)
- Population standard deviation is unknown
- Data is approximately normally distributed

Types of t-Tests:

- **One-sample t-test:** compare sample mean to population mean
- **Two-sample t-test:** compare means of two independent groups
- **Paired t-test:** compare means of the same group before and after treatment

One-Sample t-Test

Example: A coach claims that her athletes can run 100m in under 12 seconds. You test 7 athletes:

Times (in seconds): 11.8, 12.2, 11.5, 12.1, 11.9, 12.0, 11.7

Solution:

Null hypothesis H_0: $\mu = 12$

Alternative hypothesis H_1: $\mu < 12$ (one-tailed test)

Mean $(\bar{x}) = 11.89$

Standard deviation $(s) \approx 0.23$

$n = 7$

$$t = \frac{\bar{x} - \mu_0}{\dfrac{s}{\sqrt{n}}} = \frac{11.89 - 12}{\dfrac{0.23}{\sqrt{7}}} \approx -1.27$$

Degrees of freedom: $df = 6$

Critical t-value ($\alpha = 0.05$, one-tailed) ≈ -1.943

Since $-1.27 > -1.943$

Therefore, **fail to reject H_0**

Conclusion: Not enough evidence to say they run under 12 seconds.

Two-Sample t-Test (Independent Samples)

Example: Comparing scores of students taught using two different methods:

Group A ($n = 5$): 78, 74, 69, 81, 73

Group B ($n = 5$): 85, 79, 88, 84, 82

Solution:

Null hypothesis: $H_0 : \mu_1 = \mu_2$

Alternative hypothesis: $H_1 : \mu_1 \neq \mu_2$ (two-tailed test)

Steps: Mean A = 75, $s_1^2 = 22.5$ Mean B = 83.6, $s_2^2 = 13.3$

Use pooled t-test (equal variances assumed):

$$|t| = \left| \frac{\bar{x}_1 - \bar{x}_2}{\sqrt{\dfrac{\sigma_1^2}{n_1} + \dfrac{\sigma_2^2}{n_2}}} \right| = \left| \frac{\bar{x}_1 - \bar{x}_2}{\sqrt{\dfrac{s_1^2}{n} + \dfrac{s_2^2}{n}}} \right| = \left| \frac{75 - 83.6}{\sqrt{\dfrac{22.5}{5} + \dfrac{13.3}{5}}} \right| = 3.22$$

$$df = 5 + 5 - 2 = 8$$

t-critical ($\alpha = 0.05$, two-tailed) $\approx \pm 2.306$

Since $3.22 > 2.306 \rightarrow$ **reject H_0**

Conclusion: The two teaching methods result in significantly different scores.

Paired t-Test (Dependent Samples)

Example: A group of 6 students takes a math test **before and after** a tutoring program.

Student	Before	After
A	70	75
B	65	68
C	72	76
D	60	65
E	68	70
F	75	77

Differences (D = After-Before): 5, 3, 4, 5, 2, 3

$$\text{Mean of } D = 3.67, \; SD = 1.21, \; n = 6$$

$$t = \frac{\overline{D}}{\dfrac{\sigma_D}{\sqrt{n}}} = \frac{3.67}{\dfrac{1.21}{\sqrt{6}}} \approx 7.43$$

$$df = 5$$

t-critical ($\alpha = 0.05$, one-tailed) $\approx$ 2.015

Since 7.43 > 2.015

Therefore, **reject H_0**

Conclusion: The tutoring program significantly improved scores.

3.7.5 Chi-Square Test

The Chi-Square Test is a non-parametric statistical test used to determine if there is a significant association between categorical variables or if a sample fits a theoretical distribution.

Two Main Types:

Type I. Chi-Square Test of Independence

Tests whether two categorical variables are independent.

Type II. Chi-Square Goodness-of-Fit Test

Tests whether the observed frequency distribution matches the expected distribution.

Type I: Chi-Square Test of Independence:

Example: A teacher wants to check whether gender and preference for subject are related.

She surveys **40 students:**

	Maths	Science	Total
Male	10	10	20
Female	5	15	20
Total	15	25	40

Is subject preference **independent** of gender? Given $\chi^2_{0.05,1} = 3.84$.

Solution:

Step 1: Set Hypotheses

Null Hypothesis (H_0): Gender and subject preference are **independent**.

Alternative Hypothesis (H_1): Gender and subject preference are **dependent**.

Step 2: Calculate Expected Frequencies

$$E_{ij} = \frac{(\text{Row Total}) \times (\text{Column Total})}{\text{Grand Total}}$$

	Maths	Science	Total
Male	$\dfrac{20 \times 25}{40} = 12.5$	$\dfrac{20 \times 25}{40} = 12.5$	20
Female	$\dfrac{20 \times 15}{40} = 7.5$	$\dfrac{20 \times 25}{40} = 12.5$	20
Total	15	25	40

Step 3: Use the Chi-Square Formula

$$\chi^2 = \sum \left[\frac{(O - E)^2}{E} \right]$$

where: O = Observed frequency $\qquad$ E = Expected frequency

	O	E	$\dfrac{(O - E)^2}{E}$
Male–Math	10	7.5	0.833
Male–Science	10	12.5	0.5
Female–Math	5	7.5	0.833
Female–Science	15	12.5	0.5

$$\chi^2_{cal} = \sum \left[\frac{(O - E)^2}{E} \right] = 0.833 + 0.5 + 0.833 + 0.5 = 2.666$$

Step 4: Determine Degrees of Freedom

$$df = (r-1)(c-1) = (2-1)(2-1) = 1$$

Step 5: The level of significance is at 0.05

At $\alpha = 0.05$, and $df = 1$, the critical value is $\chi^2_{tab} = \chi^2_{0.05,1} = 3.84$

Step 6: Compare and Decide

$$\chi^2_{tab} = 3.84 \text{ and } \chi_{cal} = 2.666$$

Since $2.666 < 3.84$, we fail to reject H_0

Conclusion: There is not enough evidence to suggest that gender and subject preference are related. They are independent.

Use it when:
You want to test relationships between categories.
You have data in the form of counts/frequencies.
Sample size is small, but each expected cell ≥ 5 (important assumption).

Type II. Chi-Square Goodness-of-Fit Test

Example: A dice is rolled 60 times. The observed outcomes are:

Face	1	2	3	4	5	6
Observation	10	9	11	8	12	10

Is this die fair? Given $\chi^2_{0.05,5} = 11.07$

Solution:

Step 1: Set Hypotheses
Null Hypothesis (H_0): The die is **fair** (all outcomes equally likely).

Alternative Hypothesis (H_1): The die is **not fair** (some outcomes are more likely than others).

Step 2: Calculate Expected Frequencies

If the die is fair and rolled 60 times, each face should appear:

$$E = \frac{60}{6} = 10$$

So expected frequency for all faces = 10

Step 3: Use the Chi-Square Formula

$$\chi^2 = \sum \left[\frac{(O-E)^2}{E} \right]$$

where: O = Observed frequency and E = Expected frequency

Face	O	E	$\dfrac{(O-E)^2}{E}$
1	10	10	0
2	9	10	0.1
3	11	10	0.1
4	8	10	0.4
5	12	10	0.4
6	10	10	0

$$\chi^2_{cal} = \sum \left[\frac{(O-E)^2}{E} \right] = 0 + 0.1 + 0.1 + 0.4 + 0.4 + 0 = 1$$

Step 4: Determine Degrees of Freedom

$$df = k - 1 = 6 - 1 = 5$$

Step 5: The level of significance is at 0.05

$$\text{Critical value } \chi^2_{tab} = \chi^2_{0.05,5} = 11.07$$

Step 6: Compare and Decide

$$\chi^2_{tab} = \chi^2_{0.05,5} = 11.07$$

$$\chi^2_{cal} = 1$$

Since $1.0 < 11.07$, we fail to reject H_0

Conclusion: There is no evidence to suggest the die is unfair. The data fits the expected uniform distribution.

When to Use the Goodness-of-Fit Test?

Use it when:

You want to compare **observed vs. expected frequencies in one categorical variable**.
The expected frequency in each category is at least **5.**
Data categories are **mutually exclusive**.

F-Test: The **F-test** is used to determine whether **two populations have equal** variances. It compares the ratio of two sample variances and is commonly used:

- Before conducting a **t-test** (to check equal variances)
- In **ANOVA** (Analysis of Variance)

Assumptions of the F-Test

- The populations are **normally distributed**
- The samples are **independent**
- The data is **continuous**

If these conditions are not met, use non-parametric alternatives like Levene's test or Bartlett's test.

Formula:

$$F = \frac{s_1^2}{s_2^2}$$

Where:

- s_1^2 = Variance of sample 1 (larger)
- s_2^2 = Variance of sample 2 (smaller)

We assume:

- The samples are **independent**
- The data is **normally distributed**

Example: check whether two machines produce parts with **similar variability** in length.

Machine	Sample size(n)	Sample variance(s^2)
A	10	4.0
B	12	2.0

Is there a significant difference in variability between Machine A and Machine B? Given $. F_{0.05,9,11} = 3.29$

Solution:

Step 1: Set Hypotheses

Null Hypothesis H_0: The variances are equal $\left(\sigma_1^2 = \sigma_2^2\right)$

Alternative Hypothesis H_1: The variances are not equal $\left(\sigma_1^2 \neq \sigma_2^2\right)$

Step 2: Calculate F: There is **no significant difference** between the variances of the two machines.
Their variability is **statistically equal**.
The test statistic is

$$F = \frac{s_1^2}{s_2^2} = \frac{0.4}{0.2} = 2$$

Make sure **larger variance** is in the numerator to ensure $F \geq 1$.
Step 3: Determine Degrees of Freedom

$$df_1 = n_1 - 1 = 10 - 1 = 9$$

$$df_2 = n_2 - 1 = 12 - 1 = 11$$

Step 4: The level of significance is at 0.05% Find Critical Value
From the F-table at α = **0.05**, df_1 = 9 and df_2 = 11:
Critical F-value (two-tailed test): $F_{0.05,9,11} = 3.29$
Reciprocal critical value: $1/3.29 \approx 0.304$

Decision Rule:

If $F < 0.304$ or $F > 3.29$, reject H_0
Otherwise, fail to reject H_0

Step 5: Compare and Conclude

Our $F = \mathbf{2.0}$
Since $0.304 < 2.0 < 3.290.304 < 2.0 < 3.290.304 < 2.0 < 3.29$, we **fail to reject** H_0

Conclusion: There is **no significant difference** between the variances of the two machines.
Their variability is **statistically equal**.

Wrap-up

In this chapter, the basics of statistics were explained. The center of data was described using mean, median, and mode, while the spread was shown through variance, standard deviation, and interquartile range. Patterns in data were displayed with histograms, box plots, and scatter plots. Methods of sampling were introduced, and the idea of sampling distributions was discussed to show how samples represent populations. Confidence intervals were presented to express the level of certainty in estimates. Hypothesis testing was explained, where null and alternative hypotheses were compared, and possible errors were outlined. The chi-square test was introduced as a way to analyse categorical data. Through these topics, the process of describing and making conclusions from data was made clear.

QUESTIONS FOR PRACTICE

1. Define measures of central tendency. Explain mean, median, and mode with examples.   *SRM Institute of Science and Technology, 2022*

2. What are measures of dispersion? Discuss variance, standard deviation, and range.   *Manipal University, 2023*

3. Explain sampling methods and sampling distributions with practical examples.   *IIT Delhi, 2022*

4. Define random variables. Explain the difference between discrete and continuous random variables.   *BMS College of Engineering, 2021*

5. Describe common discrete and continuous probability distributions with examples.   *Amity University, 2022*

6. Explain the Central Limit Theorem and its importance in statistics.   *Anna University, 2023*

7. Define joint, marginal, and conditional distributions of random vectors with examples.   *IIT Madras, 2021*

8. Explain how joint, marginal, and conditional distributions help in understanding the relationship between two or more variables in Data Science applications.

Vellore Institute of Technology (VIT), 2022

9. What is hypothesis testing? Explain Type I and Type II errors with examples.

Jadavpur University, 2023

10. Define confidence intervals. Describe how to construct a confidence interval for a population mean with example.

University of Mumbai, 2021

4

Data Science Tools

There are multiple tools and technologies available for Data Scientists. Data scientists uses these as decision makers to analyze and manage large amounts of informal and systematic data.

In pervious chapters you have observed that a Data Science Project typically has multiple phases like–Data Cleansing, EDA, Model Building, Visualization ,etc. In the below section we will discuss some of the tools to make you familiar, which toll is used in which phase.

4.1 PYTHON FOR DATA SCIENCE

Python is one of the most powerful and versatile tools used in Data Science. Its simplicity, extensive library ecosystem, and community support make it a top choice for data analysis, visualization, and machine learning.

4.1.1 Why Python for Data Science

Feature	Description	Benefit for Data Scientists
Ease of Learning	Simple syntax and readable code	Quick learning curve for beginners
Open Source	Freely available with strong community	Cost-effective and constantly updated
Cross-Platform	Runs on Windows, macOS, and Linux	Flexibility in deployment
Extensive Libraries	Libraries for every data task	Reduces development time
Integration Support	Works with C, C++, R, and SQL	Enables hybrid workflows

4.1.2 Core Libraries Used in Data Science

Category	Library	Purpose/Functionality
Data Handling	NumPy, Pandas	Numerical computing, data manipulation
Data Visualization	Matplotlib, Seaborn, Plotly	Creating static and interactive plots
Machine Learning	Scikit-learn, TensorFlow, PyTorch	Model training and prediction
Statistical Analysis	SciPy, StatsModels	Probability and hypothesis testing
Big Data Processing	PySpark, Dask	Handling large-scale datasets
Automation and Scripting	os, sys, re, argparse	Automating workflows and preprocessing

4.1.3 Typical Libraries in Data Science Project Phases

Step	Description	Common Libraries/Tools
1. Data Collection	Reading data from files, APIs, or databases	requests, pandas, sqlite3
2. Data Cleaning	Handling missing values and duplicates	pandas, numpy
3. Data Exploration	Summarizing and visualizing data	matplotlib, seaborn
4. Feature Engineering	Creating meaningful variables	pandas, sklearn. preprocessing
5. Model Building	Training and testing predictive models	scikit-learn, tensorflow
6. Evaluation	Assessing model accuracy and performance	sklearn.metrics, yellowbrick
7. Deployment	Integrating model into applications	flask, fastapi, streamlit

Example: *Simple Data Analysis with Python*

Code Example

```python
import pandas as pd
import seaborn as sns
import matplotlib.pyplot as plt

# Load Dataset
df = pd.read_csv('data.csv')

# Summary Statistics
print(df.describe())

# Visualize Relationships
sns.pairplot(df)
plt.show()
```

> **Output Summary:**
> - Generates descriptive statistics (mean, median, std, etc.)
> - Creates a pairwise scatter plot for feature relationships.

4.1.4 Advantages of Using Python in Data Science

Aspect	Python's Edge
Community Support	Huge developer community and open-source contributions
Scalability	Works for small datasets and large enterprise systems
Integration	Easy to integrate with web apps, APIs, and cloud platforms
Visualization Power	Supports advanced 2D/3D visualizations and dashboards
Reproducibility	Notebooks like Jupyter enable step-by-step reproducible research

With its simplicity, versatility, and powerful ecosystem, Python is the backbone of modern Data Science. Every stage of the process—data cleaning, visualization, and machine learning—has efficiently reusable tools available in Python.

4.1.5 Data Science Tool: R Programming

Overview

R is a language for statistical computing and data analysis. It is used broadly for academic research, used for analyzing data statistically and data visualization, and in private industry for statistical modelling and machine learning.

4.2 THE R PROGRAMMING LANGUAGE

R is a programming language that is majorly used for statistical computing and data analysis. This was developed in the early. It has gained popularity among statisticians, data scientists and researchers because of its capabilities and the vast array of packages available.

> **‼ FACTS**
>
> R was born from frustration with S. In the early 1990s, statisticians Ross Ihakaand Robert Gentleman developed R at the University of Auckland because they wanted a free, more flexible alternative to the proprietary S language.

4.2.1 Why R

Feature	Description	Benefit
Statistical Focus	Built for data analysis and statistics	Ideal for data scientists and researchers
Open Source	Free to use and modify	Cost-effective and community-driven
Data Visualization	Strong graphical capabilities	High-quality plots and dashboards

(*Contd.*)

Feature	Description	Benefit
Comprehensive Packages	CRAN repository with 18,000+ packages	Ready-to-use tools for every task
Integration	Works with Python, SQL, and Hadoop	Flexibility for hybrid data workflows

4.2.2 Core Libraries Used in Data Science

Category	Package	Purpose/Functionality
Data Manipulation	dplyr, tidyr, data.table	Cleaning and transforming data
Data Visualization	ggplot2, plotly, lattice	Graphs, charts, and interactive plots
Statistical Analysis	stats, MASS, car	Regression, testing, and inference
Machine Learning	caret, randomForest, xgboost	Model training and evaluation
Reporting	knitr, rmarkdown, shiny	Report generation and web dashboards

4.2.3 Typical R Libraries

Step	Description	Common Packages/Tools
1. Data Import	Reading from CSV, Excel, or databases	readr, readxl, RODBC
2. Data Cleaning	Removing missing or incorrect data	dplyr, tidyr
3. Data Exploration	Summaries, visualization	summary(), ggplot2
4. Modeling	Building predictive models	caret, lm(), glm()
5. Evaluation	Model accuracy and validation	caret, Metrics
6. Reporting	Presenting results interactively	shiny, R markdown

Sample Code Snippet

Code Example

```r
library(ggplot2)

# Load Data
data <- read.csv("data.csv")

# Summary Statistics
summary(data)

# Visualization
ggplot(data, aes(x = Age, y = Income)) +
  geom_point(color = "blue") +
  theme_minimal()
```

Explanation: This code loads a dataset, displays basic statistics, and plots a scatter chart using ggplot2.

4.2.4 Advantages of R in Data Science

Aspect	R's Advantage
Statistical Strength	Best suited for complex statistical modeling
Visualization Power	Highly customizable and publication-quality graphics
Community Support	Large academic and research-based ecosystem
Integration	Works well with Python, SQL, and Excel
Reproducibility	Supports literate programming with R markdown

4.2.5 Summary

R continues to be one of the most reliable tools in Data Science due to its extensive statistical capabilities, ability for visualization, and reproducible reporting features. It is most commonly used for academic and analytical research settings.

4.3 TABLEAU

Overview

Tableau is a premier data visualization and business intelligence (BI) application employed to analyze and visualize data in a creative and interactive manner. It helps transform raw data into insightful information with the use of dashboards, charts, and reports, while minimizing coding requirements.

4.3.1 Key Features of Tableau

Feature	Description	Benefit
Drag-and-Drop Interface	Intuitive and user-friendly	Enables quick visual analysis
Real-Time Data Connectivity	Connects to databases, spreadsheets, and cloud sources	Live and updated dashboards
Interactive Dashboards	Dynamic visuals with filters and actions	Encourages data exploration
Advanced Visual Analytics	Trend lines, forecasting, clustering	Deeper analytical insights
Collaboration Tools	Shareable dashboards via Tableau Server or Public	Enhances teamwork and reporting

4.3.2 Multiple Tableau Versions

Product	Purpose/Use Case
Tableau Desktop	For creating visualizations and reports
Tableau Public	Free version for publishing work online
Tableau Server	Enterprise-level sharing and collaboration
Tableau Online	Cloud-hosted analytics platform
Tableau Prep	Data cleaning and preparation tool

4.3.3 Typical Data Science Workflow in Tableau

Step	*Description*	*Example/Tool*
1. Data Connection	Import data from Excel, SQL, or web sources	Connect using "Data Source" tab
2. Data Preparation	Clean, rename, and merge datasets	Tableau Prep or built-in data pane
3. Visualization	Create charts, maps, and graphs	Drag-and-drop interface
4. Dashboard Design	Combine multiple visuals into one view	Interactive dashboards
5. Sharing and Collaboration	Publish to Tableau Server or Public	Enables data sharing and embedding

4.3.4 Common Visualization Types

Chart Type	*Used For*	*Example Use Case*
Bar Chart	Compare categories	Sales by region
Line Chart	Show trends over time	Monthly revenue growth
Pie Chart	Show part-to-whole ratio	Market share distribution
Heat Map	Show intensity or frequency	Customer activity by location
Scatter Plot	Display correlations	Income vs. spending pattern

4.3.5 Advantages of Tableau

Aspect	*Tableau's Advantage*
Ease of Use	No programming required
Speed	Processes large datasets efficiently
Visual Power	Highly interactive and aesthetic visuals
Integration	Works with Excel, SQL, R, and Python
Sharing	Easy publishing via Server or Cloud

4.4 SQL

Structured Query Language (SQL) is the standardized language used for administration of relational databases and manipulation of the data held and stored in those databases. In data science, it may also be used for data extraction, data transformation, data aggregation, and data summarization prior to the analysis or modeling of data.

4.4.1 Key Features of SQL

Feature	Description	Benefit
Data Retrieval	Query and extract specific information	Efficient access to large datasets
Data Manipulation	Insert, update, and delete records	Full control over database contents
Data Filtering	Use conditions (WHERE, LIKE, IN)	Precise data selection
Aggregation Functions	SUM(), AVG(), COUNT()	Quick statistical summaries
Joins and Relationships	Combine multiple tables	Enables multidimensional analysis

4.4.2 Common SQL Databases

Database System	Type	Special Features
MySQL	Open-source	Fast and widely used in web and analytics projects
PostgreSQL	Open-source	Supports advanced analytics and GIS data
SQLite	Lightweight	Ideal for small-scale projects and prototyping
MS SQL Server	Commercial	Enterprise-level data management
Oracle Database	Commercial	Robust, secure, and used in large organizations

4.4.3 Typical Data Science Workflow Using SQL

Step	Purpose	Example SQL Operation
1. Data Extraction	Retrieve relevant data from database	SELECT * FROM sales;
2. Data Filtering	Apply conditions to isolate data	WHERE region = 'East';
3. Data Aggregation	Summarize values	GROUP BY product;
4. Data Joining	Combine multiple tables	JOIN customers ON sales.cust_id = customers.id;
5. Data Export	Transfer results to Python/R for modeling	Use CSV export or connectors

4.4.4 Common SQL Commands

Category	Command	Purpose
Data Retrieval	SELECT, WHERE, ORDER BY	Fetch and organize data
Data Aggregation	GROUP BY, HAVING	Summarize grouped results
Data Manipulation	INSERT, UPDATE, DELETE	Modify existing records
Table Management	CREATE TABLE, DROP TABLE	Define or remove structures
Joins	INNER JOIN, LEFT JOIN	Merge data from multiple tables

Example SQL Query

Code Example

```sql
SELECT region,
       SUM(sales) AS total_sales,
       AVG(profit) AS avg_profit
FROM sales_data
WHERE year = 2024
GROUP BY region
ORDER BY total_sales DESC;
```

Explanation:

- Retrieves sales data by region for 2024
- Calculates total and average profit
- Displays results sorted by total sales (highest first)

4.4.5 Advantages of SQL in Data Science

Aspect	SQL Advantage
Speed	Fast data retrieval even from millions of rows
Integration	Connects easily with Python, R, and BI tools
Simplicity	Declarative syntax—easy to read and write
Scalability	Handles enterprise-scale data efficiently
Universality	Standardized and works across multiple platforms

SQL remains an essential skill for data scientists, **providing the foundation for** data extraction, cleaning, and pre-analysis. **Its ability to handle structured data efficiently makes it a** core component of every data-driven workflow.

4.5 EVOLUTION OF DATA SCIENCE TOOLS: FROM PROGRAMMING LANGUAGES TO INTEGRATED PLATFORMS

Data science has been through a great change over the last few decades and has come to the point of using very complex integrated platforms as tools to perform simple programming languages. In the beginning, there were only a few tools like Python, R, and SQL that helped data scientists and analysts to do their work. They could do calculations, manipulate data, and run queries in relational databases.

The traditional programming approaches could not keep up with the growing data and its complexity and pain points started to surface. Consequently, the BI (Business Intelligence) tools like Tableau and Power BI came to the scene offering graphical interfaces for the new data visualization, and front-end reporting tools which led to the non-technical users getting their share of data access. These tools provided an easy way to get data by asking questions and through that analytics got further into the organization's hierarchy as decision-making support.

The introduction of cloud computing was another big step forward in the field. Google Cloud Platform, Microsoft Azure, and Amazon Web Services (AWS) are some of the infrastructures that were built up because of the large-scale data that was removed from on-premises hardware racks. This migration not only allowed easier access and lower prices but also quickened the cycle of application of data-driven technologies.

Over the last couple of years, the use of Artificial Intelligence (AI) and Machine Learning (ML) in data science processes has gained acceptance. H_2O.ai and Google AutoML are the examples of the new tools that provide the user with little or no programming skills, depending on the user's choice, to create a predictive model through automated machine learning capabilities. Further, the introduction of Low-Code/No-Code platforms has allowed business analysts to build data applications through picture-based interfaces, thus making the collaboration between technical and non-technical parties more effective.

4.6 PYTHON DEVELOPER TOOLKIT FOR DATA SCIENCE

In this section, we list out Python libraries in detail since it is one of the most versatile and widely-used programming languages in the field of data science. Python makes it possible to do everything from data collection and cleaning to analysis, visualization, and even machine learning. Its extensive library support—consisting of pandas, numpy, scikit-learn, matplotlib, and tensorflow among others—provides a good environment for both novices and professionals alike. Python will be visited again in the form of hands-on coding examples in several chapters thereby allowing the readers to not only master the concepts but also through acquiring practical skills that carry high esteem in both academia and industry. The very same reasons of its popularity, simplicity, and cross-platform support would mean that a project done using techniques acquired here would be easily transferable to a real-world project or another modern tool.

Stage/Task	*Tool/Library*	*Purpose/Use Case*	*When & How to Use*
	`pandas, openpyxl`	Import structured datasets from CSV, Excel, or JSON	Use at the start to load tabular datasets into a DataFrame for exploration, cleaning, and analysis.
Data Collection	`requests, beautifulsoup4, scrapy`	Collect data from websites or APIs (web scraping, REST API calls)	Use when data is not available as a local file or database; handle pagination, rate limits, and HTML parsing.
	`sqlite3, SQLAlchemy`	Connect to relational databases and extract structured data	Use for querying production or test databases; integrate SQL queries directly into Python workflows.

(Contd.)

Stage/Task	*Tool/Library*	*Purpose/Use Case*	*When & How to Use*
Data Cleaning and Preprocessing	`pandas, numpy`	Handle missing values, duplicates, filtering, and transformations	Always perform after data collection; ensures consistency, prevents errors in analysis and ML modeling.
	`regex, re`	Pattern-based text cleaning and extraction	Use for cleaning text columns (emails, phone numbers, codes) or extracting structured info from unstructured strings.
	`scikit-learn.preprocessing`	Scaling, encoding categorical variables, normalization	Use before training ML models to ensure numerical stability and correct input formats for algorithms.
Exploratory Data Analysis (EDA)	`pandas-profiling, sweetviz`	Automated data profiling and summary statistics	Use at the beginning to quickly understand dataset size, missing values, correlations, and distributions.
	`matplotlib, seaborn`	Visual exploration of distributions, trends, and relationships	Use for custom plots (histograms, scatter plots, boxplots) to identify patterns, outliers, and correlations.
	`plotly, bokeh`	Interactive plots for dashboards or presentations	Use for web-ready visualizations, interactive dashboards, or when you want to allow users to explore data dynamically.
Statistical Analysis	`scipy, statsmodels`	Hypothesis testing, regression, statistical validation	Use when performing t-tests, ANOVA, linear/multiple regression, or validating assumptions before ML modeling.
Machine Learning	`scikit-learn`	Regression, classification, clustering, model evaluation	Use for classical ML tasks; includes preprocessing, cross-validation, and pipeline support.
	`xgboost, lightgbm`	Gradient boosting models for tabular datasets	Use when high accuracy is needed for structured data; supports feature importance and missing value handling.
	`tensorflow, keras, pytorch`	Neural networks and deep learning	Use for NLP, image recognition, time series, or complex models; supports GPU acceleration for faster training.

(Contd.)

Stage/Task	Tool/Library	Purpose/Use Case	When & How to Use
Natural Language Processing (NLP)	`nltk, spaCy`	Text preprocessing, tokenization, stopwords, POS tagging	Use for cleaning and preparing text data for analysis or ML pipelines.
	`transformers`	Pre-trained language models (BERT, GPT) for NLP	Use for advanced NLP tasks like text classification, summarization, or question-answering; accelerates model development.
Big Data and Distributed Computing	`pyspark`	Distributed processing for very large datasets	Use when datasets exceed memory of a single machine; supports SQL queries, MLlib, and data pipelines.
	`dask`	Parallelized pandas workflows on large datasets	Use as a drop-in replacement for pandas on large data; works on multicore or cluster environments.
Automation and Workflow	`airflow, prefect`	Workflow orchestration and scheduling	Use to automate ETL pipelines, periodic model training, or complex multi-step processes reliably.
	`joblib, pickle`	Save/load models, preprocessors, and pipelines	Use for persisting trained models or preprocessing objects; ensures reproducibility and deployment readiness.
Visualization and Reporting	`matplotlib, seaborn`	Static charts for reports or exploratory analysis	Use when you need reproducible, publication-quality charts embedded in notebooks or reports.
	`plotly, dash, streamlit`	Interactive dashboards for stakeholders	Use to create web-based dashboards that allow users to explore data without coding; supports filters and dynamic updates.
Version Control and Collaboration	`git, GitHub, GitLab`	Track code changes, collaborate with teams	Use for team projects, maintaining code history, branching experiments, and enabling reproducibility.

(Contd.)

Stage/Task	Tool/Library	Purpose/Use Case	When & How to Use
Cloud and Deployment	`AWS Sage-Maker,` `GCP AI Platform,` `Azure ML`	Cloud-hosted model development, training, and deployment	Use when scaling ML models, enabling production deployment, or leveraging GPU/TPU compute without local hardware.
	`flask, fastapi`	REST API creation for ML models	Use to serve trained models as web endpoints; allows integration into apps, dashboards, or external systems.

Wrap-up

 In addition to concepts, data science also depends on strong tools that enable modeling, analysis, and visualization. This chapter explores the essential technologies used by data practitioners—from programming languages like Python and R to platforms like Tableau and SQL for managing and interpreting data. You'll learn how each tool works with various phases of a data project and how picking the appropriate one can greatly increase productivity and understanding. You will have a thorough understanding of the current data science toolkit and how it supports practical workflows by the end.

QUESTIONS FOR PRACTICE

1. Why is Python preferred for Data Science? List core libraries and their purposes.
   Anna University, 2022

2. Explain the role of R in Data Science. Mention important R libraries.
   Vellore Institute of Technology, 2021

3. Describe a typical Data Science workflow using SQL.
   IIT Bombay, 2022

4. Explain the advantages of using Tableau for data visualization.
   SRM Institute of Science and Technology, 2023

5. List essential Python libraries for different phases of a Data Science project.
   Manipal University, 2022

6. Compare Python and R in the context of Data Science projects.
   IIT Delhi, 2021

7. What are the key features of SQL databases used in Data Science?
   BMS College of Engineering, 2022

8. Describe the evolution of Data Science tools from programming languages to integrated platforms.
   Amity University, 2023

9. Explain the typical workflow in Tableau including data import, visualization, and sharing.
   Anna University, 2021

10. List the essential development tools and best practices for Python developers in Data Science.
    IIT Madras, 2022

5

Understanding Data: Types, Sources, and Structures

5.1   SOURCES OF DATA: PRIMARY, SECONDARY, AND TERTIARY

Knowing Data sources are very important in judging whether the information is correct, up to date, or suitable for the task. These sources are generally classified into primary, secondary, and tertiary data sources in varied respects on how remotely the data were collected.

Primary Data implies original data collected for a given purpose, which means it goes right from the source by way of surveys, experiments, observations, or sensors. Hence this data is fresh and very much tailored but requires time and costs to gather.

Primary Data	Secondary Data	Tertiary Data
Data collected directly from original sources for a specific purpose, usually by the researcher.	Data collected by someone else for a different Data that summarizes, indexes, or organizes purpose but is reused.	Data that summarizes, indexes, or organizes primary and secondary sources.
Examples: Conducting a survey to gather opinions on a new product. Recording temperature readings using loT sensors in a factory. Performing laboratory experiments to test a hypothesis.	**Examples:** Government datasets like census or health statistics from data.gov Research papers and reports from organizations like WHO or McKinsey	**Examples:** Wikipedia articles summarizing various studies. Textbooks consolidating information from multiple research papers. Bibliographies and meta-analysis reports. Statistical yearbooks compiling data from various sources.

(Contd.)

Primary Data	Secondary Data	Tertiary Data
Use Case: Ideal for answering specific research questions when accuracy and relevance are required.	**Use Case:** Suitable when relevant primary data is hard to obtain or expensive.	**Use Case:** Useful for getting quick overviews or starting points.

Secondary Data is the data collected earlier by some other party, which differs in its objective. Examples are research reports, government results, statistics, etc. Secondary Databases are easier to reach and more cost-efficient but may not exactly suit the present needs.

Tertiary Data is a compilation or summary of secondary sources of data. Being located in encyclopedias, indexes, review articles, or curated datasets, tertiary data can give a brief idea, whereas they lack detail and depth.

5.2 STRUCTURED, SEMI-STRUCTURED, AND UNSTRUCTURED: A DATA PERSPECTIVE

As a data scientist, structuring the data pipeline efficiently begins with understanding the nature of the data you're working with. Is data structured, semi-structured, or unstructured? Such classification will automatically govern the choice of tools and storage systems that will be used, the methods used in data preparation, the choice of models, and strategies for scalability.

Knowledge of the structural type of data you are handling is fundamental to efficient processing, analysis, and integration of data. As much as structured data provides simplicity and high performance in querying, semi-structured data gives room for flexibility and versatility and, therefore, works well for adaptive applications. The unstructured data has great promise but requires sophisticated tools and approaches for extracting insightful information. In contemporary data science processes, all three forms—commonly described as hybrid data—are increasingly becoming the norm, as companies aim to take advantage of every available piece of valuable information.

The three data types have been previously examined in earlier sections of this book. The Table given below provides additional insightful information for further understanding.

Data Type	Use Case	Advantages	Challenges
Structured Data	Ideal for traditional business applications, transactional systems, and real-time analytics.	Easy to process, query, and integrate; has high data integrity.	Not suitable for high-volume unstructured data; schema rigidity can limit flexibility.

(Contd.)

Data Type	Use Case	Advantages	Challenges
Semi-Structured Data	Typically used in IoT applications, web analytics, and sensor-based data collection.	More flexible than structured data; accommodates complex data types like JSON and XML.	Requires significant transformation to be used for analytics; involves hybrid systems and complex ETL pipelines.
Unstructured Data	Critical for tasks like image recognition, NLP, and voice processing.	High-value insights are often hidden in unstructured formats, such as text, video, and audio.	Requires specialized techniques (e.g., deep learning, NLP, computer vision) and large compute resources for meaningful analysis.

5.3   NOMINAL, ORDINAL, DISCRETE, AND CONTINUOUS DATA

NOMINAL DATA EXAMPLE	
Category	*Nominal Values*
Gender	Male, Female, Other
Blood Group	A, B, AB, O
Favourite Color	Red, Blue, Green, Yellow
City	Kolkata, Delhi, Mumbai, Chennai
Marital Status	Single, Married, Divorced, Widowed

ORDINAL DATA EXAMPLE	
Category	*Ordinal Values*
Education Level	Primary, Secondary, Graduate, Postgraduate

(Contd.)

ORDINAL DATA EXAMPLE	
Category	*Ordinal Values*
Satisfaction	Very Unsatisfied, Unsatisfied, Neutral, Satisfied, Very Satisfied
Socio-economic Status	Low, Middle, High
Class Rank	1st, 2nd, 3rd, 4th
Pain Severity	None, Mild, Moderate, Severe
Movie Rating	1 Star, 2 Stars, 3 Stars, 4 Stars, 5 Stars
Agreement Scale	Strongly Disagree, Disagree, Neutral, Agree, Strongly Agree

CONTINIOUS DATA EXAMPLE	
Category	*Continuous Values (Examples)*
Height (cm)	152.5, 160.2, 175.8, 180.0
Weight (kg)	45.3, 60.0, 72.8, 85.6
Temperature (°C)	22.1, 25.5, 30.0, 33.7
Time (hours)	1.25, 2.5, 3.75, 4.0
Distance (km)	2.3, 5.0, 7.8, 10.6

DISCRETE DATA EXAMPLE	
Category	*Discrete Values (Examples)*
Number of Students	20, 25, 30, 35
Cars in a Parking Lot	5, 12, 18, 22
Books on a Shelf	10, 15, 21, 28
Children in a Family	1, 2, 3, 4
Goals Scored in Match	0, 1, 2, 3, 4

5.3.1 Qualitative Data (Categorical Data)

Qualitative Data generally speaks about features or attributes about the data in statistics. Qualitative Data is referred as Categorical Data too, because it divides the data into categories or groups. A person's favourite colour, their job, or their hometown are examples of qualitative data. Qualitative data is sub-divided into two types.

- Nominal Data
- Ordinal Data

5.3.2 Nominal Data

Nominal data is a qualitative data type consisting of labels or categories that are not orderable or rankable. Nominal data is utilized to group observations into categories, and the categories possess no ranking or order.

Some examples of nominal data are:

- Favorite Color (Red, Blue, Green)
- Animal Species (Dog, Cat, Rabbit)
- Payment Methods (Cash, Credit Card, Digital Wallet)
- Marital Status (Single, Married, Divorced)

Nominal data can be expressed in the form of frequency tables and bar charts, which indicate the number or percentage of observations for each category. For instance, a frequency table of favorite colors can indicate the number of people who like red, blue, or green.

Non-parametric tests, which do not assume a specific data distribution, are typically used to analyze nominal data. Fisher's Exact Tests and Chi-Squared Tests are two popular non-parametric tests for nominal data that can be used to relate the frequency or proportion of observations for different categories.

5.3.3 Ordinal Data

Ordinal data is one form of qualitative data that represents categories that may be ranked or ordered, though the distances among categories are not always equal. Ordinal data is frequently applied to measure subjective characteristics or feelings where there exists a natural ranking to the replies.

Bar charts or line charts work best if ordinal data are represented. These two charts show the ranking or order of categories, but they also do not imply that the intervals between categories are equal.

Usually, non-parametric tests are used with ordinal data that make no assumptions with regard to the distribution of the data. Two of the most common ones are the Wilcoxon Signed-Rank Test and the Mann-Whitney U-Test.

5.3.4 Quantitative Data (Numerical Data)

Quantitative Data is the data type that indicates the numerical value of the data. It is also referred to as Numerical Data. This data type is employed to depict measurements like height, weight, temperature, and other numeric values. Quantitative data is again divided into two types:

- Discrete Data
- Continuous Data

5.3.5 Discrete Data

Discrete data is one of the types of quantitative data that are made up of distinct, quantifiable values. Such types of data are in the form of whole numbers, and the values cannot be subdivided into fractions meaningfully.

Examples of discrete data are:

- Number of Children in a Family
- Number of Cars in a Parking Lot
- Number of Students in a Class
- Number of Defective Products in a Batch

Discrete data is usually depicted with bar graphs, which show the frequency of occurrence of each unique value. These values are finite and countable.

5.3.6 Continuous Data

Continuous data is quantitative data that describes measurements in a continuous interval. The values can have any value within the specified range, and they can be subdivided infinitely.

Examples of continuous data are:

- Height (e.g., 5.6 feet, 5.61 feet, 5.611 feet)
- Temperature (e.g., 98.6°F, 98.62°F, 98.623°F)
- Time (e.g., 3.5 seconds, 3.55 seconds, 3.555 seconds)
- Weight (e.g., 68.5 kg, 68.55 kg, 68.555 kg)

Continuous data is usually presented in histograms to indicate the number of values within a given range. It is also appropriate for regression models and continuous analysis operations.

5.4 DATA COLLECTION TECHNIQUES

5.4.1 What is Data Collection?

Data collection refers to the process of acquiring data from different sources in order to analyze and derive insights. In Data Science, it is the initial step that allows model creation, pattern identification, and decision-making. The quality of data obtained largely determines the results of any data-based project.

5.4.2 Key Terms Related to Data Collection

Population vs. Sample

Population: The entire collection of items or people a data scientist would like to investigate.

Sample: A part of the population that is chosen for examination. Sampling is applied when it is not feasible to take data from the whole population.

For example, a population includes all members of a group, while a sample is a smaller subset chosen for analysis.

Raw Data vs. Processed Data

Raw Data: Information taken directly from the source without any adjustments. It might include noise, errors, or missing values.

Processed Data: Data that has been cleaned, formatted, and transformed for analysis or modeling.

Accuracy, Reliability, and Validity

Accuracy: The extent to which the data gathered represents the actual values. High accuracy indicates low error or distortion.
Reliability: Consistency in data gathering over time. Reliable data provides repeated results under similar conditions.
Validity: The degree to which the data collection method measures what it is supposed to measure. High validity guarantees relevance and appropriateness.

5.5 COMMON DATA COLLECTION TECHNIQUES IN DATA SCIENCE

5.5.1 Ethical Considerations in Data Collection

It is not optional but a responsibility of data scientists to ensure the ethics and legality of the data collection process. Upholding the privacy of the user, obtaining informed consent, knowledge of regulatory compliance (such as GDPR and CCPA), is trust building and legally defending in Data Science activity.

5.5.2 Data Privacy and Consent

Data Privacy is the right of an individual to manage how their personal data is being gathered and used. Consent implies that individuals need to willingly agree to share their data, knowing how it will be utilized.

Key Points:

Informed Consent: Users must be explicitly told about:

- What data is being gathered
- Why it is being gathered
- How it will be stored and utilized
- Who will access it

For example, an e-commerce site collecting user feedback must inform customers that their responses may be used for marketing analysis, and must offer the option to participate voluntarily.

Adherence to Data Protection Regulations (GDPR, CCPA)

Data scientists and organizations have to comply with local and global laws governing how personal data is processed, stored, and collected. Two major regulations are:

General Data Protection Regulation (GDPR)–EU Law

Applies to any organization which processes data of EU citizens, irrespective of location.

- **Right to Access:** Users can request their data.
- **Right to Erasure:** Users can ask for data deletion.
- **Data Minimization:** Only necessary data should be collected.
- **Purpose Limitation:** Data must be used only for its intended purpose.

California Consumer Privacy Act (CCPA)–US (California) Law

Gives residents of California control over their personal data.

- **Right to Know:** Users must be informed about collected data.
- **Right to Delete:** Users can request data removal.
- **Right to Opt-Out:** Users can refuse the sale of their data.

Example: A mobile app collecting data on European users must:

- Get clear permission before tracking.
- Inform users about how long data will be stored.
- Allow users to delete their data upon request (as per GDPR).

5.6 DATA CLEANING AND PREPROCESSING

5.6.1 Dataset Setup

Data cleaning and preprocessing are vital steps prior to any data analysis or machine learning project. Real-world data tends to be dirty with **missing values, inconsistencies, duplicates,** and **outliers**. To illustrate these ideas practically, we will create a synthetic dataset first and then will use the dataset to demonstrate the cleaning process.

The dataset simulates **Urban E-Scooter Usage** and includes fields like user age, ride duration, distance, payment method, and user rating. This dataset intentionally includes:

5.6.2 Code: Creating the Dataset

Code Example

```python
import pandas as pd
import numpy as np
import random

np.random.seed(42)
random.seed(42)

# Create the synthetic dataset
data = {
    "Ride_ID": [f"RS{1000 + i}" for i in range(15)],
    "User_Age": [25, 34, None, 19, 45, 22, 102, 29, 38,
None, 27, 33, 260, 31, 21],  # Outliers: 102, 260
    "Bike_Model": ["X1", "X1", "X2", "x2", "X3", "X3", "X1",
"X2", "X3", "X4", "X4", "x4", "X2", None, "X3"],
    "Trip_Duration_min": [12, 8, 15, 200, 7, None, 20, 35,
60, 5, 3, 500, 14, 9, None],  # Outliers: 200, 500
    "Distance_km": [2.5, 1.8, 3.0, 25.0, 1.2, 2.0, None, 5.5,
10.0, 0.8, 0.5, 50.0, 3.2, 1.5, None],  # Outliers: 25, 50
    "Payment_Method": ["Credit Card", "credit", "Cash",
"cash", "Wallet", None, "Credit", "Wallet", "Wallet",
                       "Cash", "Cc", "CASH", "Credit Card",
"credit card", "None"],
    "Rating": [5, 4, 4, 3, None, 5, 2, 3, 5, None, 4, 5, 10,
3, -1]  # Outliers: 10, -1
}

# Create DataFrame
df = pd.DataFrame(data)

# Add a duplicate row
df = pd.concat([df, df.iloc[[2]]], ignore_index=True)

# Save to CSV
df.to_csv("urban_e_scooter_usage.csv", index=False)

# Show first few rows
print(df.head())
```

```
OUTPUT

...    Ride_ID  User_Age Bike_Model  Trip_Duration_min  Distance_km Payment_Method  \
0   RS1000     25.0       X1              12.0              2.5      Credit Card
1   RS1001     34.0       X1               8.0              1.8           credit
2   RS1002      NaN       X2              15.0              3.0             Cash
3   RS1003     19.0       x2             200.0             25.0             cash
4   RS1004     45.0       X3               7.0              1.2           Wallet

     Rating
0       5.0
1       4.0
2       4.0
3       3.0
4       NaN
```

The dataset is now ready and saved as a CSV file: urban_e_scooter_usage.csv. We will use this for all upcoming sections of the article.

5.7 IDENTIFYING DATA QUALITY ISSUES

Before cleaning a dataset, we must identify common data quality problems that hinder analysis.

- Missing data
- Inconsistent or incorrect entries
- Duplicates
- Outliers

We'll use the **Urban E-Scooter Usage** dataset to demonstrate each of these.

5.7.1 Missing Data: Types and Implications

```
missing_data = df.isnull().sum()
print("Missing values per column:\n", missing_data)t's de-
tect where data is missing.
```

```
Missing values per column:
Ride_ID 0
User_Age 3
Bike_Model 1
Trip_Duration_min 2
Distance_km 2
Payment_Method 1
Rating 2
dtype: int64
```

These missing values can skew analysis (e.g., average age or ride time).

We'll later demonstrate imputation and deletion techniques.

5.7.2 Inconsistent and Duplicate Data

Inconsistent data often appears in text fields like Bike_Model or Payment_Method

```
print("Unique Bike Models:", df['Bike_Model'].unique())
print("Unique Payment Methods:", df['Payment_Method'].
unique())
```

```
Unique Bike Models: ['X1' 'X2' 'x2' 'X3' 'X4' 'x4' None]
Unique Payment Methods: ['Credit Card' 'credit' 'Cash'
'cash' 'Wallet' None 'Credit' 'Cc' 'CASH' 'credit card'
'None'
```

You can see inconsistencies in case, formatting, and spelling. These need standardization.

Now let's investigate duplicate rows:

```
duplicates = df[df.duplicated()]
print("Printing Duplicate Rows:\n", duplicates)
```

```
Printing Duplicate Rows:
Ride_ID User_Age Bike_Model Trip_Duration_min Distance_km \
15 RS1002 NaN X2 15.0 3.0
Payment_Method Rating
15 Cash 4.0
```

5.7.3 Outliers and Anomalies

Outliers can seriously affect mean-based statistics. Let's check for them visually and numerically.

```
print(df[['User_Age', 'Trip_Duration_min', 'Distance_km',
'Rating']].describe())
Techniques for Cleaning Data
Data Normalization and Standardization
Feature Engineering Basics
```

	User_Age	Trip_Duration_min	Distance_km	Rating
count	13.000000	14.000000	14.000000	14.000000
mean	52.769231	64.500000	7.857143	4.000000
std	65.802930	135.305779	13.692430	2.353394
min	19.000000	3.000000	0.500000	-1.000000
25%	25.000000	8.250000	1.575000	3.000000
50%	31.000000	14.500000	2.750000	4.000000
75%	38.000000	31.250000	4.925000	5.000000
max	260.000000	500.000000	50.000000	10.000000

We see:

- User_Age with 260 — likely invalid.
- Trip_Duration_min has 200 and 500 — extremely high.
- Distance_km up to 50.
- Rating values like -1 and 10 — ratings are usually between 1–5.

5.7.4 Summary of Issues Identified

Problem Type	Example(s)	Column(s) Affected
Missing Data	None, NaN	User_Age, Trip_Duration_min
Inconsistent Values	'credit', 'CASH', 'x2', 'x4'	Payment_Method, Bike_Model
Duplicates	One found	Entire row
Outliers	Age: 260, Duration: 500, Rating: –1	Numeric fields

5.8 TECHNIQUES FOR CLEANING DATA

5.8.1 Handling Missing Data (Deletion, Imputation Techniques)

We will learn below two topics here

- **Deletion** of rows or columns
- **Imputation** using statistics like mean/median/mode

View current missing data

```
print(df.isnull().sum())
```

```
Ride_ID 0
User_Age 3
Bike_Model 1
Trip_Duration_min 2
Distance_km 2
Payment_Method 1
Rating 2
dtype: int64
```

Deletion Example: Dropping rows where missing values exists

```
df_dropped = df.dropna()

print(df_dropped.isnull().sum())

print("Shape after dropping rows with any NaNs:", df_
dropped.shape)
```

```
Ride_ID 0
User_Age 0
Bike_Model 0
Trip_Duration_min 0
Distance_km 0
Payment_Method 0
Rating 0
dtype: int64
Shape after dropping rows with any NaNs: (8, 7)
```

Imputation Example: Fill missing values with sensible defaults

```python
# Impute numeric fields with median
df['User_Age'].fillna(df['User_Age'].median(), inplace=True)
df['Trip_Duration_min'].fillna(df['Trip_Duration_min'].medi-
an(), inplace=True)
df['Distance_km'].fillna(df['Distance_km'].median(), in-
place=True)
df['Rating'].fillna(df['Rating'].median(), inplace=True)
# Impute categorical fields with mode

df['Bike_Model'].fillna(df['Bike_Model'].mode()[0], in-
place=True)
df['Payment_Method'].fillna(df['Payment_Method'].mode()[0],
inplace=True)
# Check if any missing values remain
print("Here are the Missing values after imputation:\n",
df.isnull().sum())

Here are the Missing values after imputation:
Ride_ID 0
User_Age 0
Bike_Model 0
Trip_Duration_min 0
Distance_km 0
Payment_Method 0
Rating 0
dtype: int64
```

5.8.2   Correcting Inconsistent Data (Standardization and Validation)

Let's clean inconsistent **text fields**.

```python
df['Payment_Method'] = df['Payment_Method'].str.lower().str.strip()
# Manual mapping to standard categories
payment_map = {
'credit card': 'Credit Card',
'credit': 'Credit Card',
'cc': 'Credit Card',
'cash': 'Cash',
'wallet': 'Wallet',
'none': 'Unknown',
}
df['Payment_Method'] = df['Payment_Method'].map(payment_map).fill-
na('Unknown')
print("Cleaned Payment Methods:\n", df['Payment_Method'].value_
counts())

Cleaned Payment Methods:
Payment_Method
Credit Card 6
Cash 6
Wallet 3
Unknown 1
Name: count, dtype: int64
```

Standardize Bike_Model

```
df['Bike_Model'] = df['Bike_Model'].str.upper().str.strip()
print("Cleaned Bike Models:\n", df['Bike_Model'].value_
counts())

Cleaned Bike Models:
Bike_Model
X2 6
X3 4
X1 3
X4 3
Name: count, dtype: int64
```

5.9 DATA NORMALIZATION AND STANDARDIZATION

After cleaning the data, it's important to **scale** numeric features to make them suitable for machine learning algorithm especially ones that are sensitive to feature magnitudes like KNN, SVM, or logistic regression.

Importance of Scaling Data

- Raw values like Trip_Duration_min (ranging 3 to 500) can dominate over features like Rating (1 to 5).
- **Normalization** scales values to a 0–1 range.
- **Standardization** rescales values to a mean of 0 and standard deviation of 1.

We'll demonstrate both using:

- User_Age
- Trip_Duration_min
- Distance_km
- Rating

5.9.1 Techniques: Min-Max Scaling and Z-Score Normalization

```
from sklearn.preprocessing import MinMaxScaler, Standard-
Scaler
numeric_cols = ['User_Age', 'Trip_Duration_min', 'Distance_
km', 'Rating']
df_numeric = df[numeric_cols]
df_numeric.head()
```

5.9.2 Min-Max Scaling (Normalization)

```
scaler_minmax = MinMaxScaler()
df_minmax_scaled = pd.DataFrame(scaler_minmax.fit_trans-
form(df_numeric), columns=numeric_cols)
print("Normalized (Min-Max Scaled) Data:\n", df_minmax_
scaled.head())
```

```
Normalized (Min-Max Scaled) Data:
User_Age Trip_Duration_min Distance_km Rating
0 0.024896 0.018109 0.040404 0.285714
1 0.062241 0.010060 0.026263 0.142857
2 0.000000 0.396378 0.494949 0.000000
3 0.041494 0.064386 0.101010 0.000000
4 0.078838 0.114688 0.191919 0.285714
```

5.9.3 Z-Score Standardization

```
scaler_standard = StandardScaler()
df_zscore_scaled = pd.DataFrame(scaler_standard.fit_trans-
form(df_numeric), columns=numeric_cols)
print("Standardized (Z-Score Scaled) Data:\n", df_zscore_
scaled.head())

Standardized (Z-Score Scaled) Data:
User_Age Trip_Duration_min Distance_km Rating
0 -0.433012 -0.569588 -0.611129 0.059868
1 -0.315363 -0.594353 -0.654726 -0.419079
2 -0.511444 0.594353 0.790186 -0.898027
3 -0.380724 -0.427191 -0.424287 -0.898027
4 -0.263075 -0.272412 -0.144024 0.059868
```

5.10 FEATURE ENGINEERING BASICS

Feature engineering is a vital step when prepping data for machine learning. It includes converting raw data into features which more accurately capture the underlying issue to predictive models, enhancing their performance.

We're still with our synthetic Urban E-Scooter Usage Dataset.

Example 1: Categorize Time of Day

We'll derive a new categorical feature, Time_of_Day, from Start_Time. To do this, we'll first introduce a new column, Start_Time, into the dataset—since it's not currently available—allowing us to demonstrate the process effectively.

```
import pandas as pd
import numpy as np
# Ensure reproducibility
np.random.seed(42)
# Add Start_Time: random minutes from 2023-01-01
df['Start_Time'] = pd.to_datetime('2023-01-01') + pd.to_
timedelta(
np.random.randint(0, 1440, size=len(df)), unit='m'
)
# Preview to confirm
```

```
print(df[['Start_Time']].head())
def categorize_time(hour):
if 5 <= hour < 12:
return 'This is Morning'
elif 12 <= hour < 17:
return 'This is Afternoon'
elif 17 <= hour < 21:
return 'This is Evening'
else:
return 'Night'
df['Time_of_Day'] = df['Start_Time'].dt.hour.apply(catego-
rize_time)
print(df[['Start_Time', 'Time_of_Day']].head())
Start_Time Time_of_Day
0 2023-01-01 18:46:00 This is Evening
1 2023-01-01 14:20:00 This is Afternoon
2 2023-01-01 21:34:00 Night
3 2023-01-01 18:50:00 This is Evening
4 2023-01-01 18:15:00 This is Evening
```

5.10.1 Encoding Categorical Variables (One-Hot Encoding, Label Encoding)

Many ML models (e.g., linear regression, decision trees, neural networks) require the input data to be **numeric**. Thus, categorical variables (e.g., Payment_Method, Bike_Model) must be converted to numeric representations.

One-Hot Encoding

One-Hot Encoding is a method of converting categorical variables into a set of binary columns, where each column represents one possible category.

For example, for the Payment_Method feature with categories ['UPI', 'Cash', 'Card'], One-Hot Encoding will create three columns:

- Payment_Method_UPI
- Payment_Method_Cash
- Payment_Method_Card

If a user paid via UPI, only the Payment_Method_UPI column will be 1, and others will be 0.

```
df_encoded = pd.get_dummies(df, columns=['Payment_Method',
'Bike_Model'], drop_first=True)


# Display the encoded dataset
df_encoded.head()
```

Interpretation: This will transform the Payment_Method and Bike_Model columns into binary columns (one for each category). The drop_first = True option is used to avoid the "dummy variable trap," where multicollinearity can occur if all categories are included.

Label Encoding (Alternative Approach)

In some cases, especially with ordinal variables, we might use **Label Encoding**, where each category is assigned a unique integer. For example:

- UPI $\rightarrow$ 0
- Cash $\rightarrow$ 1
- Card $\rightarrow$ 2

```
from sklearn.preprocessing import LabelEncoder

le = LabelEncoder()

df['Payment_Method_Label'] = le.fit_transform(df['Payment_
Method'])

# Display the dataset with encoded labels
df[['Payment_Method', 'Payment_Method_Label']].head()
```

```
Payment_Method    Payment_Method_Label
    0        UPI       2
    1        Wallet    3
    2        Cash      1
    3        Wallet    3
    4        UPI       2
```

Interpretation: Label Encoding is often used for ordinal data, where the categories have a meaningful order (e.g., Low, Medium, High). However, for nominal categorical data (e.g., Payment_Method), **One-Hot Encoding** is generally preferred.

Feature selection and encoding categorical variables are key steps in data preprocessing. **Feature Selection** helps us reduce redundancy and irrelevant features, improving model performance. **Encoding Categorical Variables** transforms non-numeric data into a format that machine learning models can interpret.

- **One-Hot Encoding** is suitable for nominal categories.
- **Label Encoding** is a quick method for ordinal categories but can introduce unintended relationships in some cases.

Both techniques ensure that your dataset is ready for machine learning model training.

5.11 EXPLORATORY DATA ANALYSIS (EDA)

Exploratory Data Analysis (in short EDA) is one of the initial and most important steps of a data science project. It's similar to getting familiar with the story behind the dataset prior to delving into sophisticated analysis or machine learning. The wonderful thing about EDA is that it allows you to discover patterns, detect outliers, and have insights that lead the way towards the direction of your analysis.

This section, we'll guide you through the significance and role of EDA, the tools available to you for doing it, and some of the standard techniques applied to analyze datasets. We'll apply the process to the Penguins dataset from seaborn. This dataset is ideal because it has multiple features such as species, bill length, and flipper length that we can visualize and analyze.

5.11.1   Purpose and Importance of EDA

EDA is similar to the "diagnostic scan" of your data - it reveals problems that are not obvious and inform all the next steps of your data science or machine learning project. If you skip EDA, it would be almost like prescribing a drug with a diagnosis.

The primary aim of EDA is to probe the data visually and statistically. In doing this, you can:

- **Identify patterns:** Understand trends and structures in your data.
- **Spot anomalies:** Find outliers or incorrect data points that might skew the analysis.
- **Get to know the variables:** Understand the relationships between different variables.

5.11.2   Why is EDA Important?

1. **Data Quality Check:** EDA helps identify missing, inconsistent, or incorrect data that could mislead your analysis.

2. **Better Decision-Making:** By understanding the data, you can choose the right preprocessing, algorithms, and modeling strategies.

3. **Feature Understanding:** It allows you to evaluate the distribution and importance of variables, and detect multicollinearity or skewness.

4. **Hypothesis Generation:** Helps formulate meaningful hypotheses or insights that can be tested later using statistical or machine learning models.

5. **Visualization for Communication:** Plots and summaries from EDA make it easier to explain data characteristics to stakeholders or teammates.

5.11.3   Understanding Data Distributions and Patterns

To demonstrate this effectively, we'll use a synthetic dataset we created that mimics the digital lifestyle of Gen Z users, capturing screen time, app usage, sleep hours, and more. This makes the learning process not only relevant but also relatable and fun for the new-age learner.

Setting up the Dataset

We created the dataset using Python and saved it as a CSV named genz_activity_data.csv.

```python
import pandas as pd
import numpy as np
import random

np.random.seed(42)

# Generate synthetic Gen Z behavior dataset
n = 150
data = {
    'Age': np.random.randint(18, 25, size=n),
    'Daily_Screen_Time_hrs': np.random.normal(6, 1.5,
size=n).round(1),
    'Productivity_App_Usage_hrs': np.random.normal(2, 0.5,
size=n).round(1),
    'Preferred_Payment': np.random.choice(['UPI', 'Card',
'Cash'], size=n, p=[0.6, 0.3, 0.1]),
    'Top_Social_App': np.random.choice(['Instagram', 'Snap-
chat', 'YouTube', 'WhatsApp'], size=n),
    'Weekly_Online_Spend_USD': np.random.normal(75, 20,
size=n).round(2),
    'Sleep_Hours': np.random.normal(7, 1, size=n).round(1)
}

df = pd.DataFrame(data)

df.to_csv('genz_activity_data.csv', index=False)

df.head()
```

5.12   COMMON TECHNIQUES IN EDA

5.12.1   Univariate Analysis

Histogram: Online Spending

```python
sns.histplot(df['Weekly_Online_Spend_USD'], kde=True, col-
or='coral')
plt.title('Weekly Online Spending Distribution')
plt.xlabel('USD')
plt.show()
```

You can easily see whether spending is skewed, for example, more users spend between $50 and $100 weekly.

Boxplot: Productivity App Usage

```
sns.boxplot(y=df['Productivity_App_Usage_hrs'], color='or-
chid')
plt.title('Boxplot of Productivity App Usage')
plt.show()
```

Are people really productive, or do most spend under 2 hours a day on tools like Notion or Google Docs? This helps answer that.

5.12.2 Bivariate Analysis

```
plt.figure(figsize=(10, 6))
sns.heatmap(df.corr(numeric_only=True), annot=True,
cmap='coolwarm')
plt.title('Correlation Matrix')
plt.show()
```

This reveals which features move together. For instance, **daily screen time** might be positively correlated with **online spending**, but negatively correlated with **sleep hours**.

Scatterplot: Sleep vs Productivity

```
sns.scatterplot(x='Sleep_Hours', y='Productivity_App_Usage_
hrs', data=df)
plt.title('Sleep vs Productivity App Usage')
plt.show()
```

You might expect more sleep leads to higher productivity—or not. Let the data speak.

5.12.3 Multivariate Analysis

```
sns.pairplot(df, hue='Top_Social_App')
plt.suptitle('Pairplot of Gen Z Digital Behavior', y=1.02)
plt.show()
```

This multi-dimensional plot helps us spot patterns between every numeric pair of variables. The hue adds more insight based on app preference.

5.13 WHAT IS THE USE OF EDA FOR A DATA SCIENTIST?

EDA is the most important phase in any data science or machine learning project. It is the method of carefully going through the dataset by means of statistical summaries, visualizations, and correlation patterns to uncover the underlying trends, identify anomalies, and find out relationships between variables. EDA provides a Data Scientist with insights that inform feature engineering, model choice, and even business decision-making. Without good EDA, the danger is modeling on noisy, biased, or poorly known data—and consequently weak results.

Avoiding Exploratory Data Analysis (EDA) jeopardizes a data science project considerably. Without it, you're likely to lose out on unsuspected patterns, outliers, and missing values which will skew the performance of your model. Including unnecessary or confounding features easily happens, misunderstandings about the type of the data occur, or data leakage traps are avoided—resulting in incorrect forecasts and bad decision-making. EDA assists you in grasping the data structure and quality prior to modeling, and it is therefore an essential initial step in any data-driven process. In short, without EDA, you're speculating—not analyzing.

EDA is generally done after cleaning and collecting data, but prior to modeling or algorithmic processing. It is a test for diagnosing the dataset that allows one to ask the right questions and formulate the problem correctly. In short, EDA is where evidence meets intuition—an intersection of statistics, creativity, and domain expertise.

EDA Tools Across Languages and Platforms

Platform/Language	Tool/Library	Strengths
Python	pandas, matplotlib, seaborn, pandas-profiling, plotly.	Rich ecosystem, integration with ML libraries, interactivity.
R	ggplot2, dplyr, tidyverse, DataExplorer, plotly.	Excellent for statistics, elegant plots.
Excel/Power BI	Pivot Tables, Charts, Power Query, DAX.	Business-friendly, low-code visual analysis.
Tableau	Tableau Desktop & Public.	Drag-and-drop visual exploration, dashboards.
SAS	PROC UNIVARIATE, PROC CORR.	Used in enterprises, advanced statistical EDA.

Wrap-up

 Finding significant insights begins with understanding the data. This chapter explains the various forms of data, their sources, and their structures, which serve as the cornerstone of all analytical work. In order to uncover patterns and get data ready for modeling, you will discover how data is gathered, cleaned, transformed, and examined. Armed with these ideas, you will be able to evaluate the quality of the data, design practical features, and conduct efficient exploratory data analysis, which is the first step in any data science project.

QUESTIONS FOR PRACTICE

1. Explain the difference between primary, secondary, and tertiary sources of data. Give examples for each.   *Anna University, 2022*

2. Define structured, semi-structured, and unstructured data. How does their storage differ? *Vellore Institute of Technology, 2021*

3. Describe nominal, ordinal, discrete, and continuous data types with real-life examples. *SRM Institute of Science and Technology, 2023*

4. What is data collection? Explain the key terms and challenges involved in collecting data in Data Science projects. *Amity University, 2022*

5. Discuss data privacy and consent considerations during data collection in the context of Indian regulations. *IIT Bombay, 2022*

6. Explain missing data, inconsistent data, duplicate data, and outliers. How can these issues be identified? *Manipal University, 2021*

7. Describe techniques for handling missing and inconsistent data. Provide examples for each technique. *BMS College of Engineering, 2023*

8. Explain the difference between data normalization and standardization. Discuss Min-Max scaling and Z-Score normalization.

   Anna University, 2022

9. What is feature engineering? Explain encoding of categorical variables with an example. *Amrita Vishwa Vidyapeetham, 2021*

10. Define Exploratory Data Analysis (EDA). Discuss univariate and bivariate analysis with examples. *IIT Delhi, 2023*

6

Data Visualization

6.1 DATA VISUALIZATION: AN OVERVIEW

6.1.1 What is Data Visualization and Why is it Important?

Displaying data through visual aids such as maps, graphs, and charts is data visualization. It transforms numerical, higher-dimensional, or voluminous data into a visual form that can be easily interpreted. The data visualization software itself carries out certain enhancements or ensures automated accurate visual communication. The visual representation's purpose is to formulate some actionable insights from the raw data.

The raw data are tough to work with and comprehend. Therefore, data scientists duly clean and prepare the data, provide a visualized form, so decision-makers can associate the data to each other and identify any background trend or pattern. It gives data visualization stories that best honed business intelligence, strategic planning, and data-driven decision-making.

6.1.2 Data Visualization in Data Science

The story is the reason why data visualizations are done. The data scientist talks to multiple stakeholders about what they need to do with data analysis. For instance, they might need to track key performance indicators or forecast sales volumes. Data scientists and business users work together to determine the story they need the data to convey to them.

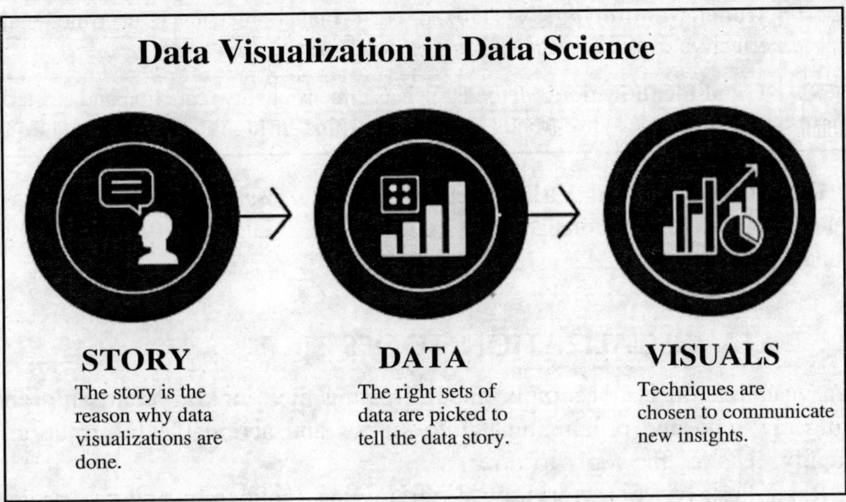

Data

Data analysts then pick the right sets of data which will assist them in telling the data story. They transform raw data into proper formats, prepare the data for analysis, strip out outliers, and conduct further analysis. Upon data preparation, they schedule various ways of visualization.

Visuals

Data scientists next choose the visualization techniques most appropriate to communicate new insights. They make charts and graphs pointing out major data points and breaking down complex sets of data.

6.1.3   The Role of Data Visualization in Data Science

Data visualization is a key aspect of data science because it helps to convert complex raw data in a visual representation that can be comprehended and interpreted such as charts and graphs. The known advantage of this, is that it adds to understanding, exposes the hidden patterns in the data and helps communicate to both technical and non-technical audience. The following Table shows a number of advantages:

	**Increased Clarity:** Visualization makes big and messy datasets more accessible so that pattern detection happens in a shorter time with quicker insight extraction.
	**Pattern Detection:** Visualizations such as scatter plots, heatmaps, and histograms assist in the detection of correlations, clusters and outliers.

(Contd.)

	**Effective Communication:** Visualizations close the gap between decision-makers and data scientists, enhancing understanding and impact.
	**Model Monitoring:** Visualized performance metrics over time enable effective evaluation and tuning of machine learning models.
	**Trend Identification:** Methods such as dimensionality reduction and clustering uncover underlying trends and relationships in high-dimensional data.

Data Cleaning and Validation: Visual aids assist in detecting missing values, outliers, and inconsistencies, guaranteeing data quality and reliability of analysis.

6.2 DATA VISUALIZATION TOOLS

Data visualization is not simply about creating nice looking charts-it's about taking raw data and organizing it into stories and actionable information. In actuality, it takes the tools to do it.

Regardless of your workflow programming inclination and the project's complexity, we can categorize visualization tools into two general categories:

Code-based Tools	*GUI Tools*
Provide low-level control and embedding into data pipelines.	Works well with drag-and-drop visual analysis, dashboards, and business reporting.
Examples • Matplotlib • Seaborn • Plotly • ggplot2	**Examples** • Tableau • Power BI

Each tool is designed for a certain type of task; some tools are best-suited for customization and automation, while others are more geared towards rapid and interactive visual exploration. The following sections will introduce these tools through hands-on examples, highlighting the key features that will help you choose the best one for your data storytelling needs.

6.2.1 Python Libraries: Matplotlib, Seaborn, Plotly

Python is favourite among data scientists because of its rich ecosystem. Python visualization libraries range from the low-level drawing libraries to the high-level interactive dashboards.

Matplotlib

Matplotlib is the base plotting library for Python. It provides low-level control over plot components (axes, grids, labels, markers) and is thus best for creating specialized visualizations from scratch. It is the base 2D plotting library for Python. It provides complete control over all features of a plot and is best for low-level customization.

Core Concepts	*Use Case*
<ul><li>Object-oriented structure: figures, axes, and artists.</li><li>Render layer-by-layer similar to constructing a painting.</li><li>Static plots good for publications and reports.</li></ul>	<ul><li>Ideal for developers who desire lexibility.</li><li>Ideal for plot embedding in PDFs or apps.</li></ul>

How to Code?

```
pip install matplotlib
import matplotlib.pyplot as plt


# x-values: [1, 2, 3]
# y-values: [4, 5, 6]
plt.plot([1, 2, 3], [4, 5, 6])   # Draws a line between the
points
plt.show()                       # Displays the plot
```

Explanation:

- `import matplotlib.pyplot as plt` imports the plotting module.
- `plt.plot()` creates a line plot using X and Y values.
- `plt.show()` pops up a window to display the plot.

Think of `plt.plot()` like drawing a basic line chart by hand—you tell it what points to connect, and it draws the line.

Seaborn

Seaborn builds on top of Matplotlib that offer a higher-level interface for statistical plots with fewer lines of code and better default aesthetics.

Core Concepts	*Use Case*
<ul><li>Works directly with Pandas DataFrames.</li><li>Encodes statistical relationships between variables.</li><li>Automates axis labeling, color palettes, and plot types.</li></ul>	<ul><li>Useful in EDA (Exploratory Data Analysis).</li><li>Great for quickly uncovering relationships in data.</li></ul>

How to Code?

```
import seaborn as sns
import matplotlib.pyplot as plt

sns.histplot([1, 2, 2, 3])
plt.show()# Displays the plot
```

Explanation:

- `sns.histplot()` creates a histogram—a bar chart of frequency.
- It automatically bins values (like how many 2s there are).
- `plt.show()` is still required to display it.

Think of `plt.plot()` like drawing a basic line chart by hand—you tell it what points to connect, and it draws the line.

Plotly (Python)

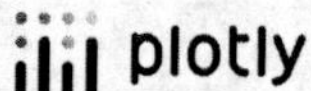

Plotly presents a new paradigm—interactivity as a default. It's designed for web contexts and is capable of zooming, panning, and tooltips out of the box.

Core Concepts	*Use Case*
• Declarative plotting: plots are defined via JSON-like structures. • Browser-based rendering (via D3.js/ WebGL). • Integrates well with Dash for full-stack data apps.	• Ideal for dashboards and presentations. • Preferred when user interaction with data is required.

How to Code?

```
pip install plotly
import plotly.express as px

# Creates a basic scatter plot (X vs Y)
fig = px.scatter(x=[1, 2, 3], y=[4, 5, 6])
fig.show()  # Opens the plot in your web browser
```

Explanation:

- `px.scatter()` makes a scatter plot of *X* vs *Y*.
- `fig.show()` opens an interactive window in your default browser.

Think of `plt.plot()` like drawing a basic line chart by hand—you tell it what points to connect, and it draws the line.

6.2.2 R Libraries: ggplot2, Plotly

R has been the statistical computing powerhouse for decades. Its visualization libraries are especially tuned to **statistical rigor** and **layered composition** of graphics.

ggplot2

 ggplot2 is based on the Grammar of Graphics, which conceptualizes every chart as a set of components—data, aesthetics, geometries, scales, and layers.

Core Concepts	Use Case
• Declarative syntax: you describe what to show, not how. • Layered grammar: add elements one by one (+ operator). • Strong default settings for statistical data.	• Widely used in academic and scientific communities. • Encourages thinking in terms of data structure and semantics.

How to Code?

```
install.packages("ggplot2")
library(ggplot2)

# Create data frame with x and y
ggplot(data.frame(x = c(1, 2, 3), y = c(4, 5, 6)), aes(x,
y)) + geom_point()
```

Explanation:

- `data.frame(...)` creates a small table of data.
- `aes(x, y)` sets up the *X* and *Y* axes.
- `geom_point()` adds points (scatter plot) as a graphical layer.

Plotly (R)

 Plotly for R extends ggplot2 into the realm of interactivity. It supports both direct plotting and ggplotly() conversions.

Core Concepts	Use Case
• Built on the same engine as Plotly in Python. • Bridges static ggplot2 visualizations into web-ready formats. • Provides a Shiny-compatible interface for interactivity.	• Perfect for those who want to build R Shiny apps. • Allows R users to create professional-grade interactive visuals.

How to Code?

```r
install.packages("plotly")
library(plotly)

# Scatter plot with Plotly
plot_ly(x = ~c(1, 2, 3), y = ~c(4, 5, 6), type = 'scatter',
mode = 'markers')
```

Explanation:

- `plot_ly()` creates an interactive plot.
- `type = 'scatter'` means it's a scatter plot.
- `mode = 'markers'` specifies that it should show dots (not lines).

6.2.3 Tableau and Power BI

For users who favor a visual interface to code, the current leading tools are Tableau and Power BI. These GUI-oriented apps enable users to build complex dashboards through drag-and-drop, as well as having the ability to connect and integrate data pipelines and business logic.

Tableau

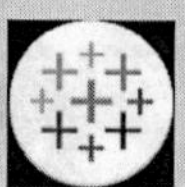

Tableau is built around the philosophy of visual exploration. It lets users drill down into data using filters, hierarchies, and interactive elements—without writing any code.

Core Concepts	*Use Case*
• Workbook-based structure (sheets, dashboards, stories).	• Common in business intelligence, analytics teams.
• Visual drag-and-drop interface for dimensions/measures.	• Great for storytelling and self-service data analysis.
• Extract-based and live connections to data.	

Power BI

Power BI, a Microsoft product, is deeply integrated with the Microsoft ecosystem (Excel, Azure, SQL Server), offering strong enterprise-grade capabilities.

Core Concepts	Use Case
• Uses DAX (Data Analysis Expressions) for custom logic.	• Enterprise reporting and operational dashboards.
• Seamless integration with MS Office tools.	• Strong candidate for Excel users transitioning to BI.
• Includes Power Query for data transformation.	

Visualization Tools: Comparison

Tool	Language/ platform	Code required	Ideal for
Matplotlib	Python	✓ Yes	Custom, scientific plotting
Seaborn	Python	✓ Yes	Statistical exploration
Plotly (Py)	Python	✓ Yes	Interactive dashboards
ggplot2	R	✓ Yes	Statistical/academic plots
Tableau	GUI	✗ No	Web-ready visuals in R
	GUI (MS)	✗ (DAX)	Storytelling with visual drag-n-drop
Power BI	GUI (MS)	✗ (DAX)	Enterprise reporting and analytics

6.3 EXPLORING DIFFERENT TYPES OF VISUALIZATIONS

Data visualization is a key component of any data analysis enterprise. It allows us to see trends, identify outliers, and understand the relationships between factors in the data that we can't see just by looking at the numbers. Different visualizations are better suited for different data and questions you are asking.

The chart below illustrates a comprehensive taxonomy of types of visualizations that are useful in Data Science for exploring, analyzing, and communicating your insights with the data. While the chart provides a quick visualization of a lot of types of visualizations, we will illustrate some of most commonly used visualizations below, recognizing that we cannot possibly discuss all of the visualizations in this format.

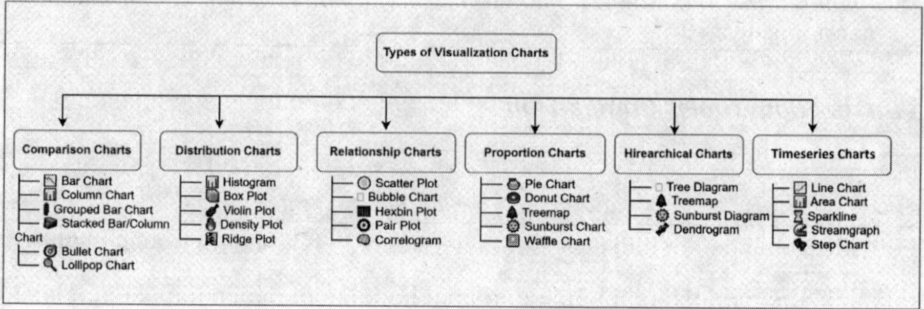

Creating Synthetic Dataset: Customer Behavior Snapshot

Here is a quick overview of the dataset we'll use throughout this article. It contains **300 customer records**, and each row represents one customer.

Column Name	Description
Age	Age of the customer
Gender	Male or Female
Spending Score	A score (1–100) indicating how much a customer typically spends
Annual Income	Customer's estimated yearly income (in local currency)
Customer Segment	Category like Budget, Mid-range, or Premium
Visit Frequency	How many times the customer visits per month
Satisfaction Level	Rating between 1 and 5 based on surveys
Days Since Last Purchase	Number of days since the last purchase

Code Example

```python
import pandas as pd
import numpy as np

# Set a seed for reproducibility
np.random.seed(42)

# Number of samples
n = 300
```

```python
# Create the dataset
df = pd.DataFrame({
'Age': np.random.randint(18, 70, size=n),
'Gender': np.random.choice(['Male', 'Female'], size=n),
'Spending Score': np.random.randint(1, 101, size=n),
'Annual Income': np.random.randint(20000, 120000, size=n),
'Customer Segment': np.random.choice(['Budget', 'Mid-range',
'Premium'], size=n, p=[0.4, 0.4, 0.2]),
'Visit Frequency': np.random.poisson(3, size=n),
'Satisfaction Level': np.round(np.random.uniform(1, 5,
size=n), 1),
'Days Since Last Purchase': np.random.randint(0, 180, size=n)
})

# Display the first few rows
df.head()
```

Output

	Age	Gender	Spending Score	Annual Income	Customer Segment	Visit Frequency	Satisfaction Level	Days Since Last Purchase
0	56	Female	94	33456	Mid-range	5	4.2	103
1	69	Male	23	76397	Mid-range	1	3.3	22
2	46	Male	10	58765	Budget	3	3.6	8
3	32	Male	69	54816	Budget	0	2.0	33
4	60	Male	100	65106	Mid-range	1	1.9	173

This code generates a synthetic customer dataset of 300 entries with attributes like age, gender, income, spending score, and satisfaction level using NumPy's random functions. It then stores the data in a pandas DataFrame and displays the first few rows.

6.3.1 Bar Chart

What is a Bar Chart? 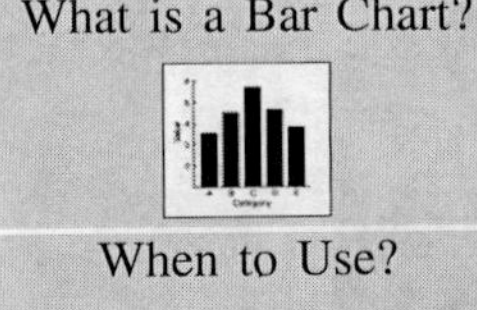	A Bar chart represents categorical data by rectangular shaped bars, with each bar's height/length showing the occurrence of each category in the dataset. It is used to understand how the data is spread across different groups.
When to Use?	• You have categorical variables. • You want to compare the frequency of category. • You want to identify imbalance or pattern in the size of groups.

Below example craetes a bar chart that shows the count of customers by gender from a dataset (df), using Seaborn for styling and plotting.

```python
import matplotlib.pyplot as plt
import seaborn as sns
sns.set(style="whitegrid")
plt.figure(figsize=(6, 4))
sns.countplot(x='Gender', data=df, palette='pastel')

plt.title('Customer Count by Gender')
plt.xlabel('Gender')
plt.ylabel('Number of Customers')

# Show plot
plt.tight_layout()
plt.show()
```

Code	Explanation
`sns.set(style="whitegrid")`	Sets the overall visual style of the plot to include a white background with a grid.
`plt.figure(figsize=(6, 4))`	Creates a figure with 6 inches width and 4 inches height.
`sns.countplot(x='Gender', data=df, palette='pastel')`	Creates a bar chart showing the count of each unique value in the Gender column from the DataFrame df. The palette='pastel' gives light, soft colors.
`plt.title('Customer Count by Gender')`	Adds a title to the chart.
`plt.xlabel('Gender')`	Labels the x-axis as "Gender".
`plt.ylabel('Number of Customers')`	Labels the y-axis as "Number of Customers".
`plt.tight_layout()`	Automatically adjusts plot elements so nothing is cut off or overlaps.
`plt.show()`	Displays the plot on the screen.

Output

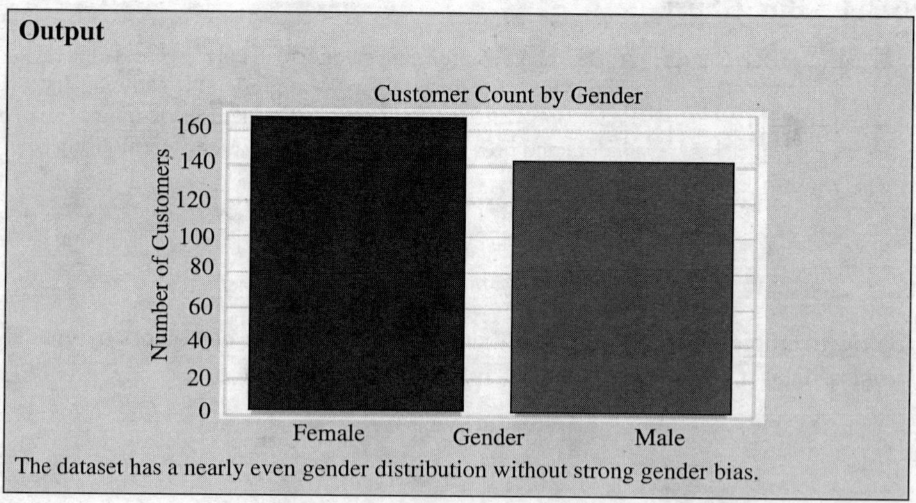

The dataset has a nearly even gender distribution without strong gender bias.

6.3.2 Histogram

What is a Histogram? 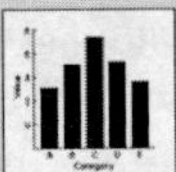	A histogram is one type of bar chart that shows the distribution of numerical data. A histogram divides the data into intervals (known as bins) and counts how many values fall into each bin. The height of each bar represents the frequency of data points within each range.
When to use a Histogram	• You have continuous numerical data • You want to understand the distribution of your data • You need to identify outliers, skewness, or patterns in data
A Histogram Answers	• Is the data normally distributed (bell-shaped curve)? • Are there outliers or peaks? • How is the data spread out across ranges?

Below code creates a **histogram** showing the **distribution of Age** using Seaborn. A histogram helps us understand how frequently age values occur in the dataset.

Code Example

```python
import matplotlib.pyplot as plt
import seaborn as sns

sns.set(style="whitegrid")

plt.figure(figsize=(8, 5))

sns.histplot(df['Age'], bins=20, kde=True, color='skyblue',
edgecolor='black')

plt.title('Distribution of Age', fontsize=16, font-
weight='bold', color='darkblue')
plt.xlabel('Age', fontsize=14, fontweight='bold', col-
or='darkblue')
plt.ylabel('Frequency', fontsize=14, fontweight='bold', col-
or='darkblue')

plt.tight_layout()
plt.show()
```

Code Example

Code	Explanation
`sns.histplot(df['Age'], bins=20, kde=True, color='skyblue', edgecolor='black')`	Creates a histogram from the Age column in the DataFrame df. Each parameter customizes how the plot looks and behaves. See breakdown below.

Parameter	Explanation
`df['Age']`	This selects the Age column from the dataset df.
`bins=20`	Divides the age range into 20 equal-sized intervals (bins). Each bar shows how many people fall into that age range.
`kde=True`	Adds a smooth curve (Kernel Density Estimate) over the histogram to show distribution trend.
`color='skyblue'`	Sets the color of the bars to a sky-blue shade.
`edgecolor='black'`	Adds black borders around each bar, making them more distinguishable.

Output

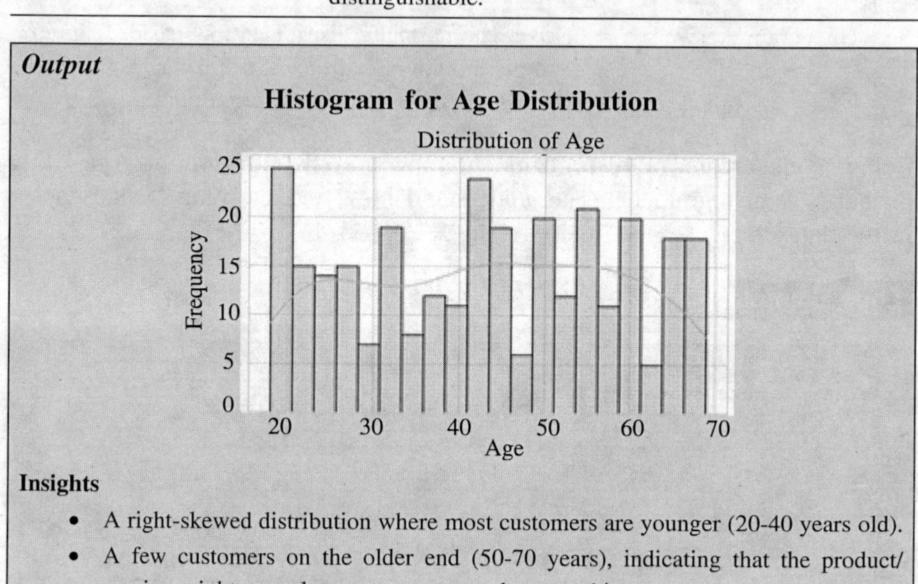

Insights

- A right-skewed distribution where most customers are younger (20-40 years old).
- A few customers on the older end (50-70 years), indicating that the product/service might appeal more to younger demographics.

6.3.3 Box Plot

What is a Box Plot?	A box plot (also popularly known as box-and-whisker plot) is a graphical representation which displays the distribution of a dataset. It summarizes the data based on five summary statistics: • **Minimum:** The smallest data point in the dataset. • **First Quartile (Q_1):** The 25th percentile, or the median of the lower half of the data. • **Median (Q_2):** The middle value of the dataset. • **Third Quartile (Q_3):** The 75th percentile, or the median of the upper half of the data. • **Maximum:** The largest data point in the dataset, excluding outliers.

When to use?	• You want to visualize the distribution of numerical data. • You need to identify outliers and the spread of the data. • You need to compare distributions across.
A Histogram Answers	• You want to visualize the distribution of numerical data. • You need to identify outliers and the spread of the data. • You need to compare distributions across.
How to Read a Box Plot?	When you look at a box plot, you should be able to interpret the following: • The box represents the interquartile range (IQR), that includes 50% of the data, between the first and third quartiles (Q_1 and Q_3). • The line inside the box is the median (Q_2), which divides the data into two halves. • The whiskers (lines extending from the box) represent the range of data, excluding outliers. The whiskers typically extend to 1.5 times the IQR. • Any data points which are outside the whiskers are actually outliers and are plotted as individual points.

Let's create a **Sales Data** dataset and visualize the **Sales Amount** distribution across different **Customer Segments** using a box plot.

Code Example

```python
import pandas as pd
import numpy as np

np.random.seed(42)

# Generate synthetic data
n = 1000
data = {
    'Sales Amount': np.random.randint(100, 5000, size=n),
    'Profit': np.random.randint(50, 1000, size=n),
    'Customer Segment': np.random.choice(['Budget', 'Mid-
range', 'Premium'], size=n),
    'Region': np.random.choice(['North', 'South', 'East',
'West'], size=n),
    'Product Category': np.random.choice(['Electronics',
'Furniture', 'Clothing'], size=n)
}

df = pd.DataFrame(data)

# Display first few rows of the dataset
df.head()
```

	Sales Amount	Profit	Customer Segment	Region	Product Category
0	960	205	Premium	West	Furniture
1	3872	931	Mid-range	East	Furniture
2	3192	518	Premium	South	Furniture
3	566	98	Mid-range	East	Electronics
4	4526	898	Mid-range	West	Clothing

Now that we have our dataset, let's visualize the Sales Amount distribution across the Customer Segment using a box plot. This will allow us to see how the sales are spread out and if there are any outliers based on different customer segments.

```python
import matplotlib.pyplot as plt
import seaborn as sns

sns.set(style="whitegrid")

plt.figure(figsize=(8, 5))

# Create the box plot for Sales Amount distribution by Customer Segment
sns.boxplot(x='Customer Segment', y='Sales Amount', data=df,
palette='Set3')

# Add chart title and labels
plt.title('Sales Amount Distribution by Customer Segment',
fontsize=16, fontweight='bold', color='darkblue')
plt.xlabel('Customer Segment', fontsize=14, font-
weight='bold', color='darkblue')
plt.ylabel('Sales Amount ($)', fontsize=14, font-
weight='bold', color='darkblue')

# Show plot
plt.tight_layout()
plt.show()
```

What this box plot tells us:

- **X-Axis (Customer Segment):** These are the categories you're comparing: Premium, Mid-range, Budget.
- **X-Axis (Customer Segment):** Tells you how much money was spent.
- **The Box (Rectangle):**

  ◆ Represents the middle 50% of the data (called the Interquartile Range, or IQR).

  ◆ Bottom of box = 25th percentile (Q_1) $\rightarrow$ 25% of data points are below this.

  ◆ Top of box = 75th percentile (Q_3) $\rightarrow$ 75% of data points are below this.

  ◆ So, the height of the box shows how spread out the "middle half" of the sales amounts are.

A **taller box** means more variability among typical sales; a **shorter box** means most people spend around the same.

- The Line Inside the Box:

  ◆ This is the **Median (50th percentile)**—the **middle value** of the data.

  ◆ 50% of values are below it, 50% are above.

It helps you see where the center of the spending is for each group. If it's not centered in the box, the data is **skewed**.

- The "Whiskers" (Vertical Lines Above and Below the Box):

  ◆ These show the **range of the data**, but only up to a point:

  ◆ Lower whisker: smallest data point within 1.5 × IQR below the 25th percentile.

  ◆ Upper whisker: largest data point within 1.5 × IQR above the 75th percentile.

If whiskers are longer in one direction, the data is more **spread out** in that direction.

- Outliers (Not Visible in This Plot):

  ◆ Dots outside the whiskers (if any) would be considered outliers—values that are unusually high or low.

  ◆ Since they're not visible here, it means no extreme sales amounts fell outside the 1.5 × IQR range.

6.3.4 Scatter Plot

What is a Scatter Plot?	One of the most effective visualizations for identifying relationships between two numeric variables is a scatter plot. Each dot on the scatter plot represents a data point (or row) where: • The x-axis represents one variable (independent or input). • The y-axis represents the other variable (dependent or output). Scatter plots assist in identifying trends, clusters, correlations, and outliers, making them a critical part of Exploratory Data Analysis (EDA). Scatter plots are useful for identifying trends, identifying relationships, and detecting possible detractors (e.g., losing customers), and when combined with shape encoding they also enhance the discoverability and accessibility of the visualization as well.
When to Use?	• You want to check if two numerical variables are **correlated**. • You want to spot **patterns** across different categories. • You're exploring **causal relationships** (e.g., does more spending lead to higher profit?).

We simulate a retail scenario with customers belonging to **three segments—** Budget, Mid-rang-e, and Premium. Premium customers tend to generate **higher sales and profit**, whereas Budget customers may even cause **losses**.

Code Example

To explore correlation visually, we simulate a dataset that reflects **real-world business logic**—particularly, sales and profit patterns across three customer segments:

• **Budget** (Low-cost, low-profit or even loss)
• **Mid-range** (Moderate sales and profit)
• **Premium** (High-value transactions with high margins)

Step 1: Creating the Dataset

```python
import pandas as pd
import numpy as np

np.random.seed(42)

# Generate synthetic data
n = 150
segments = ['Budget', 'Mid-range', 'Premium']
segment_distribution = np.random.choice(segments, size=n,
p=[0.3, 0.4, 0.3])
sales = []
profit = []
```

```python
for seg in segment_distribution:
    if seg == 'Budget':
        s = np.random.normal(200, 50)
        p = s * np.random.uniform(-0.05, 0.10)
    elif seg == 'Mid-range':
        s = np.random.normal(500, 100)
        p = s * np.random.uniform(0.05, 0.15)
    else:  # Premium
        s = np.random.normal(900, 120)
        p = s * np.random.uniform(0.10, 0.30)
    sales.append(round(s, 2))
    profit.append(round(p, 2))

# Create DataFrame
df = pd.DataFrame({
    'Customer Segment': segment_distribution,
    'Sales Amount': sales,
    'Profit': profit
})
df.head()
```

	Customer Segment	Sales Amount	Profit
0	Mid-range	480.76	31.00
1	Premium	936.19	185.26
2	Premium	1037.14	153.01
3	Mid-range	575.19	70.65
4	Budget	270.14	12.16
...	...	...	...
145	Budget	220.09	17.67
146	Mid-range	522.41	29.98

Step 2: Visualizing with a Scatter Plot

We'll now plot Sales Amount vs Profit, and differentiate customer segments using different shapes:

- Circle (o) for Budget
- Square (s) for Mid-range
- Triangle (^) for Premium

```python
import matplotlib.pyplot as plt

# Define marker shapes for each customer segment
marker_shapes = {
    'Budget': 'o'
```

```python
            # Circle
        'Mid-range': 's'
         # Square
        'Premium': '^'            # Triangle
} # Set figure size and grid

plt.figure(figsize=(10
 7))
plt.grid(True
 linestyle='--'
 alpha=0.6)


# Plot each customer segment using a different shape
for segment
 marker in marker_shapes.items():
        data = df[df['Customer Segment'] == segment]
        plt.scatter(
            data['Sales Amount']
            data['Profit']
            label=segment
            marker=marker
            s=100
            edgecolors='black'
            alpha=0.75
        )
# Labels and title
plt.title('Sales vs Profit by Customer'
 fontsize=16
 fontweight='bold'
 color='darkgreen')
plt.xlabel('Sales Amount ($)'
 fontsize=14)
plt.ylabel('Profit ($)'

 fontsize=14)
plt.legend(title='Customer Segment')
plt.tight_layout()
plt.show()
import matplotlib.pyplot as plt
# Define marker shapes for each customer segment
marker_shapes = {
    'Budget': 'o'

        # Circle
    'Mid-range': 's'

     # Square
    'Premium': '^'            # Triangle
}


# Labels and title
plt.title('Sales vs Profit by Customer Segment (Shapes for
Clarity)'
```

```
 fontsize=16
 fontweight='bold'
 color='darkgreen')
plt.xlabel('Sales Amount ($)'
 fontsize=14)
plt.ylabel('Profit ($)'
 fontsize=14)
plt.legend(title='Customer Segment')
plt.tight_layout()
plt.show()
```

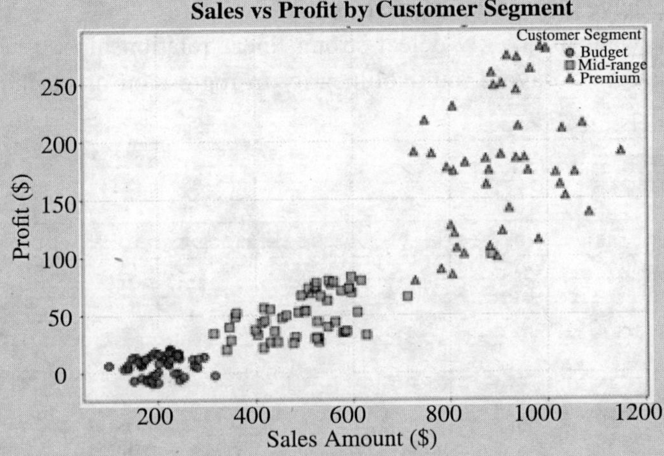

Insight

The scatter plot illustrates the relationship between sales and profit across three customer segments—Budget, Mid-range, and Premium.

- The **Budget** segment (circles) shows low and scattered profit values with some losses, indicating little to no correlation.
- The **Mid-range** segment (squares) displays a moderate positive correlation, where profit gradually increases with sales.
- The **Premium** segment (triangles) demonstrates a strong positive correlation, with profit rising sharply as sales increase.

Overall, the plot reveals that Premium customers contribute the most consistent and high profits, while Budget sales may be less profitable or even loss-making.

6.3.5   Correlation Matrix

A correlation matrix is a square table showing correlation coefficients (typically Pearson's r) between several numeric variables. It tells us how strongly two variables are related and in which direction (positive or negative).

- Values range from –1 to 1:
    - ♦ +1: Perfect positive correlation
    - ♦ –1: Perfect negative correlation
    - ♦ 0: No correlation

This is very helpful in data analysis when selecting features for modeling or detecting multicollinearity.

When to Use a Correlation Matrix

Use it when:

- You have 3 or more numeric features.
- You want to quickly detect strong linear relationships.
- You want to avoid multicollinearity in regression or machine learning models.

Code Example

```python
# Step 1: Import necessary librarieimport pandas as pd
import numpy as np
import seaborn as sns
import matplotlib.pyplot as plt

# Step 2: Create the base synthetic dataset
np.random.seed(42)

# Define customer segments and probabilities
segments = ['Budget', 'Mid-range', 'Premium']
n = 150  # Total records

# Assign random segments
segment_distribution = np.random.choice(segments, size=n,
p=[0.3, 0.4, 0.3])

# Generate Sales and Profit based on segment
sales = []
profit = []
for seg in segment_distribution:
    if seg == 'Budget':
        s = np.random.normal(200, 50)
        p = s * np.random.uniform(-0.05, 0.10)
    elif seg == 'Mid-range':
        s = np.random.normal(500, 100)
        p = s * np.random.uniform(0.05, 0.15)
    else:
        s = np.random.normal(900, 120)
        p = s * np.random.uniform(0.10, 0.30)
    sales.append(round(s, 2))
    profit.append(round(p, 2))
```

```python
df = pd.DataFrame({
    'Customer Segment': segment_distribution,
    'Sales Amount': sales,
    'Profit': profit
})

# Step 3: Add more numeric features
df['Customer Age'] = np.random.normal(35, 10, size=n).as
type(int)
df['Product Rating'] = np.clip(np.random.normal(4, 0.5,
size=n), 1, 5).round(1)
df['Discount Applied'] = np.where(df['Customer Segment'] ==
'Budget',
        np.random.uniform(10, 30,n),
        np.random.uniform(0, 15,n)).d(2)

# Step 4: Compute and visualize the correlation matrix
corr_matrix = df[['Sales Amount', 'Profit', 'Customer Age',
'Product Rating', 'Discount Applied']].corr()

plt.figure(figsize=(10, 7))
sns.heatmap(corr_matrix, annot=True, cmap='coolwarm',
fmt=".2f", linewidths=0.5)
plt.title('Correlation Matrix of Customer Metrics', fon-
tsize=16, fontweight='bold')
plt.tight_layout()
plt.show()
```

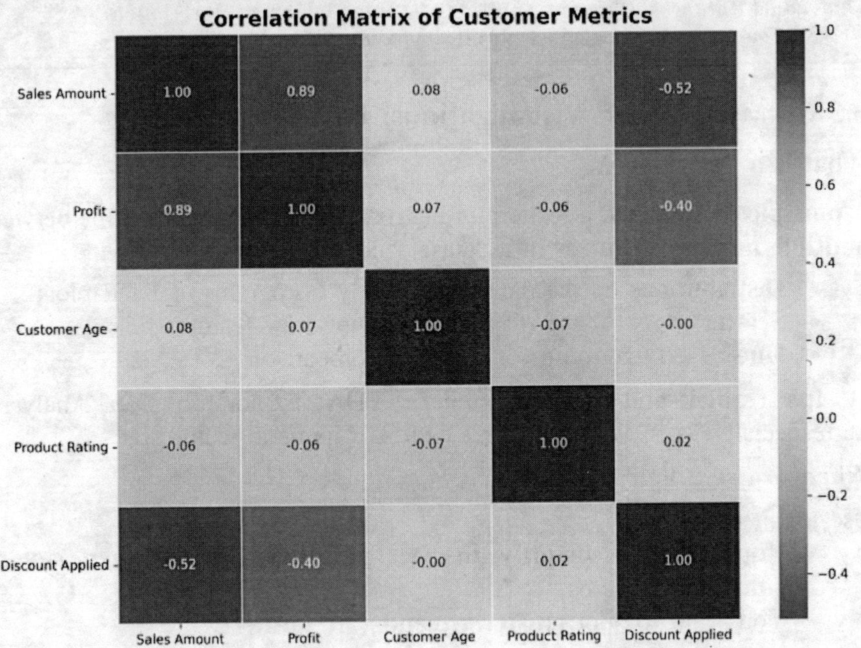

> **Insight**
>
> The **heatmap** visualizes the correlation between different customer metrics. Here is the explanation:
>
> Each cell in the matrix represents the **correlation coefficient** between two variables:
>
> 1. **Sales Amount vs. Profit (0.89 - Strong Positive Correlation)**
>   - Since **Profit is derived from Sales,** this high correlation is expected.
>   - Higher sales generally lead to higher profits, but the exact profit depends on the **profit margin**.
> 2. **Sales Amount vs. Discount Applied (-0.52 - Moderate Negative Correlation)**
>   - **Budget customers receive higher discounts,** while **Premium customers receive lower discounts.**
>   - Since **Budget customers have lower sales,** the correlation between **Sales Amount and Discount Applied** is **negative.**
>   - This means that **higher discounts are associated with lower sales amounts.**
> 3. **Profit vs. Discount Applied (-0.40 - Moderate Negative Correlation)**
>   - Discounts reduce profit margins, but the effect varies across customer segments.
>   - **Premium customers get lower discounts but contribute higher profits, while Budget customers get higher discounts but contribute lower profits.**
>   - This results in a **moderate negative correlation.**
> 4. **Customer Age vs. Product Rating (-0.07 - Weak Negative Correlation)**
>   - Older customers might prefer **higher-rated products,** but the correlation is weak.
>   - This suggests that **age does not strongly influence product ratings.**
> 5. **Sales Amount vs. Product Rating (-0.06 - Weak Negative Correlation)**
>   - Higher-rated products might be **more expensive,** leading to a slight negative correlation.
>   - However, since ratings are **bounded between 1 and 5,** the correlation is not strong.
> 6. **Customer Age vs. Discount Applied (-0.00 - No Correlation)**
>   - This means that **age does not influence discount application.**
> 7. **Product Rating vs. Discount Applied (0.02 - No Significant Correlation)**
>   - Discounts do not significantly affect product ratings.

6.3.6 Multivariate Visualizations: Pair Plots

What is a Pair Plot?

A **pair plot** (also called a scatterplot matrix) shows the **relationships between multiple numeric features** in a dataset, plotted **pairwise**. It provides:

- **Distributions** on the diagonal (usually histograms or KDE plots)
- **Scatter plots** off the diagonal (showing how features relate)
- **Hue-based grouping** for category comparison

It's a **quick and powerful tool** for EDA (Exploratory Data Analysis), especially when you're dealing with 3–6 numeric features.

When to Use a Pair Plot?

Use a pair plot when:

- You want to **visually inspect relationships** between several numerical features.
- You want to spot **clusters, trends, or outliers.**
- You want to see if categories (via hue) separate clearly.

Code Example

```python
import seaborn as sns
import matplotlib.pyplot as plt
import pandas as pd
import numpy as np

# --- Synthetic dataset creation (same as your code) ---
np.random.seed(42)
segments = ['Budget', 'Mid-range', 'Premium']
n = 150
segment_distribution = np.random.choice(segments, size=n, p=[0.3,
0.4, 0.3])

sales, profit = [], []
for seg in segment_distribution:
    if seg == 'Budget':
        s = np.random.normal(200, 50)
        p = s * np.random.uniform(-0.05, 0.10)
    elif seg == 'Mid-range':
        s = np.random.normal(500, 100)
        p = s * np.random.uniform(0.05, 0.15)
    else:
        s = np.random.normal(900, 120)
        p = s * np.random.uniform(0.10, 0.30)
    sales.append(round(s, 2))
    profit.append(round(p, 2))

df = pd.DataFrame({
    'Customer Segment': segment_distribution,
    'Sales Amount': sales,
    'Profit': profit
})
df['Customer Age'] = np.random.normal(35, 10, size=n).astype(int)
df['Product Rating'] = np.clip(np.random.normal(4, 0.5, size=n),
1, 5).round(1)
df['Discount Applied'] = np.where(df['Customer Segment'] == 'Bud-
get',
        np.random.uniform(10, 30, n),
        np.random.uniform(0, 15, n)).round(2)

# --- Plotting ---
sample_df = df.sample(100, random_state=42)

sns.set(style="whitegrid")  # no color palette

plt.figure(figsize=(12, 10))
pairplot = sns.pairplot(
    sample_df,
    vars=['Sales Amount', 'Profit', 'Customer Age', 'Product
Rating', 'Discount Applied'],
    hue='Customer Segment',
    height=2.5,
    plot_kws={'alpha': 0.7, 's': 40},
    palette=['black'],  # force monochrome
    markers=["o", "s", "D"]  # circle, square, diamond for seg-
ments
)
pairplot.fig.suptitle("Pair Plot of Customer Metrics by Segment",
    y=1.02, fontsize=16, fontweight='bold')
plt.savefig("pairplot_customer_metrics.png", dpi=300, bbox_
inches='tight')
plt.show()
```

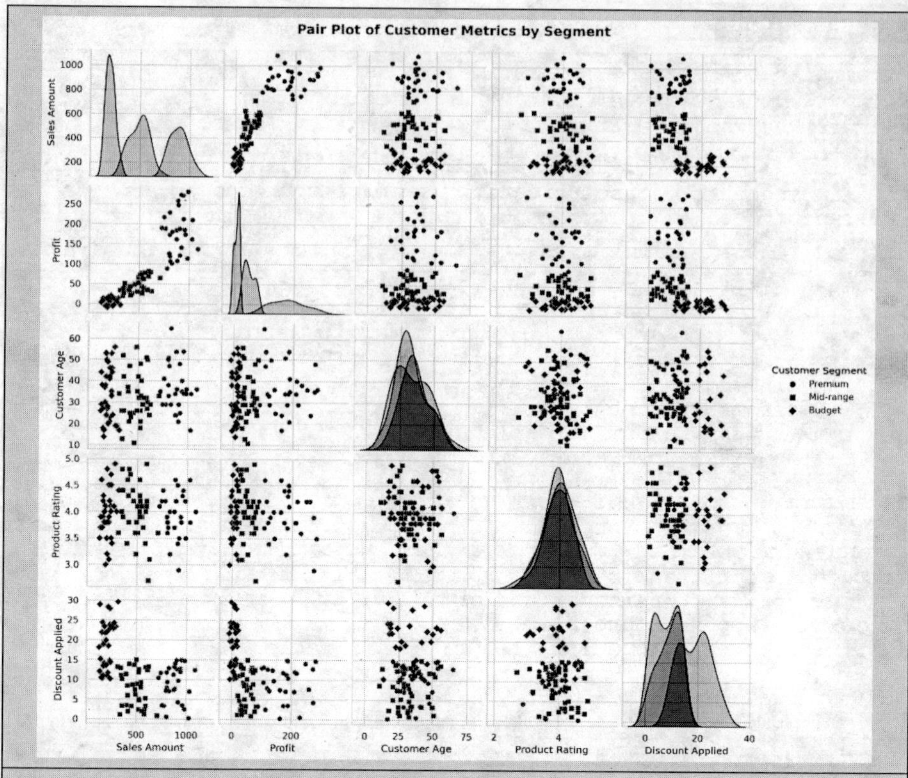

How to Read the Output

- **Diagonals:** Each plot along the diagonal shows the distribution of a feature (histogram. For example, you may observe that Profit is moderately right-skewed, with a few high-profit outliers.
  - For example, you may observe that Profit is moderately right-skewed, with a few high-profit outliers.
- **Off-Diagonals:** These are scatter plots of feature pairs.
  - For instance, Sales Amount vs Profit likely shows a positive trend.
  - Discount Applied vs Profit may show a negative correlation for some segments.
- **Shape (marker type)** shows separation by Customer Segment: Clusters are visibly distinct by shape—triangle (Premium), square (Mid-range), circle (Budget)—it suggests that segment is a useful predictive feature.

6.3.7 Violin Plots

What is a Violin Plot?

A violin plot combines features of a box plot and a Kernel Density Estimate (KDE) plot. It helps you understand both:

- The distribution shape (like a histogram turned sideways)
- The summary statistics (median, quartiles—like a box plot)

It's especially useful when you want to compare distributions across categories and see where most data points are concentrated.

When to Use a Violin Plot?

Use a violin plot when you want to:

- Compare distributions across multiple groups.
- See data spread and concentration more clearly than a box plot.
- Understand skewness and multi-modal distributions (multiple peaks).

Below example code simulates customer sales data by segment and visualizes the distribution of profit across customer segments using a violin plot, helping to compare profitability patterns among Budget, Mid-range, and Premium buyers.

Code Example

```python
import pandas as pd
import numpy as np
import seaborn as sns
import matplotlib.pyplot as plt

# For consistent results
np.random.seed(42)

# Define customer segments and sample size
segments = ['Budget', 'Mid-range', 'Premium']
n = 150

# Assign random customer segments
segment_distribution = np.random.choice(segments, size=n,
p=[0.3, 0.4, 0.3])

# Generate Sales and Profit based on segment
sales = []
profit = []
for seg in segment_distribution:
    if seg == 'Budget':
        s = np.random.normal(200, 50)
        p = s * np.random.uniform(-0.05, 0.10)
    elif seg == 'Mid-range':
        s = np.random.normal(500, 100)
        p = s * np.random.uniform(0.05, 0.15)
    else:  # Premium
        s = np.random.normal(900, 120)
        p = s * np.random.uniform(0.10, 0.30)
    sales.append(round(s, 2))
    profit.append(round(p, 2))
```

```python
# Assemble the DataFrame
df = pd.DataFrame({
    'Customer Segment': segment_distribution,
    'Sales Amount': sales,
    'Profit': profit
})

# Add additional features
df['Customer Age'] = np.random.normal(35, 10, size=n).as-
type(int)
df['Product Rating'] = np.clip(np.random.normal(4, 0.5,
size=n), 1, 5).round(1)
df['Discount Applied'] = np.where(df['Customer Segment'] ==
'Budget',
    np.random.uniform(10, 30, n),
    np.random.uniform(0, 15, n)).round(2)

# Plotting
plt.figure(figsize=(10, 6))
sns.set(style="whitegrid")
sns.violinplot(
    x='Customer Segment',
    y='Profit',
    data=df,
    inner='box',
    scale='count',
    palette='Set2'
)

plt.title('Profit Distribution by Customer Segment', fon-
tsize=16, fontweight='bold')
plt.ylabel('Profit')
plt.xlabel('Customer Segment')
plt.tight_layout()
plt.show()
```

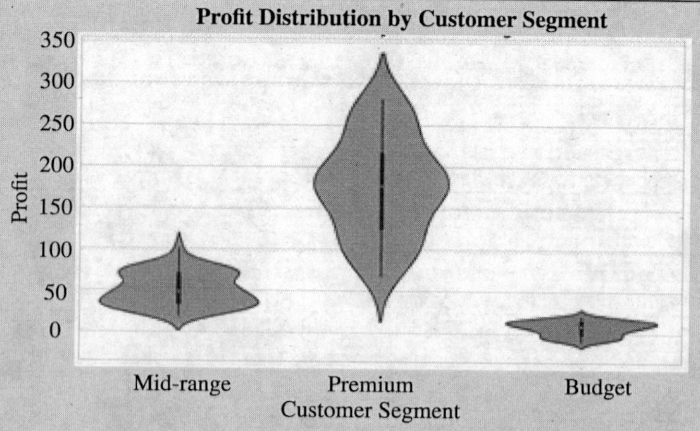

> **Insight**
> The output is a **violin plot** showing the **profit distribution across different customer segments**—*Budget*, *Mid-range*, and *Premium*.
>
> - Each "violin" represents the **distribution density** of profit values within that segment.
> - **Wider sections** of the violin indicate **higher concentration** of data points (i.e., more customers with profits in that range).
> - **Narrower sections** indicate fewer customers at that profit level.
> - Premium-Has the **widest spread and highest profits**
> - **Profitability increases with customer segment level**, with Premium being most lucrative.
> - **Budget** segment is least profitable and carries risk (losses).
> - Violin plots here give a visual summary of **profit consistency and variability** within each segment.

6.3.8   Treemaps

What is a Treemap?

A treemap that displays hierarchical data as a nested rectangles. The size of each rectangle represents a numeric value and optionally, the colour that can show a second variable. It's perfect when you want to compare the parts of a whole at once—like revenue of per product category or the profit of per segment.

When to Use a Treemap?

Use treemaps when:

- You want to show relative sizes of subcategories.
- You want a compact view of all data categories.
- You want to show both value and proportion in one chart.

Example Use Case

We will visualize:

Total Sales by Customer Segment, with color representing average profit.

Code Example

```python
import squarify  # For treemaps
# Summarize the data
treemap_data = df.groupby('Customer Segment').agg({
    'Sales Amount': 'sum',
    'Profit': 'mean'
}).reset_index()
# Normalize values for display
labels = treemap_data['Customer Segment'] + '\nSales: $' +
treemap_data['Sales Amount'].round(0).astype(str)
sizes = treemap_data['Sales Amount']
colors = treemap_data['Profit']
```

```python
# Plot the treemap
plt.figure(figsize=(10, 6))
squarify.plot(
    sizes=sizes,
    label=labels,
    color=sns.color_palette("YlGnBu", len(sizes)),
    alpha=0.8
)

plt.title("Sales by Customer Segment (Color = Avg Profit)",
fontsize=16, fontweight='bold')
plt.axis('off')
plt.tight_layout()
plt.show()
```

This treemap displays three customer segments:

- **Largest area** in the chart, indicating it generates the highest total sales.
- **Color:** Medium tone suggests **moderate average** profit. This segment is contributing significantly to sales with decent profitability.
- **Color:** Lighter shade, which may indicate lower average profit. Suggests this segment is both low in volume and low in profitability.
- **Premium customers** are your most valuable segment — high sales and high profit. Consider focusing marketing and retention strategies here.
- **Mid-range** segment offers a good balance — don't ignore them. Upselling or cross-selling here could boost both sales and profit.
- **Budget** segment contributes the least — low return. It may need targeted strategies if the profit margins are too thin.

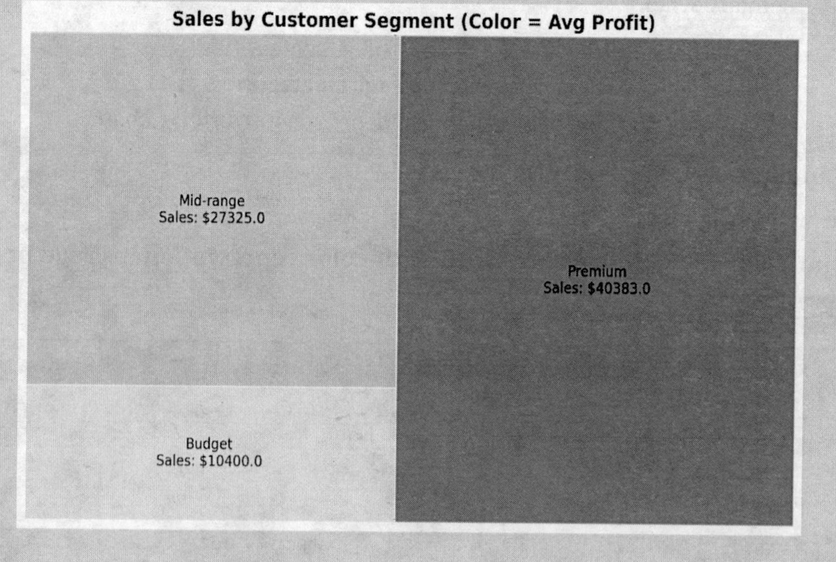

6.3.9 Bubble Chart

A bubble chart is an extension of a scatter plot every data point is represented by a bubble:

- X-axis shows one numeric variable.
- Y-axis shows another.
- Bubble size shows a third variable.
- (Optional) Color can represent a fourth.

It's ideal for visualizing multidimensional relationships in a compact way.

When to Use a Bubble Chart?

Use a bubble chart when:

- You want to visualize three or more variables simultaneously.
- You need to see how volume (size) relates to two other features.
- You want an intuitive overview of clusters and outliers.

As of now, the graphs and plots discussed was non-interactive. Unlike static graphs, interactive visualizations allow users to zoom, pan, filter, and hover over elements, making it easier to explore patterns and details. Below section will demonstrate an interactive bubble chart implementation.

Here's an example of an interesting graph for visualization that's both visually appealing and insightful

- **X-axis:** Number of COVID-19 cases per country.
- **Y-axis:** Number of COVID-19 deaths per country.
- **Bubble size:** Population of the country (or vaccination rate).
- **Bubble color:** Continent or income group.
- **Optional:** Animation over time to see the progression of the pandemic.

Code Example

```python
import plotly.express as px
import pandas as pd

# Sample data frame structure
data = {
    'Country': ['USA', 'India', 'Brazil', 'Russia', 'UK'],
    'Cases': [33000000, 31000000, 20000000, 6000000, 4500000],
    'Deaths': [590000, 410000, 570000, 150000, 128000],
    'Population': [331000000, 1380000000, 213000000,
    146000000, 67000000],
    'Continent': ['North America', 'Asia', 'South America',
    'Europe', 'Europe']
}

df = pd.DataFrame(data)
```

```
fig = px.scatter(df, x='Cases', y='Deaths',
                size='Population', color='Continent',
                hover_name='Country', size_max=60,
                title='COVID-19 Cases vs Deaths by Coun-
                try',
                labels={'Cases': 'Total Cases', 'Deaths':
                'Total Deaths'})
fig.show()
```

Insights

- Countries with higher COVID-19 cases tend to have higher deaths, showing a general positive correlation.
- However, the ratio of deaths to cases can vary, indicating differences in healthcare quality, testing, or reporting.
- Larger bubbles mean bigger populations. A large bubble with relatively fewer cases or deaths might indicate effective containment or under-reporting.
- Countries far from the main cluster (either high deaths despite fewer cases, or vice versa) highlight anomalies.
- These outliers could suggest unique situations like healthcare system collapse, data inaccuracies, or demographic factors.

Wrap-up

Data visualization is more than aesthetic—it's a cognitive bridge between raw data and human understanding. By transforming numbers into visual narratives, it empowers analysts, scientists, and decision-makers to uncover patterns, communicate insights, and drive action with clarity and precision. As we advance into deeper analytical territories, mastering visualization tools and techniques becomes essential for storytelling, exploration, and impactful data-driven decisions.

QUESTIONS FOR PRACTICE

1. Define Data Visualization. Explain why it is important in Data Science projects. *Anna University, 2022*

2. Compare Python libraries (Matplotlib, Seaborn, Plotly) and R libraries (ggplot2, Plotly) for data visualization. Give examples of when each would be used. *Vellore Institute of Technology, 2021*

3. Describe the key features and workflow of Tableau for data visualization. *SRM Institute of Science and Technology, 2023*

4. Explain the difference between a bar chart, histogram, and box plot. Provide a real-world example dataset for each visualization. *Amity University, 2022*

5. What is a scatter plot? How is it used to analyze relationships between two variables? *IIT Bombay, 2022*

6. Describe a correlation matrix. How can it help in identifying relationships in multivariate data? *Manipal University, 2021*

7. Explain multivariate visualizations such as pair plots and violin plots. When would you use each type? *BMS College of Engineering, 2023*

8. Describe a treemap and a bubble chart. Provide a scenario in retail or finance where each can be applied. *Anna University, 2022*

9. List advantages of using Tableau and Power BI for business intelligence and reporting. *Amrita Vishwa Vidyapeetham, 2021*

10. Discuss the role of data visualization in communicating insights from a Data Science model to non-technical stakeholders. *IIT Delhi, 2023*

7

Machine Learning

7.1 MACHINE LEARNING: AN OVERVIEW

7.1.1 What is Machine Learning?

Machine learning (ML) is a branch of artificial intelligence (AI) that specializes in the development of algorithms and statistical models to allow computers to execute tasks without explicit directions. It is a subfield of artificial intelligence that deals with creating algorithms and models that allow computers to learn and make predictions or decisions without direct programming. Thus, rather than depending on your commands, ML systems learn from examples and get better over time through experience.

The process usually involves having you input massive amounts of data into a machine learning algorithm. A data scientist usually develops, tunes, and deploys your models. The ML algorithm processes and discovers patterns, relationships, and trends in the data and applies these findings to create a mathematical model that is capable of predicting, can fuel predictive analytics, or make decisions when it receives new, unseen data.

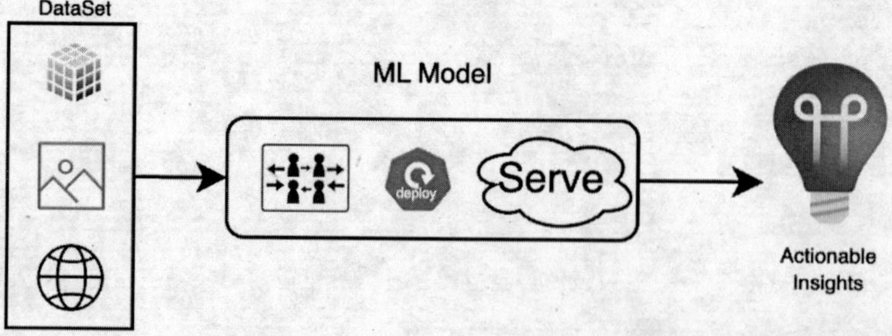

Imagine explaining the difference between cats and dogs to a friend—not by listing features like ear size or tail shape, but by simply showing many pictures of each. Over time, your friend begins to recognize the patterns and tell them apart on their own.

Machine Learning works in the same way. Instead of being explicitly programmed with rules, it is given large amounts of examples, from which it learns patterns and makes decisions independently.

7.1.2 How are ML and Data Science Related?

Machine Learning is a subset of Data Science focused on the creation of predictive models to forecast or identify patterns in data. Data Science covers all aspects of collecting, analyzing, and interpreting data, frequently utilizing machine learning to uncover insights and make automated decisions. Both disciplines collaborate to transform raw data into actionable information.

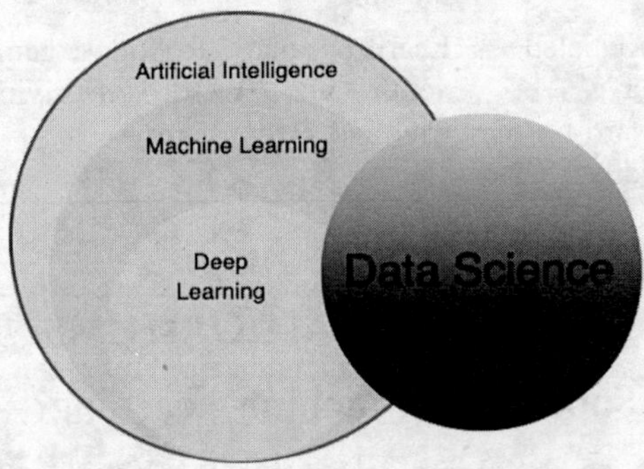

7.1.3 Types of Machine Learning

Machine learning algorithms are broadly divided into four types—supervised learning, unsupervised learning, semi-supervised learning, and reinforcement learning.

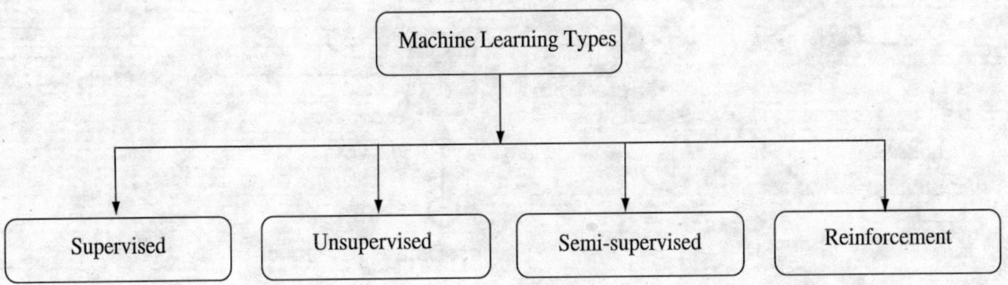

Type	Input Data	Goal	Common Use Cases	Example Algorithms
Supervised Learning	Labeled data (input-output pairs)	Predict outputs for new, unseen inputs	Spam detection, fraud detection, diagnostics	Linear Regression, Decision Trees, SVM
Unsupervised Learning	Unlabeled data	Discover hidden patterns or groupings	Market segmentation, clustering, anomaly detection	K-Means, PCA, Hierarchical Clustering
Semi-Supervised Learning	Small labeled + large unlabeled data	Improve learning accuracy with minimal labeling	Medical imaging, text classification	Modified supervised algorithms
Reinforcement Learning	No labeled data; reward-based feedback	Learn optimal actions via trial and error	Robotics, game AI, self-driving cars	Q-Learning, Deep Q-Networks (DQN), SARSA

7.2 SUPERVISED LEARNING ALGORITHMS

7.2.1 What is Supervised Machine Learning?

Supervised learning as the name indicates is similar to learning with your instructor (supervisor) who supplies answers during the learning process. In supervised machine learning, the machine learns relationships and patterns between the target and input variables using labeled data. The machine applies its learning based on given labeled data to predict new unseen data.

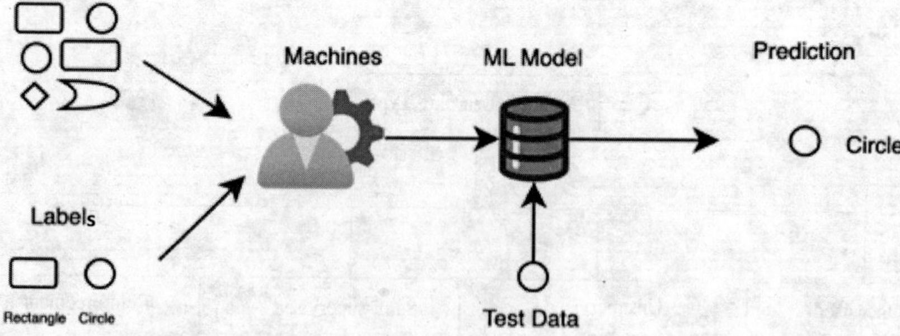

Note: Input variables are also referred to as independent variables or features and target variables are also referred to as dependent variables. Let us take the example of distinguishing between an apple and a banana. The teacher presents you with a number of pictures of the fruits. Below each picture is written whether it is an apple or banana. You see the pictures and their annotations, and gradually you figure out how to tell them apart. This is exactly what happens in supervised learning.

The computer in supervised learning is shown a plethora of examples. Each example consists of data (for example, fruit image) and a label (for example, apple or banana). Over time, the computer learns to give the right label to new data that it had never seen before.

The applications of supervised learning are numerous. For example:

- To know if a message is a spam or not in e-mail services.
- Face detection in photo apps using labelled images.
- Predicting rain or no rain using weather analysis.

In a nutshell, this is how supervised learning basically operates: A teacher shows a student answers during practice, and after the kid has learned enough, he can make a good guess, all by himself!

7.2.2 What is Labelled Data?

Dataset of input-output pairs in which every input is associated with its correct output value. For instance, in a classification problem to label pictures as cat or dog, labelled data would be example pictures and their correct label as a cat or a dog.

Why are input variables referred to as independent variables and target variables are referred to as dependent variables?

This nomenclature originates from the connection of these variables in the training set and the predictive problem being tackled.

- **Independent Variables (Input Variables):** Independent variables are input attributes or features in machine learning models, denoting factors or features thought to have an impact on the outcome (target variable) and are usually unaffected by other variables in the context of the model.
- **Dependent Variable (or Target Variable):** The dependent variable is the variable that the machine learning model needs to predict or estimate using the input variables. It is referred to as "dependent" since its value depends on the independent variables' values. The model learns to predict the dependent variable using patterns and relationships identified in the independent variables.

7.2.3 How Supervised Learning Works?

Indeed, you are training on data up to October 2023. An example of Supervised Learning is picture demonstration with cats and dogs: Suppose you are learning the difference between two animals—a cat and a dog—at the initial stage. You would, however, know little about them at first. If, however, your instructor was to share many pictures with you, one showing a cat and the other a dog, they might be able to help you by specifying that it shows a cat or a dog.

So, in Supervised Learning, just like that! Here is how it works:

- **Training with Examples:** To get the same, the teacher gives examples of either cats or dogs; a computer gets lots of such examples too. These are called labeled data because each picture is given a label, i.e., a cat or a dog.
- **Learning the Pattern:** The more you see, the more you get to recognize patterns. For instance, cats are usually known to have pointed ears, while dogs are rounder faces. A computer does the same thing; it generally checks the data and figures out the patterns.
- **Making Predictions:** As soon as you've learned enough, if the teacher shows you a new picture of an animal, you can guess which animal it is—a cat or a dog. The computer does this too; it looks at new, previously unseen data and tries to come up with an educated guess on the basis of the learned patterns.
- **Feedback and Improvement:** If you call a cat a dog or do something as ignorant, the teacher will say it is not so. Thus, the mistake is done, and learning occurs. Also, in Supervised Learning, the computer gets feedback and gradually improves in the predictions.

7.2.4 Key Characteristics of Supervised Learning

Characteristic	Description
Labeled Data	Uses input data that is paired with the correct output (labels).
Teacher-like Learning	Learns with guidance—just like a student learns with answers from a teacher.
Prediction Focused	The goal is to make accurate predictions on new, unseen data.
Training Phase	The model learns from a training dataset that includes both inputs and outputs.
Common Algorithms	Examples include Linear Regression, Decision Trees, and Support Vector Machines.
Applications	Spam detection, image classification, speech recognition, and more.

7.2.5 Applications of Supervised Learning in Real-World Scenarios

Unique Application Area	Description	Example
Crop Disease Detection	Identifies plant diseases from leaf images labeled with disease types	Mobile apps helping farmers detect crop issues
Loan Approval in Banks	Predicts if a loan applicant is likely to repay based on labeled financial data	Automated loan risk assessment systems
Wildlife Monitoring	Classifies animal species from camera trap images using labeled examples.	AI in national parks to track animal populations
Industrial Defect Detection	Detects defects in products using labeled images of faulty vs. non-faulty items	Quality control in manufacturing
Personalized Learning Tools	Adapts lessons based on student performance data labeled by skill level	AI tutors like Carnegie Learning, Squirrel AI

We have seen some of the widely used applications of Supervised Learning in the above table, now let's implement one of the applications.

7.2.6 Practical Implementation

Code Example

Loan Approval Prediction using Logistic Regression (Supervised Learning)

```python
import pandas as pd
import numpy as np
from sklearn.model_selection
import train_test_split from sklearn.linear_model
import LogisticRegression
from sklearn.metrics
import accuracy_score, confusion_matrix, classification_report
#Create or Load Dataset
data = { 'Income': [50000, 60000, 35000, 120000, 40000,
75000, 100000], 'Credit_Score': [700, 720, 580, 800, 600,
750, 770], 'Loan_Amount': [20000, 25000, 12000, 40000,
10000, 30000, 35000], 'Approved': [1, 1, 0, 1, 0, 1, 1]
# 1 = Approved, 0 = Rejected }
df = pd.DataFrame(data)
#Print(df)
```

```
#Split Features and Target
X = df[['Income', 'Credit_Score', 'Loan_Amount']] # Features
y = df['Approved'] # Target label

#Train-Test Split
X_train, X_test, y_train, y_test = train_test_split(X, y, test_
size=0.3, random_state=42)

#Train the Logistic Regression Model
model = LogisticRegression() model.fit(X_train, y_train)

#Make Predictions
y_pred = model.predict(X_test)

#Evaluation Metrics
print("Model Evaluation")
print("Accuracy:", accuracy_score(y_test, y_pred))
print("Confusion Matrix:\n", confusion_matrix(y_test, y_
pred))
print("Classification Report:\n", classification_report(y_test,
y_pred))

#Predict on New Applicant Data
new_applicant = np.array([[85000, 740, 25000]]) # [Income,
Credit_Score, Loan_Amount] prediction = model.predict(new_
applicant)

print("\nNew Application Result:")print("Loan Approved" if
prediction[0] == 1 else "Loan Rejected")

OUTPUT
Model Evaluation
Accuracy: 1.0
Confusion Matrix:
[[2 0]
[0 1]]
Classification Report:
```

Class	Precision	Recall	F1-Score	Support
0	1	1	1	2
1	1	1	1	1
accuracy	—	—	1	3
macro Avg	1	1	1	3
weighted Avg	1	1	1	3

7.3   LINEAR REGRESSION

7.3.1   What is Linear Regression?

Linear regression is the most fundamental technique in statistics and machine learning applied to model relationships between a dependent variable and one or more independent variables. It often predicts a continuous outcome based on input data. The simplicity and interpretability of linear regression have made it extremely popular in multiple fields, such as economics, healthcare, etc. Let's understand linear regression by taking an example. Suppose you are a real estate agent. You want to predict the price of a house based on the size of that house in square feet. Here, the price of the house is your dependent variable, and the size of the house is the independent variable. You have the data of many houses: sizes and their respective prices.

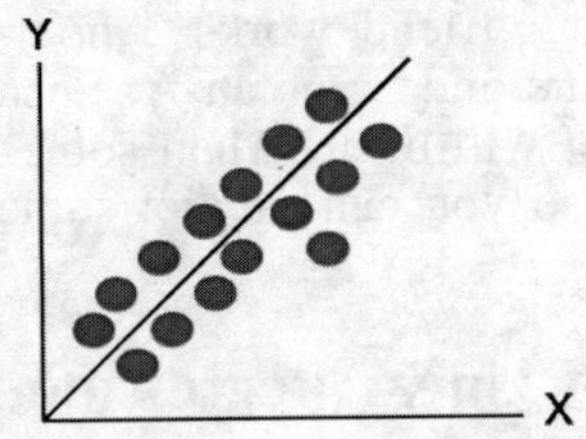

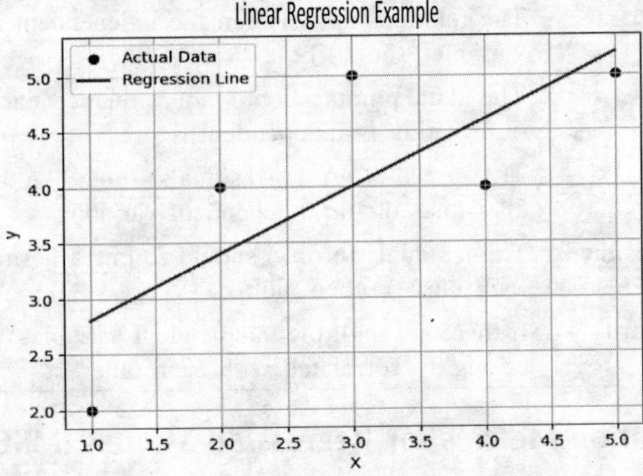

Linear regression enables you to build a model that predicts the price of a house given its size. The model will try to find a relationship, usually a straight line, that best fits the data points. The goal is to figure out how much the price changes when the size of the house increases. For instance, if it finds that the price of a house increases by $10,000 for every 100 square feet, then you can use this relationship to estimate the prices of other houses based on their sizes.

This is an example of a simple linear regression. In such a case, only one independent variable is available. If, however, more than one variable was considered—including the number of bedrooms and where the house was located—those other variables would be considered using multiple linear regression.

7.3.2 Concept and Mathematical Foundations

Linear regression is a method of determining the best-fitting straight line through a collection of points on a graph. Suppose you're examining how many hours you study and your grades. If you plot a graph with "hours studied" on one axis and "grades" on the other, the points will typically slope upward—that is, more studying tends to result in higher grades.

Linear regression assists in plotting a straight line through those points to indicate the overall trend. Once we have that line, we can then use it to estimate what type of grade someone would receive if we knew how many hours they worked.

For example, when your friend works 3 hours and typically earns a B, another friend works 5 hours and earns an A, linear regression assists you to make a good guess of what will occur when someone works for 4 hours. It's like putting a best-fit line so you can predict something or comprehend how two things connect.

7.3.3 Assumptions of Linear Regression

Assumption	Description
Linearity	The relationship between the independent and dependent variables should be a straight line.
Independence	The data points should not influence each other (each observation is independent).
Homoscedasticity	The spread of errors (residuals) should be the same across all values of the independent variable.
Normality of Residuals	The residuals (errors) should follow a normal distribution (bell curve) when plotted.
No Multicollinearity	If there are multiple independent variables, they shouldn't be highly correlated with each other.

7.3.4 Evaluation Metrics for Regression Models (MSE, RMSE, R²)

Metric	Full Name	What it Measures	How it Works	Formula	Interpretation
MSE	Mean Squared Error	Average of the squared differences between predicted and actual values	Calculate the difference between the predicted and actual values, square each difference, and average them.	$MSE = \left(\dfrac{1}{n}\right)\sum_{i=1}^{n}\left(y_i - \hat{y}_i\right)^2$	Lower value means better fit; sensitive to large errors

(Contd.)

Metric	Full Name	What it Measures	How it Works	Formula	Interpretation
RMSE	Root Mean Squared Error	Square root of MSE, brings error to the original units	Take the square root of the MSE value to return the error to the same units as the target variable.	$RMSE = \sqrt{\left(\frac{1}{n}\right)\sum_{i=1}^{n}(y_i - \hat{y}_i)^2}$	Lower value means better fit; more interpretable than MSE
R^2	R-squared	Proportion of variance in the dependent variable explained by the model	Compare the model's prediction errors to the errors made by a simple model predicting only the average of the target.	$R^2 = 1 - \dfrac{\sum_{i=1}^{n}(y_i - \hat{y}_i)^2}{\sum_{i=1}^{n}(y_i - \overline{y})^2}$	Higher value means better fit; 1 is perfect prediction

7.3.5   Top 3 Applications and Use-Cases

Sales Forecasting (Business and Economics)

- **Why is it important:** Sales forecasting allows businesses to predict sales at any given time in the future, thereby facilitating business planning, inventory management, and allocation of resources. In other words, linear regression correlates various factors such as advertising, sales seasonality, and historical sales data into predicting future sales performance.

- **How does it work:** Linear regression analyses historical sales data and identifies patterns. Factors such as advertising spending, for example, or how a price change influences sales from a regression viewpoint are examined. In this manner, it enables the company to forecast sales in the coming months and years.

Stock Market Prediction (Finance)

- **Why is it important:** Stock price prediction, trend forecast, and valuation of other financial variables are some of the fundamental purposes for which investors and financial analysts employ linear regression. With the knowledge of how these indicators move with respect to economic indicator variables, they tend to make more informed investment decisions.

- **How does it work:** Linear regression can be applied to determine the stock price based on its past stock data (like past price trends, volume of trading, or macroeconomic variables). It helps the investor to think of different trends and make better predictions of future movements of stock price.

Property Price Prediction (Real Estate)

- **Why it's important:** The real estate market is heavily influenced by various factors such as location, property size, age, and amenities. Predicting property prices is crucial for buyers, sellers, and investors to make data-driven decisions.
- **How it works:** By using linear regression, real estate professionals can estimate property prices based on the features of the property (like square footage, number of bedrooms, proximity to schools or public transportation). The model helps predict future property prices and assess property value.

7.3.6   Practical Implementation

Code Example

```python
import numpy as np
import matplotlib.pyplot as plt
from sklearn.model_selection import train_test_split
from sklearn.linear_model import LinearRegression
from sklearn.metrics import mean_squared_error, r2_score

# Step 1: Generate sample data (Advertising Spend vs Sales)
np.random.seed(0)
# For reproducibility
advertising_spend = np.random.randint(1, 20, 50)
# Advertising spend in thousands
sales = 2 * advertising_spend + np.random.normal(0, 2, 50)
# Sales with noise

# Step 2: Split the data into training and testing sets
X = advertising_spend.reshape(-1, 1)  # Feature
y = sales  # Target variable

X_train, X_test, y_train, y_test = train_test_split(X, y, test_
size=0.2, random_state=42)

# Step 3: Train a linear regression model
model = LinearRegression()
model.fit(X_train, y_train)

# Step 4: Make predictions on the test set
y_pred = model.predict(X_test)

# Step 5: Evaluate the model's performance
mse = mean_squared_error(y_test, y_pred)
rmse = np.sqrt(mse)
r2 = r2_score(y_test, y_pred)

# Print the evaluation metrics
print(f'Mean Squared Error (MSE): {mse:.2f}')
print(f'Root Mean Squared Error (RMSE): {rmse:.2f}')
print(f'R-squared (R²): {r2:.2f}')
```

```python
# Step 6: Visualize the results
plt.figure(figsize=(10, 6))

# Scatter plot of actual data
plt.scatter(X_test, y_test, color='black', label='Actual
Sales')

# Plot the predicted values
plt.plot(X_test, y_pred, color='gray', linewidth=2, la-
bel='Predicted Sales')

# Labels and title
plt.title('Advertising Spend vs Sales')
plt.xlabel('Advertising Spend (in thousands)')
plt.ylabel('Sales')
plt.legend()

# Show the plot
plt.tight_layout()
plt.show()
```

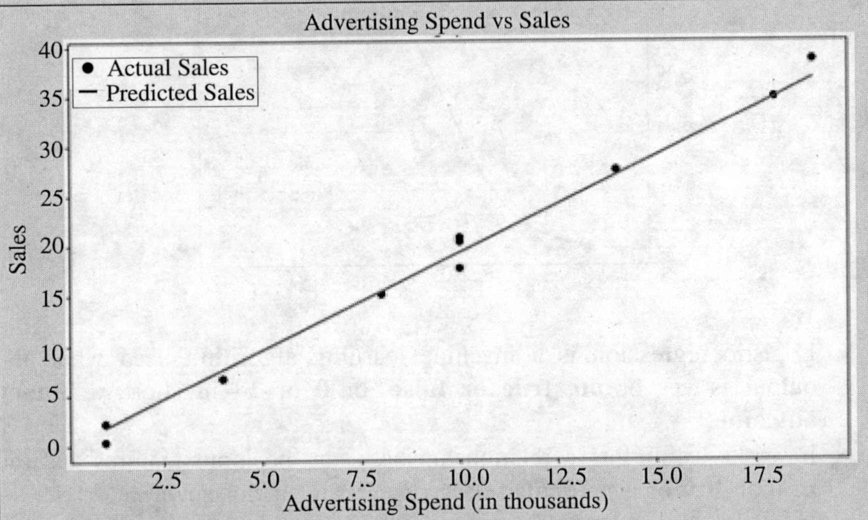

How this work: This is a statistical application through Python for linear regression in forecasting sales and using the specific parameters of an advertisement budget. First to create sample data with random advertisement spending and the considered sales that would have a linear relationship plus some noise to it. A training set created and a test set, hereafter called a train and test the linear regression model on the training operation for the model to learn and capture the relationship between advertising spend and sales. The model would predict sales in the test data, and performance evaluated through metrics like MSE, RMSE, and R^2. Finally, the actual versus predicted sales are plotted for visualizing model fit for the data.

7.4 LOGISTIC REGRESSION

7.4.1 What is Logistic Regression?

Logistic regression is a class of statistical methods for binary classification problems, which aim to predict the probability associated with an instance that belongs to one of two classes. It predicts the relationship between the input features and the probability of occurrence of certain outcomes by means of the logistic function (or sigmoid function), where the output produced is in the range between 0 and 1, that is interpretable as a probability. A model is trained to minimize a cost function (typically chosen to be binary cross-entropy) that will lead to the most suitable parameters for predicting the class labels.

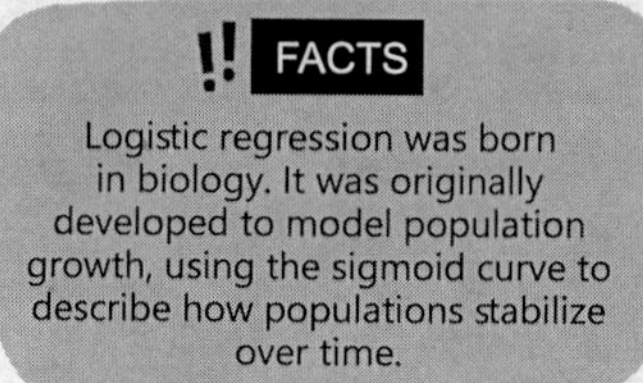

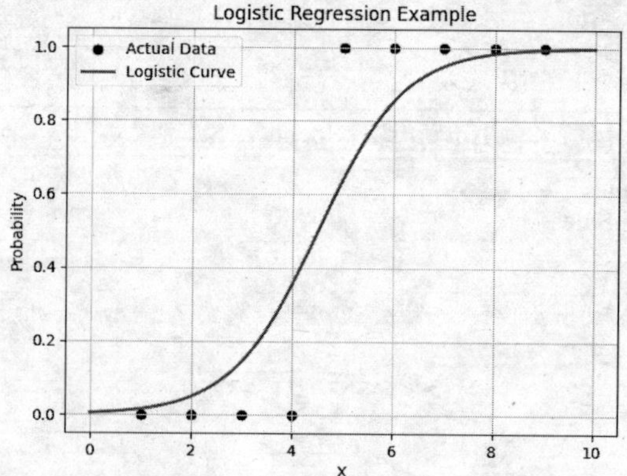

- Logistic regression is a machine learning algorithm used when the output is **yes** or **no, true or false**, or **0** or **1**—in short, a **binary outcome**.
- It works by finding a relationship between the input features and the **probability** of a particular class (like spam or not spam).
- It uses a **sigmoid function** to convert the result into a value between 0 and 1, which we treat as a probability.
- The model is trained by adjusting its internal parameters to reduce the **error in prediction**, usually using a method called **binary cross-entropy loss**.

7.4.2 Concept and Mathematical Interpretation (Sigmoid Function)

Logistic regression denotes a statistical model for binary classification problems, where the probability of an object belonging to one of the two classes is estimated. It takes input features that are linearly combined, and the resulting value is passed through a logistic function (sigmoid function). This process transforms the linear output in the interval [0; 1] to indicate the likelihood of the object belonging to the positive class. The output is mapped as class 0 or 1 based on a decision threshold (usually at 0.5). The model is trained by minimizing the cost function which is log-loss or binary cross-entropy, representing the difference between the predicted probabilities and actual label values. Optimization methods such as gradient descent are used to find the parameter values of the models that minimize this error. Logistic regression is perhaps one of the most widely used methods in machine learning because it's easy to use, interpret, and efficient for binary outcomes. The major limitation of logistic regression, however, is that it assumes a linear relationship between the input features and the log-odds of the outcome-specific event, which may not hold in a more complicated data set.

7.4.3 Type of Logistic Regression

The main types of Logistic Regression are:

- **Binary Logistic Regression:** Binary Logistic Regression can be applied to instances when the outcome variable has two possible classes, in common parlance defined as 0 or 1. Thus, the model estimates the probability of an observation falling in one of these two classes, based on the input feature(s). In the beginning, observations are subjected to the sigmoid function, mapping the output to fall between the values of 0 and 1. The next step is to classify the observations through the application of a decision threshold (0.5), thus classifying the observations as either 0 or 1. This logistic regression method is typically employed in many situations such as the detection of spam, diagnosis in the medical field, and prediction of customer churn.

- **Multinomial Logistic Regression:** It extends binary logistic regression toward multiclass problems, i.e., situations in which the outcome variable has more than two categories. The SoftMax function assigns probabilities, summing to 1, across all classes. Thus, the class with the highest probability is chosen as predicted class. It is useful in problems like image classification, analysing sentiments, and differentiating types of products or animals.

- **Ordinal Logistic Regression:** It is applied when the outcome variable appears under the form of ordered categories, such as Low, Medium, and High. It estimates the probabilities of being at or above a certain category while considering the natural ordering of the classes. This is fitting for customer satisfaction survey scenarios, where the categories bear a meaningful rank. Unlike multinomial regression, ordinal logistic regression considers the ordering of the categories, thereby improving the accuracy of the estimates when an inherent order is present among those classes.

7.4.4   Logistic Regression Implementation

Code Example

```python
#Step 1: Import necessary libraries
import pandas as pd
import numpy as np
from sklearn.model_selection
import train_test_split
from sklearn.preprocessing
import StandardScaler
from sklearn.linear_model
import LogisticRegression
from sklearn.metrics
import accuracy_score, confusion_matrix, classification_re-
port

#Step 2: Load the dataset (mock data for demonstration)
data = { 'age': [25, 30, 35, 40, 45, 50, 55, 60, 65, 70],
'account_balance': [1000, 1500, 2000, 2500, 3000, 3500,
4000, 4500, 5000, 5500], 'years_with_company': [1, 2, 3, 4,
5, 6, 7, 8, 9, 10], 'churn': [0, 0, 0, 1, 0, 1, 1, 0, 1, 1]
# 0 = No Churn, 1 = Churn }
df = pd.DataFrame(data)

#Step 3: Preprocess the data
X = df[['age', 'account_balance', 'years_with_company']]
# Features
y = df['churn']

# Target variable

#Standardizing the features
scaler = StandardScaler()
X_scaled = scaler.fit_transform(X)

#Step 4: Split the data into training and testing sets
X_train, X_test, y_train, y_test = train_test_split(X_scaled,
y, test_size=0.2, random_state=42)

#Step 5: Train the logistic regression model
model = LogisticRegression() model.fit(X_train, y_train)

#Step 6: Evaluate the model
y_pred = model.predict(X_test)

#Accuracy Score
accuracy = accuracy_score(y_test, y_pred)

#Confusion Matrix
conf_matrix = confusion_matrix(y_test, y_pred)
```

```
#Classification Report
class_report = classification_report(y_test, y_pred)

#Print the results
print(f"Accuracy: {accuracy:.2f}") print("Confusion Matrix:")
print(conf_matrix) print("Classification Report:")
print(class_report)
```

```
Accuracy:
Confusion Matrix:
 [[1 0]
  [0 1]]
```

Classification Report	Precision	Recall	F1-score	support
0	1.00	1.00	1.00	1
1	1.00	1.00	1.00	1
Accuracy			1.00	2
macro avg	1.00	1.00	1.00	2
weighted avg	1.00	1.00	1.00	2

How this code Work: This code demonstrates how a Logistic Regression model is built and evaluated for predicting customer churn. It starts by preparing a dataset and separating input features from the target variable. The data is then standardized and split into training and testing sets to ensure fair evaluation. Finally, the model is trained on the training data and its performance is measured using accuracy and a confusion matrix.

7.5   DECISION TREE

7.5.1   What is Decision Tree?

A Decision Tree is a supervised algorithm in machine learning for both classification and regression. It gives a tree-like model of decisions and their possible consequences.

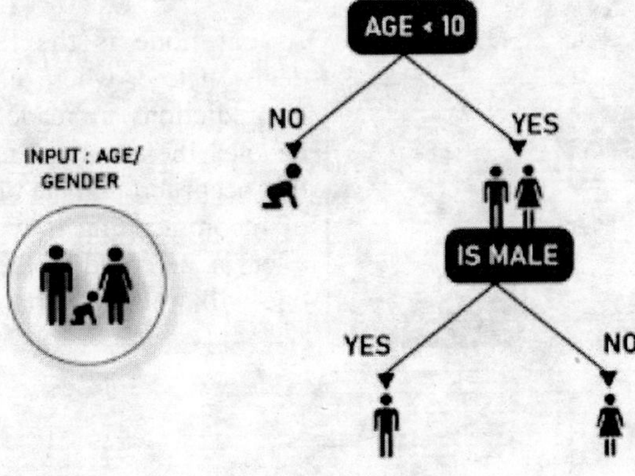

The details are as follows:

- Each internal node is a test on a feature.
- Each branch represents the outcome of a test.
- Each leaf node is a class label in classification or a continuous value in regression.

The tree is constructed by recursively splitting the dataset in a manner that yields the most informative partitions assessed by Gini Index, Information Gain, or Mean Squared Error. This makes Decision Trees easy to interpret, although they may overfit the data unless properly pruned or regularized.

7.5.2   Decision Tree Terminologies

<table>
<tr><td>

Root Node

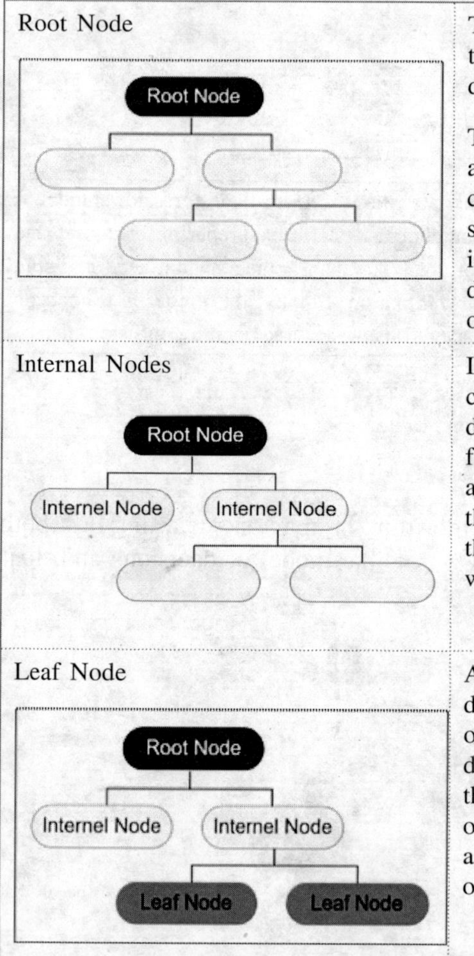

</td><td>

The root node of a decision tree represents the starting point and contains the full dataset.

This tree starts with a root node, and at every step the most relevant feature comes into focus and develops meaningful subsets of data. The first feature chosen is the most suited one for splitting the data and hence impacts the way the rest of the tree should look like.

</td></tr>
<tr><td>

Internal Nodes

</td><td>

Internal nodes in a decision tree are critical decision points at which the dataset is divided based on specific features. Each internal node acts like a question or condition and determines the direction for the further progress of the tree, indicating how that information will be split further.

</td></tr>
<tr><td>

Leaf Node

</td><td>

A leaf node is the termination of a decision tree, where ultimate decisions or predictions are made. Every leaf node denotes the result of many evaluations that occur through the tree. In the context of recommending movies, for instance, a leaf node could be the situation where one will watch a certain movie or not.

</td></tr>
</table>

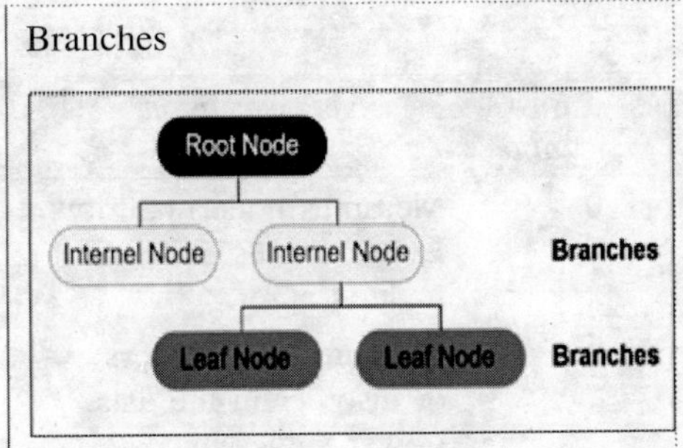

The edges that connect a node to another in a decision tree are called branches.

In simpler terms, a branch can be said to represent the possible choices or directions taken based on the discretion of feature values.

Every branch determines the path it takes based on a specific condition or criterion evaluated at some internal node.

7.5.3 How Decision Tree Algorithms Work

A **decision tree** is a model that makes decisions by asking a series of **yes/no questions** about the data.

- **Start at the Root:** It begins at the root node, which holds the full dataset. The algorithm picks the best feature to split the data—this is the feature that gives the most information gain (i.e., helps separate the data most clearly).
- **Branching:** Based on the selected feature, the data is split into groups, forming branches.
- **Node to Node:** At each node (or step), the tree asks another question based on a new feature, and this process continues—splitting the data further and further.
- **Leaf Node:** When there are no more useful questions to ask, we reach a leaf node, which gives the final prediction (like class 0 or 1).

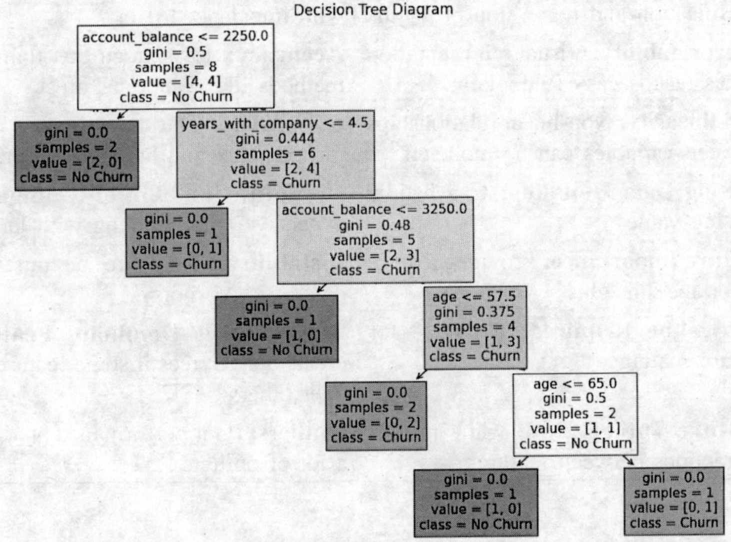

7.5.4 Key Components

Criterion	Used for	Value Range	Best Value	Description
Gini Index	Classification	0 to 0.5 (for binary)	0	Measures node impurity. Lower values mean the node is purer.
Entropy	Classification	0 to $\log_2(n)$	0	Measures randomness or disorder in the data. Lower values indicate purity.
Information Gain	Classification	≥ 0	Higher is better	Measures the effectiveness of a feature in reducing uncertainty.
Mean Squared Error	Regression	≥ 0	0	Measures the variance in prediction. Lower values mean more accurate splits.

7.5.5 Advantages and Disadvantages

Advantages	Disadvantages
Ease of Understanding: Easy to understand and interpret	**Overfitting:** Prone to overfitting if not pruned properly
Minimal Preprocessing: Requires minimal data preprocessing	**Sensitivity:** Sensitive to small changes in data
Versatility: Handles both numerical and categorical data	**Inefficiency on Large Datasets:** Not efficient for large or complex datasets
Problem Solving: Suitable for classification and regression problems	**Bias with Imbalanced Data:** Can be biased with imbalanced data
Interpretability: Visual representation makes results easy to explain	**Accuracy:** Less accurate than ensemble methods like Random Forest
Non-linearity: Non-linear relationships between variables can be modeled	**Complexity:** The tree structure can become too complex and hard to interpret
Missing Data Handling: Can handle missing values	**Computation Time:** Computationally expensive when dealing with large datasets
Feature Importance: Provides feature importance insights	**Instability:** Tends to be unstable if the dataset is too noisy
No Scaling Required: No need for feature scaling	**Bias towards Dominant Features:** May create biased trees if some features dominate over others
Feature Interaction: Can model interactions between features	**Outliers:** Poor performance on datasets with a lot of outliers

7.6 SUPPORT VECTOR MACHINE (SVM)

7.6.1 Definition of SVM

SVM is a machine learning algorithm used to separate data into two classes with the **best possible boundary**, called a **hyperplane**.

Algorithm is used to discover the optimal separation or hyperplane that segregates the different classes of data within the dataset. The "support vectors" are those data points near this boundary that are used to define how to position it. The SVM maximizes the margin, or distance, between the classes and this boundary. This maximization ensures that the separation between the two classes is best possible. In this way, the accuracy of classifications is enhanced, and this method can also be used in cases where the data is not linearly separable.

For example, whether a student will **pass** or **fail** based on two key factors: the **number of study hours** and the **number of sleep hours** they get.

Here, the support vectors are the critical data points that lie on the boundary of the **margin** (the region that separates the two classes). An SVM will be maximizing distance to its closest point with this kind of training such that its boundary produces an almost exact classification for the unseen email it needs to classify.

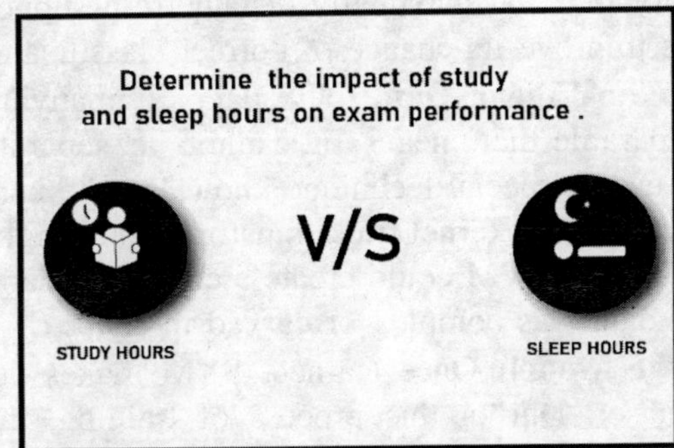

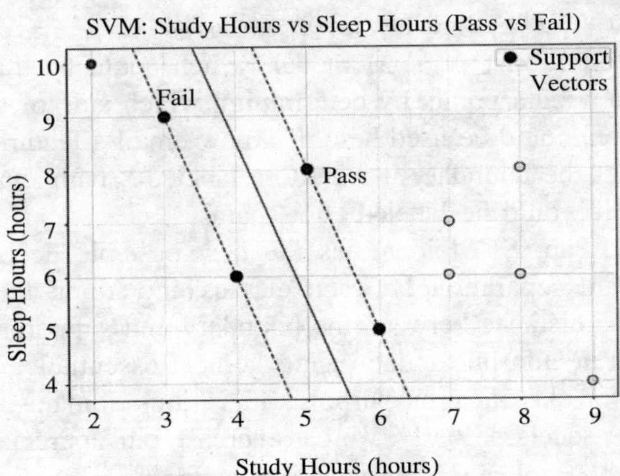

7.6.2 How SVMs Work: A Step-by-Step Overview

Support Vector Machine SVM are very strong classification algorithms used highly in machine learning. They are most applicable in scenarios where the intention of allocating data into distinct classes based on different features. But understanding how SVMs work can be a great way to admire their versatility and efficiency in solving real-world problems. Let's break down how SVM works, including some technical aspects, in a simple and coherent manner:

- **Understanding the Data:** SVM starts with a dataset containing features and labels. In the case of trying to classify emails as "spam" and "not spam," the features are the words in the email, and the labels are just the categories.

- **Finding the Decision Boundary:** An SVM determines a hyperplane that could best distinguish between the categories of data. Often, a "hyperplane" is interpreted as a line in two dimensions or a plane in three, which separates the data points of different categories.

- **Maximizing the Margin:** The idea behind SVM is to find a boundary which maximizes the margin. That is, maximizing the distance of the boundary from its nearest points in each class. These nearest points are referred to as "support vectors." Maximizing this margin means that the boundary must be maximally distant from support vectors, which again helps improve its chance of correct classification.

- **Handling Non-Linear Data:** The data, in many real cases, is not linearly separable-that means, it cannot be separated by a straight line. SVM uses a special technique known as the kernel trick to solve such a problem. The kernel trick transforms the original data to higher dimensions where SVM could create a clear boundary between classes even if the data was complex or curved in shape.

- **Training the Model:** Once learned, SVM makes decisions from the training dataset. During this process of training, the support vector finding algorithm shifts the position of the hyperplane so that new input data are classified more appropriately.

- **Make Predictions:** A SVM model, which could be trained and then classify new data points by determining which side of the hyperplane they fell on, could be used here, if a new email's features placed it on one side of the boundary it would be labeled "spam" and if it was on the other it would be labeled "not spam".

To sum it up, SVM identifies the best possible decision boundary with maximum separation between classes and along the margin also maximizes the distance between the boundary and support vectors. It can handle linear or non-linear data using kernels essentially, so that's why it is chosen for classification purposes in various domains. If we explain the technical aspects properly, we can increase our appreciation for SVM capabilities and applications in machine learning.

Hyperplane and Margin in SVM (Made Easy):

Hyperplane: A **hyperplane** is simply a **boundary** that separates different classes in the data.

- In **2D**, it's a **line**.
- In **3D**, it's a **plane**.
- In higher dimensions, it's harder to visualize but still serves the same purpose.

Margin: The **margin** is the **distance between the hyperplane and the closest data points** (called **support vectors**) from each class.

- The goal of **SVM** is to **maximize this margin** so that the data classes are as far apart as possible.
- A **larger margin** means the model is less likely to make errors on **new, unseen data**, because there's a clearer separation between classes.

Support Vectors: The **support vectors** are the data points closest to the hyperplane. They are the key points that help define where the boundary should be.

Best Hyperplane: SVM looks for the **optimal hyperplane** that maximizes this margin, ensuring that the model generalizes well and doesn't overfit.

7.6.3 Kernel Function

- A kernel function in SVM is a mathematical tool to map the original data into a higher dimension so that it will be easier to find a separating hyperplane between complex, non-linear datasets.
- Instead of directly calculating the coordinates of data in a higher dimension, the kernel function calculates the **similarity** between data points in the original space.
- This allows SVM to create more **flexible decision boundaries**.

There are different types of kernels, including:

- **Linear:** Used when the data is already separable with a straight line or hyperplane.
- **Polynomial:** Useful for data that can be separated with curves.
- **Radial Basis Function (RBF):** Effective for data with complex boundaries and non-linear separations.
- **Sigmoid:** Another way to transform data, often used in neural networks.

7.6.4 What are Kernels?

In machine learning, the data might be noisy and possibly in various shapes so that it is difficult to classify it. Not less often, a set of data we are working on cannot be linearly separated by a simple straight line or hyperplane. That's where kernels in Support Vector Machines prove to be very useful. Kernels are special functions that facilitate SVM to transform the hard data into a high-dimensional space where this data is easier to separate. Think of it as a way where you stretch and bend the data so that it may become easily separable. Utilizing kernels, therefore, SVM is able to draw proper boundaries for differentiating among categories even though the patterns may be complicated.

7.6.5   How Kernels Work in Support Vector Machines (SVM)

Kernels were very crucial in the success of Support Vector Machines in dealing with complex and non-linear data efficiently. They can be summed up in simpler terms as follows in general:

- **Data Transformation:** Kernels allow SVM to map the original space of data into a possibly much larger space without ever actually computing the coordinates in that space. This can be thought of as a "mapping." Attempt to imagine taking a two-dimensional set of data and mapping it into three dimensions where it is easier to distinguish between the categories.

- **Adding Non-Linear Boundaries:** SVMs can then introduce a linear boundary separating different categories of data points in the higher-dimensional space. In this way, for example, a pattern that is hard to separate by two dimensions can be made linear in three. The kernel function thus captures these complex relationships within the data.

- **Learning from Support Vectors:** When the SVM uses a kernel, it still focuses on the support vectors-the points in the data that lie closest to the boundary. They are crucial because they determine the position and orientation of the boundary. The kernel function lets the SVM learn from these support vectors effectively even if the space has been transformed.

- **Prediction:** One can make use of the same kernel function for new data points during classification after having trained SVM with the kernel. It assesses where the new point falls relative to the decision boundary it created in the higher-dimensional space. From this position, it can predict where the new point belongs.

Kernels help SVM by transforming complex data into a space where it's easier to draw a clear boundary. This allows SVM to handle non-linear data efficiently and make accurate predictions.

Kernel Type	Use Case
Linear Kernel	Email Classification (spam vs. not spam)
Polynomial Kernel	Image Recognition (facial features classification)

(Contd.)

Kernel Type	Use Case
Radial Basis Function (RBF) Kernel	Medical Diagnosis (classifying MRI scans)
Sigmoid Kernel	Sentiment Analysis (classifying tweets as positive/negative)
Custom Kernel	Tailored applications based on specific data relationships

7.6.6 Practical Implementation

Imagine that you work for a company providing cybersecurity and are asked to classify web traffic as either normal or malicious. We will simulate this scenario by generating a synthetic 2D dataset representing web traffic. We'll use **request size** as one feature and **request frequency** as another feature and classify the traffic as either normal or malicious.

Assumption: In a real-world cybersecurity scenario, Normal traffic may consist of regular browsing requests with lower frequency and smaller request sizes. Malicious traffic could be generated by attackers using DDoS attacks, SQL injections, or botnets, which can produce more frequent or larger requests than normal users.

So,

- **Normal traffic** has low request size and low frequency.
- **Malicious traffic** has either high request size or high frequency (or both)

Code Example

```python
#Code
import numpy as np
import matplotlib.pyplot as plt
from sklearn import datasets
from sklearn.svm import SVC
from sklearn.preprocessing import StandardScaler
import pandas as pd

# Step 1: Generate a synthetic 2D dataset (representing web traffic features)
X, y = datasets.make_moons(n_samples=300, noise=0.2, random_state=42)

# Step 2: Standardize the features (important for SVM performance)
scaler = StandardScaler()
X = scaler.fit_transform(X)

# Step 3: Create a DataFrame to display the dataset in tabular format
df = pd.DataFrame(X, columns=['Request Frequency', 'Request Size'])
df['Class'] = y  # Add the target class (0 = normal, 1 = malicious)
```

```python
# Optional: Print the first few rows of the dataset to under-
stand the structure
print(df.head())


# Step 4: Train a non-linear SVM with RBF kernel
clf = SVC(kernel='rbf', C=1, gamma='auto')
clf.fit(X, y)


# Step 5: Create a mesh grid for plotting decision boundary
h = .02  # Step size in the mesh grid
x_min, x_max = X[:, 0].min() - 1, X[:, 0].max() + 1
y_min, y_max = X[:, 1].min() - 1, X[:, 1].max() + 1
xx, yy = np.meshgrid(np.arange(x_min, x_max, h),
np.arange(y_min, y_max, h))


# Step 6: Predict the class labels for each point in the
mesh grid
Z = clf.predict(np.c_[xx.ravel(), yy.ravel()])
Z = Z.reshape(xx.shape)


# Step 7: Plot decision boundary and data points
plt.contourf(xx, yy, Z, alpha=0.8, cmap=plt.cm.coolwarm)
# Decision boundary with shading
plt.scatter(X[:, 0], X[:, 1], c=y, edgecolors='k', mark-
er='o', s=50, cmap=plt.cm.coolwarm)
# Data points


# Step 8: Add labels and title to the plot
plt.title('Non-Linear SVM Decision Boundary (RBF Kernel)')
plt.xlabel('Request Frequency')
plt.ylabel('Request Size')
plt.colorbar()  # To add a color bar indicating the class
labels


# Step 9: Show the plot
plt.show()
```

	Request Frequency	Request Size	Class
0	0.337921	-1.043549	1
1	2.026552	-0.725001	1
2	-0.874264	0.354298	1
3	0.321734	0.228366	0
4	0.765784	-1.457870	1

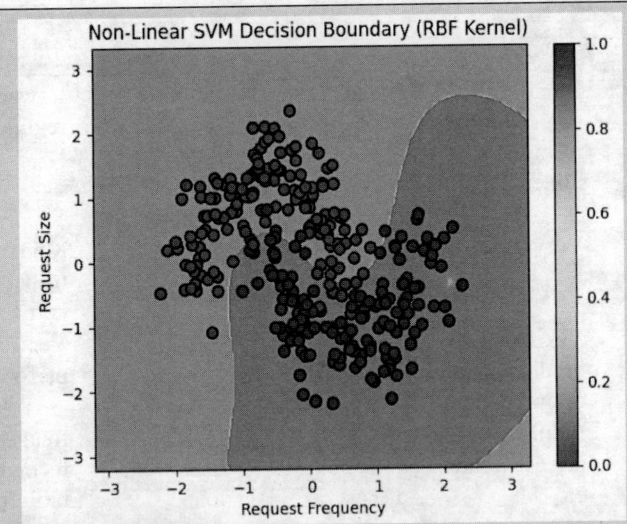

- The plot will show two interleaving crescent-shaped regions, which represent the decision boundary learned by the SVM with an RBF kernel.
- The normal traffic points will be represented in one color, say blue, and the malicious traffic points will be represented in another color, say red.
- The boundary will be curved, showing how the SVM mapped the data into a higher-dimensional space and found a non-linear boundary to separate the two classes.

7.6.7 Summary of Supervised Machine Learning

Feature/ Model	Linear Regression	Logistic Regression	Decision Tree	SVM
Type	Regression	Classification (binary/multi-class)	Both Classification and Regression	Primarily Classification (also Regression)
Output	Continuous values	Probabilities → Classes	Discrete classes or values	Discrete classes (or continuous for SVR)
Algorithm Nature	Parametric	Parametric	Non-parametric	Non-parametric
Decision Boundary	Linear	Linear (can be extended to non-linear)	Non-linear (piecewise splits)	Linear or Non-linear (with kernel)
Interpretability	High	High	Moderate to High	Low to Moderate
Handling of Non-linearity	Poor (without transformation)	Poor (unless with non-linear features)	Good	Excellent (with kernel trick)

(Contd.)

Feature/ Model	Linear Regression	Logistic Regression	Decision Tree	SVM
Overfitting Tendency	Prone (especially in high dimensions)	Prone (with many features)	High (can be controlled with pruning)	Lower (with regularization)
Scalability	Very good	Very good	Moderate	Moderate to Poor (especially with kernels)
Feature Scaling Needed	Yes (for gradient-based optimization)	Yes (for gradient-based optimization)	No	Yes (critical for performance)
Applications	Predicting prices, trends, etc.	Spam detection, disease prediction, etc.	Fraud detection, loan approval, etc.	Image recognition, bioinformatics, etc.

7.7 UNSUPERVISED LEARNING ALGORITHMS

7.7.1 Definition

Unsupervised learning is a form of machine learning in which the model is trained on input data with no labeled outputs. The objective is to discover patterns, structures, or relationships in the data, like clustering similar items (clustering) or dimensionality reduction (dimensionality reduction), without knowing the right results beforehand.

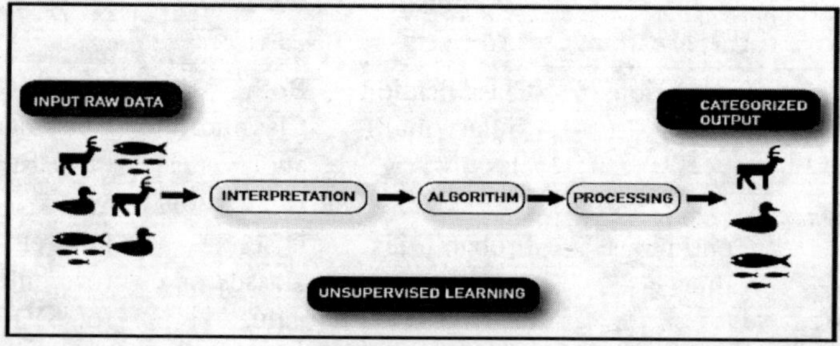

Clustering similar tunes on a music streaming application based on listening patterns is one example of Unsupervised Learning, now let's understand how this work, in a music application such as Spotify or YouTube Music, people listen to numerous songs without labelling them. Unsupervised learning techniques observe the listening patterns of millions of people and naturally form groups of similar songs into playlists or suggest songs that match the user's preference. Such groupings are performed without prior knowledge about the song genres or user preferences, only from hidden patterns in the data.

7.7.2 Key Characteristics

Characteristic	Description
No Labeled Data	Works with data that does not have predefined outputs or labels.
Pattern Discovery	Identifies hidden patterns or structures in the data.
Clustering and Association	Groups similar data (clustering) or finds relationships (association rules).
Exploratory Nature	Mainly used for exploring unknown data structures.
Dimensionality Reduction	Reduces features while retaining meaningful information (e.g., PCA).
Used for Preprocessing	Helps prepare data for supervised learning by organizing or simplifying it.
Real-Time Learning	Useful in detecting anomalies or changes in real-time systems.

7.7.3 Importance in Data Exploration and Pattern Discovery

Unsupervised learning is extremely useful for **exploring and discovering patterns** in data, especially when the data is **large** and **unstructured**. It's helpful because **it doesn't require labeled data**, which can be time-consuming or impossible to get.

Here's why unsupervised learning is important:

1. **Finding Hidden Patterns:** By identifying similarities, differences, and relationships in the data, unsupervised learning helps find patterns that may not be obvious at first glance.

2. **Clustering:** One popular use of unsupervised learning is clustering, where similar data points are grouped together. For example, in advertising, businesses can use unsupervised learning to group customers based on their buying habits. This helps in creating targeted marketing strategies.

3. **Dimensionality Reduction:** Another important application is dimensionality reduction (like PCA). This process simplifies complex data, making it easier to visualize and use with other machine learning models.

4. **Anomaly Detection:** Unsupervised learning can also be used for anomaly detection, where the model identifies unusual patterns. For example, it could detect fraud or security attacks by noticing behavior that's different from the usual pattern.

5. **Hypothesis Generation:** Finally, unsupervised learning helps generate hypotheses by uncovering unexpected trends or patterns. This can assist scientists and analysts in making better decisions.

7.8 K-MEANS CLUSTERING

K-Means Clustering Algorithm is the best suited and widely used algorithm for machine learning in unsupervised learning tasks. Its main aim is to divide the dataset into various groups, which in fact refers to the clusters that share similar characteristics within same cluster of data points. The phrase K-Means comes from the fact that the user decides the number of clusters K, and then finds their canters or centroids by computing the means of the data points in each cluster.

The ease, speed, and applicability with which this algorithm can be applied are quite evident from the fact that it is commonly applied for customer segmentation, image compressing, or anomaly detection. Unlike supervised learning algorithms that depend on labelled data, K-means uses unlabelled data to discover prospective unknown patterns or groupings useful for exploratory data analysis.

7.8.1 When to Apply the K-Means Clustering

K-Means is often favoured in finding patterns within data owing to its simplicity and efficiency. Like any other such tools, it works best in given conditions. Understanding when to apply K-Means clustering will help in utilizing its power and derive meaningful results.

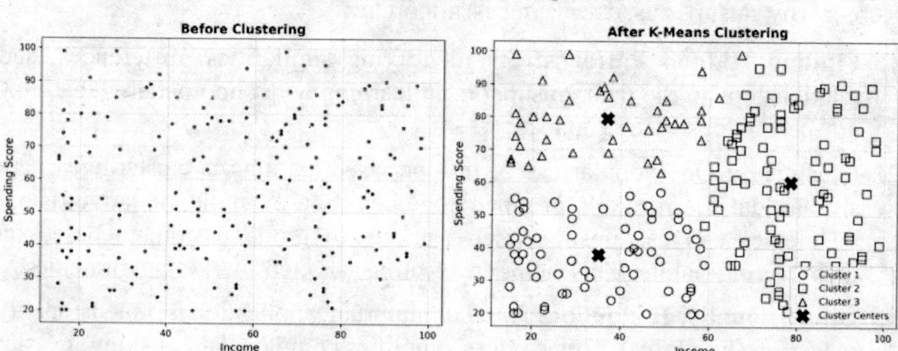

Thus, the most important factor a K-Means researcher must contemplate is the kinds of clusters present in the dataset. Most suitable data for K-Means algorithm work contains spherical or well-separated clusters in feature space; this is because K-Means uses centroid, and a centroid represents the centre point of the cluster. Thus, if they are of irregular formations or overlap within each other, it would be difficult for K-Means to capture them appropriately. For example, in customer segmentation tasks where segment categories such as high spenders are available, knowledge shoppers and K-Means will succeed in categorizing those customers under those segments.

Knowing or estimating the number of clusters K is another important consideration. In this case, the algorithm works on the fact that one must specify the number of clusters in advance; thus, this algorithm is suitable for problems in which this information is known or can be extrapolated using techniques like the Elbow Method. For example, if the dataset contains several categories (like electronics, clothing, and furniture) and the number is predefined, then K-Means can cluster well the required products, as they can be segmented in groups.

The algorithm also performs extremely well on numerical data. Because K-Means focuses on distance metrics, Euclidean distance, to allocate points to clusters, datasets with numeric features give rise to optimal results. For example, financial data.

7.8.2   Why Use K-Means Clustering?

K-Means clustering has good reasons why it's very popular in data analysis. In below section it is explained.

Ease and Efficiency: K-Means is intuitive and simple to understand; users with different levels of experience in data science may easily apply the concept. Furthermore, the algorithm can process the huge data size efficiently.

Scalability: K-Means is extremely efficient for large datasets, which makes this algorithm applicable to numerous applications. The time complexity of the algorithm is linear in the number of data points, and so it will continue to perform well as the data set grows.

Flexibility: In the algorithm, different kinds of data can be used-numerical and categorical due to distance metrics adjustment. Such flexibility gives a possibility to apply K-Means in the completely different domains—from marketing to image processing.

Versatility: K-Means is applied for very different tasks—such as customer segmentation, market basket analysis, or image compression. It offers great versatility in data exploration for both exploratory data analysis and prediction in general.

Output: It produces output in the form of clusters which is well defined and interpretable so that the results can be visualized quite easily.

It converges very quickly; therefore K-Means needs fewer numbers of iterations before the clusters settle. This improves the efficiency of the algorithm for the big data application. In brief, K-Means Clustering is one of the more powerful and efficient algorithms that tend to unveil the latent structures in the data, hence valuable for a data analyst.

7.8.3 Choosing the Right Number of Clusters (Elbow Method, Silhouette Score)

When clustering, one of the most important challenges is choosing the best number of clusters. Having too few clusters can result in general groupings, whereas having too many can overfit the model. Two popular methods to choose the best number of clusters are the Elbow Method and the Silhouette Score.

The Elbow Method: The Elbow Method is to plot the Within-Cluster Sum of Squares (WCSS) against various values of k (number of clusters). As k increases, WCSS reduces, but beyond a point, the rate of reduction slows down. The "elbow" points at which this slowing down happens indicates the ideal number of clusters. This is an easy method to use but may be tricky to interpret if the elbow is not well defined.

The Silhouette Score: The Silhouette Score gives a more numerical method by quantifying how well the clusters are separated and cohesive. The score is between −1 and 1, with higher being better-defined clusters. To apply this technique, you compute the Silhouette Score for different values of k and choose the one with the largest score, representing the best clustering quality. Although it is more precise than the Elbow Method, it might be computationally costly for larger datasets.

The two methods both work well when deciding on the best number of clusters. The Elbow Method is simpler to use and grasp, whereas the Silhouette Score gives a clearer measure of how good the clusters are. If both methods are used together, it usually means a better-quality clustering solution results, with relevant and well-defined groups.

7.8.4 Application of Clustering

Application	Description
Customer Segmentation	Groups customers with similar behaviors or demographics. for targeted marketing and personalized campaigns.
Image Segmentation	Divides images into regions based on pixel similarities for object recognition, medical imaging, or autonomous vehicles.
Anomaly Detection	Identifies outliers or abnormal patterns in data, useful in fraud detection or system security.
Document and Text Classification	Groups similar documents or text data, aiding in information retrieval, content recommendation, and organizing large datasets.
Bioinformatics	Groups genes or proteins with similar functions, aiding in understanding biological processes or disease-related genes.
Image and Video Retrieval	Organizes large media databases into clusters for faster and more accurate search results based on visual similarities.

7.9 PRINCIPAL COMPONENT ANALYSIS (PCA)

7.9.1 What is PCA

PCA is a statistical method to transform complex datasets in a way to reduce their dimensionality while keeping the most essential patterns and relationships in the data. PCA reduces the original set of features or variables into new uncorrelated variables called principal components. Principal components are arranged in such an order that the first few ones capture the maximum variance in the data. In other words, PCA identifies those directions in which the data is changing the most (principal components) and projects the original data onto them.

7.9.2 Dimensionality Reduction Concept

Dimensionality reduction is a technique of data science and machine learning to reduce the number of features or variables in the dataset in such a way that it preserves as much essential information as possible. That is, mainly, to simplify big high-dimensional data and remove noise or redundant features that have higher uncertainty or less informative values. It alleviates issues, such as overfitting and noise, or high computational requirements. The benefits of this type of dimensionality reduction are even more significant where the number of features is overwhelming and data samples are few.

7.9.3 Purpose of Dimensionality Reduction

Purpose	*Description*
Simplify Data	Reduces the number of variables, making the dataset easier to understand and analyze.
Improve Model Performance	Speeds up training and prediction time by reducing computation requirements.
Prevent Overfitting	Removes irrelevant or redundant features, reducing the risk of overfitting.
Enhance Visualization	Helps visualize high-dimensional data in 2D or 3D plots for better interpretation.
Remove Multicollinearity	Eliminates highly correlated features that can affect model accuracy.
Noise Reduction	Filters out less informative or noisy data to improve overall data quality.

7.9.4 Anomaly Detection

Anomalies can signify rare events like fraud in financial transactions, equipment failure in industrial systems, or suspicious behavior in cybersecurity logs. In many domains, the detection of such anomalies is crucial to maintaining efficiency, security, and reliability across many domains. The wide-range application of anomaly detection is its relevance to importance. The measure of anomalies can detect fraud transactions while the medical data could indicate critical health conditions in healthcare financing. Anomaly detection system launched into networks and systems enhances security by detecting potential cyberattacks and system breaches through abnormal traffic patterns. Other applications include quality control, predictive maintenance, and even analyzing consumer behaviors.

7.9.5 Practical Implementation

Problem Statement

We are building a personalized music recommendation system using PCA in order to reduce the dimensionality of user preferences on music, so that the system can provide new song recommendations based on user preferences.

What we are trying to achieve is the following:

- Use PCA to reduce the dimensionality of the music dataset and bring out the most prominent patterns in song attributes such as tempo, energy, danceability, and mood.

- Recommend similar songs to users by using these simplified patterns.

- Visualize song relationships as points in a 2D space and determine how songs relate to each other based on their features.

```python
# Importing necessary libraries
import pandas as pd
import numpy as np
from sklearn.decomposition import PCA
import matplotlib.pyplot as plt
from sklearn.preprocessing import StandardScaler
from sklearn.metrics.pairwise import cosine_similarity

# Sample dataset with real song names and some made-up features
data = {
    'Song': ['Blinding Lights', 'Shape of You', 'Levitating', 'Uptown Funk', 'Watermelon Sugar', 'Stay', 'Good 4 U'],
    'Artist': ['The Weeknd', 'Ed Sheeran', 'Dua Lipa', 'Mark Ronson ft. Bruno Mars', 'Harry Styles', 'The Kid LAROI & Justin Bieber', 'Olivia Rodrigo'],
    'Tempo': [85, 96, 103, 115, 95, 105, 138],
    'Energy': [0.8, 0.85, 0.9, 0.88, 0.92, 0.85, 0.88],
    'Danceability': [0.75, 0.85, 0.9, 0.87, 0.91, 0.88, 0.92],
    'Mood': [0.8, 0.7, 0.85, 0.85, 0.9, 0.75, 0.88]
}
```

```python
# Convert the data to a DataFrame
df = pd.DataFrame(data)

# Display the dataset
print("Original Music Dataset:")
print(df)

# Feature Selection (excluding 'Song' and 'Artist' columns
for PCA)
X = df[['Tempo', 'Energy', 'Danceability', 'Mood']]

# Standardizing the features
scaler = StandardScaler()
X_scaled = scaler.fit_transform(X)

# Applying PCA
pca = PCA(n_components=2)  # Reduce to 2 dimensions for vi-
sualization X_pca = pca.fit_transform(X_scaled)

# Add the PCA results to the original dataset for visualiza-
tion
df['PCA_1'] = X_pca[:, 0]
df['PCA_2'] = X_pca[:, 1]

# Visualize the PCA result
plt.figure(figsize=(8, 6))
plt.scatter(df['PCA_1'], df['PCA_2'], c='blue', marker='o')
for i, txt in enumerate(df['Song']):
    plt.annotate(f"{df['Song'][i]} - {df['Artist'][i]}",
(df['PCA_1'][i], df['PCA_2'][i]), fontsize=10)
plt.title('PCA of Music Features')
plt.xlabel('Principal Component 1')
plt.ylabel('Principal Component 2')
plt.grid(True)
plt.show()

# Recommending songs based on PCA
def recommend_song(song_name, n_recommendations=2):

    # Get the index of the song selected for recommendation
    song_idx = df[df['Song'] == song_name].index[0]

    # Compute cosine similarity between the selected song
and all other songs
    song_pca_values = df[['PCA_1', 'PCA_2']].iloc[song_idx].
values.reshape(1, -1) similarities = cosine_similarity(song_
pca_values, df[['PCA_1', 'PCA_2']])

    # Get the indices of the most similar songs
    similar_songs_idx = np.argsort(similarities[0])[::-1]
[1:n_recommendations+1]
    recommended_songs = df.iloc[similar_songs_idx]['Song'].
values return recommended_songs
```

```
# Example: Recommending songs similar to 'Blinding Lights'
recommended = recommend_song('Blinding Lights')

print("\nRecommended Songs for 'Blinding Lights':")

print(recommended)
```

```
Original Music Dataset:
            Song                        Artist  Tempo  Energy
0  Blinding Lights                   The Weeknd     85    0.80
1     Shape of You                   Ed Sheeran     96    0.85
2       Levitating                     Dua Lipa    103    0.90
3      Uptown Funk    Mark Ronson ft. Bruno Mars    115    0.88
4  Watermelon Sugar                 Harry Styles     95    0.92
5             Stay  The Kid LAROI & Justin Bieber    105    0.85
6           Good 4 U                Olivia Rodrigo    138    0.88

   Danceability  Mood
0          0.75  0.80
1          0.85  0.70
2          0.90  0.85
3          0.87  0.85
4          0.91  0.90
5          0.88  0.75
6          0.92  0.88
```

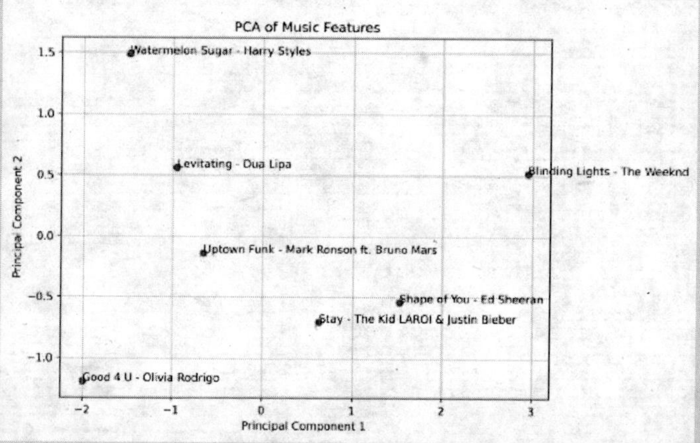

Explanation of the Code

We will compose a simple dataset with practical song names involving great artists as "Blinding Lights" by The Weeknd, "Shape of You" by Ed Sheeran, and "Levitating" by Dua Lipa. It would hold fake numerical attributes, for example, tempo, energy, danceability, and mood for mimicking actual song characteristics.

7.10 MODEL EVALUATION METRICS

Metrics for evaluation are tools that serve to evaluate the performance of a machine learning model. This gives us some way to evaluate how correct or effective a model is in predicting the output. Metrics common with classification tasks include accuracy, precision, recall, and F1 score, with those common with regression including MAE (Mean Absolute Error), MSE (Mean Squared Error), and R^2 (R-squared). For clustering, metrics like Silhouette Score help assess the appropriateness of grouping. Metrics like those are supposed to go hand in-hand with understanding how good a model is and how to make it better.

7.10.1 When are Model Evaluation Metrics Used?

Evaluation metrics are used at every stage within a machine learning project. They are used to test the performance of a model after training, to compare different models, and to steer the tuning of hyperparameters. In production, they are used to track model performance through time and detect issues such as model drift. Without evaluation metrics, it would be tricky to tell whether a model is genuinely worth using or reliable.

7.10.2 Importance of Proper Evaluation in Machine Learning

A sound evaluation, especially in machine learning, is vital to build reliable, accurate, and fair models. It seeks to understand how well a model performs, not merely on its ability to fit the training data, but more importantly, on its ability to generalize to unseen data. Without the right evaluation, a model might show successful results that are only misleading, overfitted, or biased, and hence, the model would fail to deliver the results in the real-world.

With proper evaluation methods, a data scientist would be able to detect errors at an early stage and further improve the model based on meaningful insights. By choosing appropriate metrics-the metrics of evaluation such as accuracy, precision, recall, or error rates-the developers can point out whether their models fail to recognize significant patterns, mark too many false predictions, or simply are not fitted for the task at hand.

Evaluations are also instrumental in setting up model selections and fine tunings. This evaluation will contrast different algorithms and configurations to best perform the one. Besides this, in life-critical applications like healthcare, finance, or autonomous systems, evaluation will dictate trust, safety, and ethical or regulatory compliance.

Task Type	Metric	Description
Classification	Accuracy	Ratio of correctly predicted instances to total instances.
	Precision	Proportion of true positives among predicted positives.
	Recall (Sensitivity)	Proportion of true positives among actual positives.
	F1 Score	Harmonic mean of precision and recall; balances both.

(Contd.)

Task Type	Metric	Description
	ROC-AUC Score	Measures the ability of the model to distinguish between classes.
	Confusion Matrix	A table showing true vs. predicted classifications (TP, FP, FN, TN).
Regression	Mean Absolute Error (MAE)	Average of absolute differences between actual and predicted values.
	Mean Squared Error (MSE)	Average of squared differences; penalizes large errors.
	Root Mean Squared Error (RMSE)	Square root of MSE; interpretable in original units.
	R-squared (R^2)	Proportion of variance in the target explained by the model.

7.11   CLASSIFICATION METRICS

7.11.1   Accuracy

Accuracy refers to the extent to which the measurement result matches the correct or actual value. This is an important concept in science, engineering, and data analysis, where reliability needs to be guaranteed. In simple terms, the accuracy in machine learning is referring to the ratio of valid predictions over the total number of predictions made. Also, this ratio determines how good or bad is the performance of the model.

The question of accuracy is not only for technical fields but is critical in everyday life: if we think of GPS coordinates or IDs for a financial transaction, erroneous information might even become a matter of loss! There are just too many realms in which trustworthiness is the word synonym with accuracy and give a visual for the array of issues on which accuracy is accepted as the standard for judgment and analysis.

Aspect	Description
Definition	Accuracy = (True Positives + True Negatives)/Total Predictions.
Purpose	Measures overall correctness of a classification model.
Strengths	Simple to compute and understand; effective in balanced datasets.
Limitations	Can be misleading in imbalanced datasets; may ignore minority class performance.
Example Scenario	If 95% of samples are negative, predicting all as negative gives 95% accuracy.
Better Alternatives	Use Precision, Recall, F1 Score, or ROC-AUC in imbalanced cases.

7.11.2 Precision

Precision refers to the degree of consistency in obtaining results, even if those results are not the desired ones. In the sciences, precision is mostly correlated with repeatability, whereas, in machine learning, it is related to the measure of true positives to all predicted positives. If the precision of the method is high, there will be some guarantee of reliability. This is very important where false positives can cause costly mistakes.

Precision builds trust and clarity, be it for experiments or communication; this sort of trust and clarity is essential for quality and accuracy in any field.

Aspect	*Description*
Definition	Precision = True Positives/(True Positives + False Positives)
Also Known As	Positive Predictive Value (PPV)
Purpose	Measures how many predicted positives are actually correct
Focus Area	Evaluates the quality of positive predictions
Best Used When	False positives are costly (e.g., spam detection, medical diagnosis)
Limitation	Does not consider false negatives; may be misleading alone
Complementary Metrics	Recall (Sensitivity), F1 Score
Example	If 10 emails are predicted as spam and only 7 are actual spam, precision = 70%

7.11.3 Recall

Recall measures the degree to which the system identifies all positives. The recall is defined as the truly positive cases divided by all actual positive cases. A high recall would mean few false-negatives; hence, domains like healthcare or fraud-detection in which missing a true case can be costly would highly appreciate having high recall.

Even though recall reflects how complete the predictions are, it is often necessary to weigh it against precision so that we would not consider a result that is full yet not accurate.

Aspect	*Description*
Definition	Recall = True Positives/(True Positives + False Negatives)
Also Known As	Sensitivity, True Positive Rate (TPR)
Purpose	Measures how many actual positives are correctly identified
Focus Area	Evaluates the completeness of positive predictions
Best Used When	Missing a positive case is costly (e.g., disease detection, fraud detection)
Limitation	Does not account for false positives; can be high even with many incorrect positives
Complementary Metrics	Precision, F1 Score
Example	If 100 people have a disease and the model detects 80, recall = 80%

7.11.4 F1-Score

The F1-score is the harmonic mean of precision and recall, combining both into one value. It is especially useful when dealing with imbalanced data or when both false positives and false negatives matter. A high F1-score means a model balances accuracy and completeness, making it more reliable than accuracy alone in many situations.

Aspect	Description
Definition	F1 Score = 2 × (Precision × Recall)/(Precision + Recall)
Purpose	Balances precision and recall into a single metric
Type of Mean	Harmonic mean (less influenced by extreme values than the arithmetic mean)
Best Used When	Need to balance false positives and false negatives; especially in imbalanced datasets
Strength	Useful when both precision and recall are important
Limitation	Ignores true negatives; not ideal if they are important in your problem
Complementary Metrics	Precision, Recall, Accuracy
Example	If precision = 0.75 and recall = 0.60, then F1 Score ≈ 0.67

7.11.5 Confusion Matrix

A confusion matrix is a table that shows how a classification model's predictions compare to actual results. It includes true positives, true negatives, false positives, and false negatives. This breakdown helps identify not just how accurate a model is, but what kinds of mistakes it makes—making it essential for improving and evaluating models in critical areas like healthcare or fraud detection.

Term	Description
True Positives (TP)	Correctly predicted positive cases (e.g., actual spam predicted as spam).
True Negatives (TN)	Correctly predicted negative cases (e.g., non-spam predicted as non-spam).
False Positives (FP)	Incorrectly predicted positive cases (e.g., non-spam predicted as spam).
False Negatives (FN)	Incorrectly predicted negative cases (e.g., spam predicted as non-spam).
Precision	TP/(TP + FP) – Measures the quality of positive predictions.
Recall (Sensitivity)	TP/(TP + FN) – Measures the completeness of positive predictions.
Accuracy	(TP + TN)/(TP + TN + FP + FN) – Measures overall correctness of the model.
F1 Score	2 × (Precision × Recall)/(Precision + Recall) – Harmonic mean of precision and recall.

Example Confusion Matrix for a Binary Classification Problem:

	Predicted Positive	*Predicted Negative*
Actual Positive	True Positive (TP)	False Negative (FN)
Actual Negative	False Positive (FP)	True Negative (TN)

#Let's implement the above Topics using Python

```python
from sklearn.metrics
import accuracy_score, precision_score, recall_score, f1_
score, confusion_matrix
from sklearn.model_selection
import train_test_split
from sklearn.linear_model
import LogisticRegression
from sklearn.datasets
import make_classification
import matplotlib.pyplot as plt
import seaborn as sns

#Generate sample classification data
X, y = make_classification(n_samples=100, n_features=5, n_
classes=2, random_state=42)

#Split into train and test sets
X_train, X_test, y_train, y_test = train_test_split(X, y, test_
size=0.2, random_state=42)

#Train a logistic regression classifier
model = LogisticRegression() model.fit(X_train, y_train)

#Make predictions
y_pred = model.predict(X_test)

#Evaluate metrics
accuracy = accuracy_score(y_test, y_pred)
precision = precision_score(y_test, y_pred)
recall = recall_score(y_test, y_pred)
f1 = f1_score(y_test, y_pred)
cm = confusion_matrix(y_test, y_pred)

#Print the metrics
print(f"Accuracy: {accuracy:.2f}")
print(f"Precision: {precision:.2f}")
print(f"Recall: {recall:.2f}")
print(f"F1 Score: {f1:.2f}")

#Plot confusion matrix
plt.figure(figsize=(6, 4))
sns.heatmap(cm, annot=True, fmt='d', cmap='Blues',
xticklabels=['Predicted 0', 'Predicted 1'],
```

```
yticklabels=['Actual 0', 'Actual 1'])
plt.title('Confusion Matrix')
plt.xlabel('Predicted')
plt.ylabel('Actual')
plt.show()
```

#Output

```
Accuracy: 1.00
Precision: 1.00
Recall: 1.00
F1 Score: 1.00
```

Wrap-up

Without explicit programming, computers can learn from data, identify patterns, and make predictions thanks to machine learning. The fundamental concepts of machine learning are introduced in this chapter, which also examines supervised and unsupervised learning as well as well-known algorithms like PCA, decision trees, SVMs, clustering, and regression. Additionally, you'll discover how models are assessed using crucial performance indicators to guarantee accuracy and dependability. You will have a clear, organized understanding of how machine learning drives contemporary data-driven systems with these foundations.

QUESTIONS FOR PRACTICE

1. Define Machine Learning. Explain how it relates to Data Science.

   Anna University, 2022

2. What are the main types of Machine Learning? Give examples for supervised, unsupervised, and reinforcement learning.

   Vellore Institute of Technology, 2021

3. Explain the concept of supervised learning. How does labeled data help in training a model?

   SRM Institute of Science and Technology, 2023

4. Describe linear regression. Include its assumptions, evaluation metrics (MSE, RMSE, R^2), and a real-world application.

   Amity University, 2022

5. Explain logistic regression and the role of the sigmoid function. Provide an example classification problem.   *IIT Bombay, 2022*

6. Describe the structure and working of a decision tree. List advantages and disadvantages.   *Manipal University, 2021*

7. Explain the concept of Support Vector Machine (SVM). What are kernels, and why are they used in SVM?

   BMS College of Engineering, 2023

8. Define unsupervised learning. Describe K-Means clustering and explain how to choose the number of clusters (Elbow Method, Silhouette Score).

   Anna University, 2022

9. What is Principal Component Analysis (PCA)? Explain its role in dimensionality reduction.   *Amrita Vishwa Vidyapeetham, 2021*

10. List common classification evaluation metrics (accuracy, precision, recall, F1-score). Why is evaluation important in Machine Learning?

    IIT Delhi, 2023

8

Deep Learning

8.1 INTRODUCTION TO DEEP LEARNING

8.1.1 What is Deep Learning?

Deep Learning is a revolutionary field of artificial intelligence that enables machines to think like humans and take decisions like a human. It is a form of machine learning, but the difference lies in the fact that it can work on unstructured data, such as images, text, or audio. Deep neural networks consist of multiple layers of interconnected nodes progressing through data in stages. That is, in that way, every layer capture progressively more and more complex patterns; deep learning has proven well suited to tasks in which even the best algorithms flail. At the center of deep learning lies the removal of the need for humans to separately extract features so that systems can learn from raw data. This makes deep learning an extremely powerful tool for solving real-world problems in health care, finance, entertainment, and transportation domains, among others.

8.1.2 Key Characteristics

Hierarchical Feature Learning: Learning goes from simple features to more complex features, layer-by-layer through the networks layers.
End-to-End Learning: Accepts raw data directly as input, without requiring manual coding of features.
Representation Learning: Automatically learns representations of optimal data, internally learning the features that best represent the data.
Data Hungry: Requires large amounts of labeled data to achieve a high degree of accuracy.
Computationally Intensive: Relies on high-performance computing infrastructure, such as GPUs and TPUs for the learning process.

8.1.3 Importance of Deep Learning in Data Science

Deep learning methods represent the most important tools available to data science practitioners who work with large and complex data sets. Traditionally, practitioners had to manually select the relevant features from the raw data. With deep learning methods, however, relevant features are selected, automatically, from the raw data. This is especially powerful when working with unstructured data like image, audio and text data.

Moreover, deep learning methods can obtain predictive scores much closer to perfect accuracy when compared with traditional methods in applications such as image and speech recognition and natural language processing. Their ability to learn from data without human intervention allows for greater efficiency.

Moreover, the deep learning system is very much scalable and flexible in terms of onboarding new data streams with their changing requirements. The health care, finance, and e-commerce sectors are heavily dependent on data analytics to make the right calls; thus, it is a major underpinning in real-life situations.

8.1.4 Differences between Machine Learning and Deep Learning

Aspect	*Machine Learning (ML)*	*Deep Learning (DL)*
Definition	Subset of AI that uses algorithms to parse data, learn from it, and make decisions.	Subset of ML that uses neural networks with many layers to learn from data.
Data Dependency	Performs well with smaller datasets.	Requires large volumes of data to perform effectively.
Feature Engineering	Requires manual feature extraction and domain expertise.	Automatically extracts features from raw data.
Model Complexity	Uses simpler models (e.g., decision trees, SVM).	Uses complex architectures like CNNs, RNNs, Transformers.
Computation Power	Can run on conventional CPUs.	Needs high-end GPUs or TPUs for training.
Execution Time	Faster to train on small datasets.	Slower training but more accurate on large data.
Interpretability	Easier to interpret and understand decisions.	Often considered a "black box" with less interpretability.

(Contd.)

Aspect	Machine Learning (ML)	Deep Learning (DL)
Application Examples	Spam detection, credit scoring, predictive maintenance.	Image recognition, speech translation, autonomous driving.
Training Time	Generally shorter training time.	Requires much longer training due to deep networks.
Accuracy	Good, but may plateau on complex tasks.	Higher accuracy on large, complex datasets and problems.

8.1.5 Why Deep Learning has Gained Importance

Deep learning systems are a contemporary technology that has integrated into the realm of artificial intelligence and has the capability to surpass all other methods. From the standpoint of data, deep learning is at the forefront of the technology wave along with its big data dependency. Through the minute-to-minute activities on almost every social media platform, IoT device, or mobile application, vast datasets of varying qualities ranging from semi-structured to completely uncertain are being produced. Facto, the data on which these models are trained simultaneously originates from the same source.

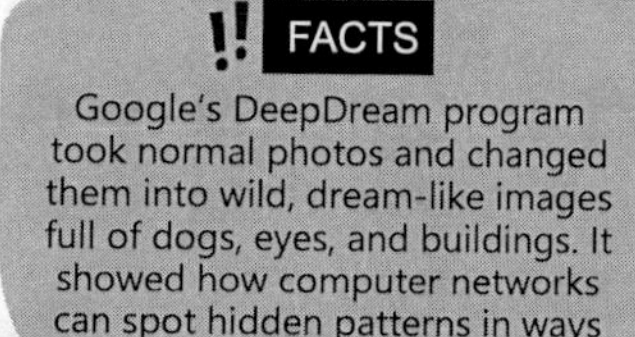

Dealing with such large datasets is no small feat and deep learning is the only technique that can handle this situation, besides the fact that it will gain more power from the data. It is said that these large datasets are necessary to train deep learning models; however, it does not necessarily mean that they will get the right outputs. The mighty and rich data gradients are still the major contributors to well-trained and accurate deep learning models in the real-world.

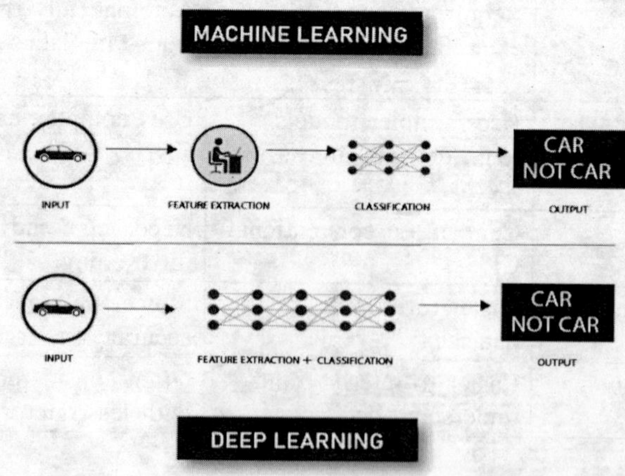

The next step was to enhance the computing power, with the best advance coming from GPUs and TPUs, which serve from being have high computing power so a large neural network can be trained very fast. Cloud services and open-sourcing frameworks like TensorFlow and PyTorch have accelerated the progress in training and deployment.

More importantly, deep learning eliminates feature extraction from several manual processes that would ordinarily require the intervention of somebody possessing a domain knowledge of the subject of interest. This makes it applicable across numerous fields, across multiple disciplines, including healthcare, finance, and autonomous systems.

8.2 APPLICATIONS OF DEEP LEARNING

8.2.1 Top Application of Computer Vision

Application	Description	Key Models	Major Use Cases
Image Classification	Assigns a label to an entire image based on its content.	CNNs (ResNet, VGG, Inception)	Medical imaging, face recognition, photo tagging (e.g., in Facebook/Instagram)
Object Detection	Identifies and localizes multiple objects within a single image.	YOLO, SSD, Faster R-CNN	Autonomous vehicles, security surveillance, retail analytics
Image Segmentation	Performs pixel-level classification to segment specific regions of interest.	U-Net, Mask R-CNN, DeepLab	Tumor segmentation, road/lane detection, satellite image analysis

Now we will implement one usecase from above table:

Use Case: Image Classification

Code Example

Problem: Imagine we have a photo of an animal, and we want a computer to identify what type of animal it is (e.g., cat, dog, elephant). Instead of manually looking at the image, we want a computer to classify the image for us automatically.

```
#ResNet50 Image Classification - All in One Cell (No Tkinter)
#Install (uncomment if needed in Colab/Kaggle)

!pip install tensorflow pillow numpy
import tensorflow as tf from tensorflow.keras.applications.
resnet50
import ResNet50, preprocess_input, decode_predictions from
tensorflow.keras.preprocessing
import image import numpy as np
```

```
#File upload (works in Colab/Jupyter)

from google.colab import files uploaded = files.upload()

#Get uploaded image filename
img_path = next(iter(uploaded.keys())) print("Image upload-
ed:", img_path)

#Load model
model = ResNet50(weights='imagenet')

#Preprocess image
img=image.load_img(img_path,target_size=(224,224))
img_array= image.img_to_array(img)
img_array=np.expand_dims(img_array, axis=0)
img_array = preprocess_input(img_array)
Predict
predictions=model.predict(img_array)
decoded_predictions=decode_predictions(predictions, top=3)
[0]

#Display results
print("\nTop 3 Predictions:")
for i, (_, label, score) in enumerate(decoded_predictions):
        print(f"{i+1}. {label}: {score:.2f}")
```

INPUT

OUTPUT

```
Top 3 Predictions:
1. zebra: 0.98
2. hartebeest: 0.00
3. cheetah: 0.00
```

8.2.2 Top Application of Natural Language Processing

Application	*Description*	*Real-World Examples*
Chatbots & Virtual Assistants	AI-driven systems that simulate human conversation, providing automated customer support and assistance.	Siri, Alexa, Google Assistant, ChatGPT
Sentiment Analysis	Analyzing text to determine the sentiment expressed, such as positive, negative, or neutral.	Monitoring social media for brand sentiment, analyzing customer reviews
Machine Translation	Automatically translating text or speech from one language to another.	Google Translate, DeepL, Microsoft Translator

Now we will implement one use case from above table:

Code Example

Objective: Determine whether a movie review expresses a positive or negative sentiment.

Approach: Utilize the TextBlob library to analyze the sentiment of a given text.

```python
#Python


from textblob import TextBlob


# Sample movie review
review = "I absolutely loved this movie! The plot was
thrilling and the acting was superb."


# Create a TextBlob object
blob = TextBlob(review)


# Get the sentiment polarity and subjectivity
polarity, subjectivity = blob.sentiment


# Display the results
print(f"Polarity: {polarity}")
print(f"Subjectivity: {subjectivity}")


# Determine the sentiment
if polarity > 0:
sentiment = "Positive"
elif polarity < 0:
sentiment = "Negative"
else:
sentiment = "Neutral"


print(f"Sentiment: {sentiment}")
```

```
#output
Polarity: 0.75
Subjectivity: 0.6
Sentiment: Positive
```

Explanation: The TextBlob object is initialized with the movie review text. The sentiment property of Text-Blob returns a named tuple of the form Sentiment(polarity, subjectivity).

- **Polarity:** A float within the range [−1.0, 1.0], where −1 indicates negative sentiment and 1 indicates positive sentiment.
- **Subjectivity:** A float within the range [0.0, 1.0], where 0.0 is very objective and 1.0 is very subjective.

8.2.3 Artificial Neural Networks

Artificial Neural Networks (ANNs) are a completely innovation copied from how the human brain works. These networks are meant to mimic the way neurons interact so that machines can treat data just like humans treat it.

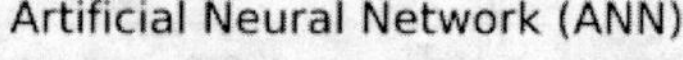

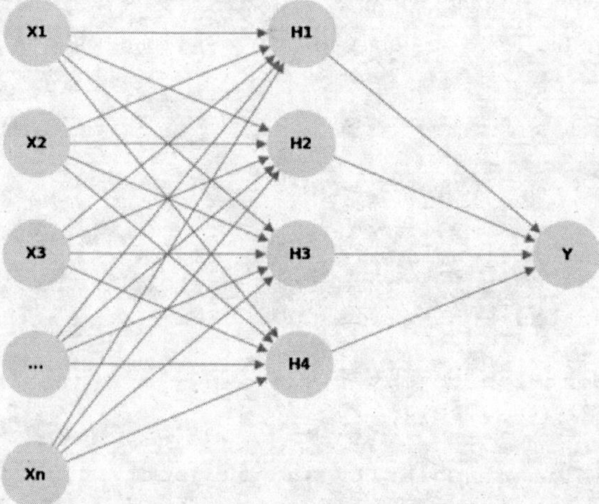

Much like the brain identifies patterns and learns from experience, ANNs are designed to recognize patterns in data, learn from them, and make informed decisions. At the core of ANNs are layers of interconnected units called neurons. Each layer has a specific role: the input layer receives raw data, the hidden layers process and analyze it, and the output layer produces the result.

8.2.4 Why ANN's are Important?

They matter because Artificial Neural Networks really do change the way we tackle and solve these really complex problems not only in data analysis, but also for making predictions-and often with an eye towards automation. What makes ANNs really special?

Mimicking the Human Brain: ANNs simulate the brain's functioning to process vast data, detect patterns, and make intelligent decisions.

Ability to Handle Non-linear Problems: ANNs effectively capture complex, non-linear relationships that traditional algorithms cannot.

Automated Feature Extraction: ANNs automatically learn key features from raw data, reducing the need for manual feature engineering.

Big Data Handling: ANNs efficiently learn from massive datasets, enhancing prediction accuracy and decision-making.

8.2.5 Definition of Artificial Neurons

An artificial neuron is a mathematical model that emulates the biological neuron in that it takes in input values, performs some calculations on that input, and eventually produces an output. An artificial neuron has input values that it receives, then applies weights to them, and finally, it takes the weighted input and inputs it into an activation function to generate the output. Artificial neural networks are made up of numerous artificial neurons, organized into layers which consist of an input layer, one or more hidden layers, and an output layer. As a result, this layered architecture allows the artificial neural network to perform difficult tasks such as classification, regression, pattern recognition, and decision-making. During training the network weight and bias shifts and consequently gets better at the problem-solving and accurate predicting by learning through the data it receives.

8.2.6 Artificial Neural Networks and their Constituents

An ANN, which abbreviates Artificial Neural Network, is one method of computing data which is able to identify the patterns and relationships in the data. Its formation is similar to that of the human brain, with the ability to process the information via the network of neurons. To be more precise, ANN can be described as a collection of algorithms which are capable of learning identification of the data patterns, relationships and features in a way similar to the human brain.

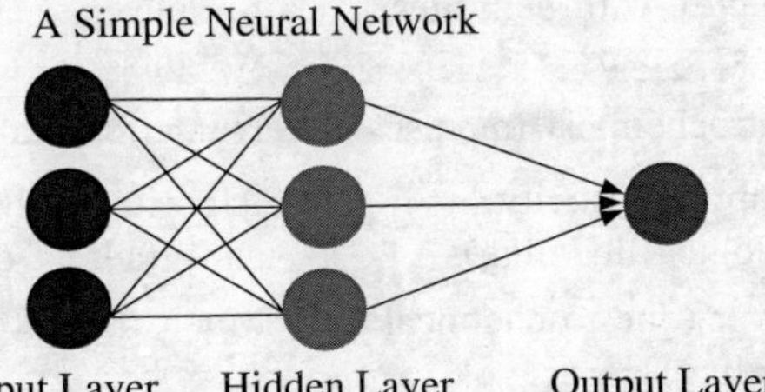

Neural networks have been largely adopted for various applications that range from image recognition to natural language understanding, passing through speech processing. The structure of networks consists of layers that collectively transform the input data into meaningful outputs. The input layer, the hidden layer(s), and the output layer are the three primary components of an artificial neural network.

Input Layer: The Input Layer is the first layer in a neural network, which receives raw data from the external environment. A neuron in this layer corresponds to a feature or characteristic of the input data. These data will just be transferred and handed on to the subsequent layers for processing. Input Layer does not transform or calculate anything; it just forwards the information to the Hidden Layer where the actual learning takes place.

Hidden Layer: The Whole Computational Work is carried out in the Hidden Layer(s). These layers contain neurons which execute the mathematical computations in the process of taking the data fed to it by the input layer. The more hidden layers a network contains, the more complex the type of patterns to which it can be trained. It is through the hidden layers' neurons that the model can capture those intricate relationships and features in the data. Depending on the architecture of the network, it can have one or even more hidden layers.

Output Layer: The result of the computation done by the network is output through the Output Layer. It is the layer where information already computed from the previous hidden layer feeds in to produce the final output or in other words a prediction. There are different numbers of neurons in this layer depending upon the type of task that network performs. For binary classification problems, that are usually based on determining spam vs. no-spam from the email the output layer commonly comprises one neuron only. With multiple-class classifications, for example, determining an image represents various digits then there are also numerous neurons of an output layer for every possibility.

8.2.7 How Artificial Neurons are Different from Biological Neurons

Aspect	Biological Neurons	Artificial Neurons
Structure	Complex with dendrites, axons, synapses	Simple mathematical model with weights and activation
Signal Type	Electrochemical impulses	Numerical values (e.g., 0.0 to 1.0)
Learning Mechanism	Synaptic plasticity (biological learning)	Algorithms like backpropagation and gradient descent
Speed	Slower (due to chemical signaling)	Much faster (electronic processing)
Energy Efficiency	Highly efficient, brain uses ~20 watts	More energy-consuming, especially in large neural networks

8.2.8   Activation Functions

An activation function is a mathematical operation applied to the output of a neuron (node) in a neural network. It determines whether a neuron should be activated (i.e., fired) or not by introducing non-linearity into the model. This non-linearity allows neural networks to learn complex patterns.

Functions	Formula	Output Range	Advantages	Disadvantages	Typical Use Cases
ReLU		$[0, \infty)$	Fast, efficient, avoids vanishing gradients	Can cause "dying ReLU" (neurons stuck at 0)	Hidden layers in most deep networks
Leaky ReLU		$(-\infty, \infty)$	Fixes dying ReLU by allowing small negative gradients	Slightly more complex, leak factor tuning required	Hidden layers when ReLU underperforms
Sigmoid		$(0, 1)$	Probabilistic output, smooth gradient	Vanishing gradient, not zero-centered	Binary classification (output layer)
Softmax		$(0, 1)$, sum = 1	Outputs probabilities over classes	Sensitive to outliers, not for binary classification	Multi-class classification (output layer)

8.2.9   When to Use Activation Functions

Activation functions are essential for making neural networks **learn complex patterns**. Without them, even deep networks would behave like simple linear models. Here's when and why you use activation functions in different parts of a neural network:

Input layer: Often linear or raw input; no activation applied.

Hidden layers: Use **ReLU** or its variants (like Leaky ReLU). It speeds up training and avoids vanishing gradients.

Output layer:

- **Sigmoid** for binary classification
- **Softmax** for multi-class classification
- **Linear** for regression problems

8.3 BACKPROPAGATION ALGORITHM

8.3.1 Concept

Backpropagation goes into the domain of learning algorithms that work on training neural networks. Neural networks learn by modifying their internal weights and biases so that the predictions they make are less erroneous.

Here is an analogy: The neural network makes a prediction → checks how wrong it is → and then uses that error to fine-tune itself so it can do better next time.

Main Idea

- Make a prediction (onward flow).
- Compare the prediction with the true answer by way of a loss function.
- Derive the extent to which each neuron contributed to the error (gradients).
- Backpropagate the error through the whole network.
- Update the weight to make a better prediction the next time (gradient descent).

8.3.2 Chain Rule and Gradient Computation

The Chain Rule: An Overview

The chain rule is a fundamental concept in calculus so that we can see how one quantity in a series of changes indirectly changes the other. Put simply, it tells us how one quantity is affected when the initial quantity goes under several layers or other intervening situations.

Here the general procedure: Suppose that input A affected B while B affected C. It's pretty easy to see how A will affect B or how B will affect C, but the chain rule tells you how to compute the effect of A on C by combining these effects together. The concept becomes especially handy when dealing with situations wherein the output depends on nested operations.

Let's say, in the real-world: For example, a production line in a factory. If raw materials pass through many stages toward becoming the final product, and if there is a mishap at the end, you would want to go back tracing through these steps to find the error. The chain rule gives you the logic to do that: how one step affects the next is considered, and then these effects are combined to see how the first step influenced the last.

Why is the Chain Rule Vital to Backpropagation?

The chain rule is at the core of the backpropagation algorithm which is the way artificial neural networks train. Backpropagation is how a neural network learns from its mistakes by simultaneously altering internal weights with the goal of ultimately making a better prediction through successful learning. But the neural network must first understand how much of the final prediction error can be accounted for by each part of the system when the prediction is wrong. This is why the inner workings of the chain rule are essential to backpropagation.

Artificial neural networks are structured with layers of processing that scaling in sorts of units where each layer passes the information on to the next set of units. The end output would be dependent on each layering ordered before it from the past outputs. When the network makes a wrong prediction, backpropagation must start at the output and effectively track back through each layer to ultimately understand what went wrong and by how much. This process is known as tracing responsibility through the layers. This tracing of responsibility is only able to take place, due to the link that the chain rule affords the network.

8.3.3 Loss Functions (MSE, Cross-Entropy Loss)

Aspect	*Mean Squared Error (MSE)*	*Cross-Entropy Loss*
Purpose	Measures average squared difference between predicted and actual values	Measures the difference between predicted probabilities and actual class labels
Used for	Regression tasks	Classification tasks (binary & multi-class)
Prediction Type	Continuous numeric output	Probabilistic output (class probabilities)
Formula (conceptual)	Average of (prediction − target)^2	$-\Sigma$ (true label $\times$ log (predicted probability))
Output Range	0 to ∞ (non-negative)	0 to ∞ (lower is better)
Sensitivity to Errors	Penalizes larger errors more due to squaring	Penalizes confident wrong predictions harshly
Effect of Outliers	Highly sensitive (large errors dominate the loss)	Less affected unless prediction is confidently incorrect
Interpretability	Error magnitude is intuitive in numeric terms	Based on information theory (entropy), less intuitive
Optimization Behavior	May lead to slow convergence for classification tasks	Encourages faster and sharper convergence in classification
Best for	Predicting values like price, temperature, etc.	Problems like image recognition, text classification
Example Use Case	Predicting house prices	Classifying emails as spam or not
When Not to Use	When dealing with probabilities or class labels	For regression tasks (outputs not in [0,1])

(Contd.)

Aspect	Mean Squared Error (MSE)	Cross-Entropy Loss
Variants	Root Mean Squared Error (RMSE), MAE	Binary Cross-Entropy, Categorical Cross-Entropy
Gradient Characteristics	Gradient decreases with smaller errors	Steeper gradients for incorrect predictions
Computation Complexity	Simple, low cost	Slightly higher due to log operations

8.4 TRAINING NEURAL NETWORKS

8.4.1 Optimization Algorithms

Machine learning and deep learning model adjustment for loss function minimization uses optimization algorithms to modify parameter values. The two major algorithms that exist for this purpose are:

- The first algorithm called **Gradient Descent** updates model parameters through an iterative process which minimizes loss functions through gradient-based parameter modifications.
- **Adam Optimizer** represents an advanced algorithm that integrates the principles of Momentum and RMSProp to adjust learning rates through gradient-based first and second moment estimation.

Importance

- Training models depends significantly on optimization algorithms because they reduce errors through learning patterns from data.
- Adam together with other efficient optimizers enable models to achieve faster convergence when compared to traditional optimization methods.
- The stability of training processes increases using adaptive optimizers which provides benefits to training deep and complex networks.
- Model accuracy along with generalization benefits from optimization processes that are implemented correctly.

8.4.2 When to Use

Scenario	Use Gradient Descent	Use Adam Optimizer
Simple linear or logistic regression	Yes	No
Large datasets with noisy gradients	Not ideal	Yes
Deep learning/neural networks	Slow, may diverge	Preferred
Memory is limited	Yes (lightweight)	No (slightly heavier)
Full control over learning dynamics	Yes (for experimenting with step sizes and momentum)	Yes (configurable, but automatically adapts learning rates)

8.4.3 Challenges: Vanishing and Exploding Gradients

The process of training deep neural networks encounters two main problems named Vanishing and Exploding Gradients. Deep networks with sigmoid or tanh activation functions experience Vanishing Gradients which result from extremely small gradients that move backward through multiple layers. The model faces difficulty in learning because small weight updates happen in the beginning layers.

Exploding Gradients emerge during backpropagation when gradients exceed proper limits and cause significant weight modifications that make training unstable.

Solutions:

- **Weight Initialization:** Both Xavier and He initialization techniques serve to properly handle gradient scale issues.
- **ReLU Activation:** Implementing ReLU activation functions serves as a solution to stop the occurrence of vanishing gradients.
- **Gradient Clipping:** The technique controls gradient size by restricting its value thus eliminating the problem of exploding gradients.

8.4.4 Techniques for Stable Training (Batch Normalization, Dropout)

Batch Normalization (BN):

- **Definition:** Training involves the process of normalizing the input to every layer through activation adjustment and scaling operations. It normalizes the current activation layer output using batch statistical parameters which involves mean subtraction and standard deviation division.
- Training benefits from accelerated performance together with enhanced convergence and reduced chances of gradient problems. The technique enables faster model training by decreasing the need for proper initialization and allowing the application of elevated learning rates.

Dropout:

- **Definition:** During training steps, the Dropout technique applies a random elimination of neurons by setting their values to zero. This technique helps prevent overfitting by making the model less dependent on single neurons.
- The usage of Dropout prevents overfitting through the random shutdown of neurons which maintains better generalization capabilities of the model.

8.5 CONVOLUTIONAL NEURAL NETWORKS (CNNS)

8.5.1 Introduction to CNNs

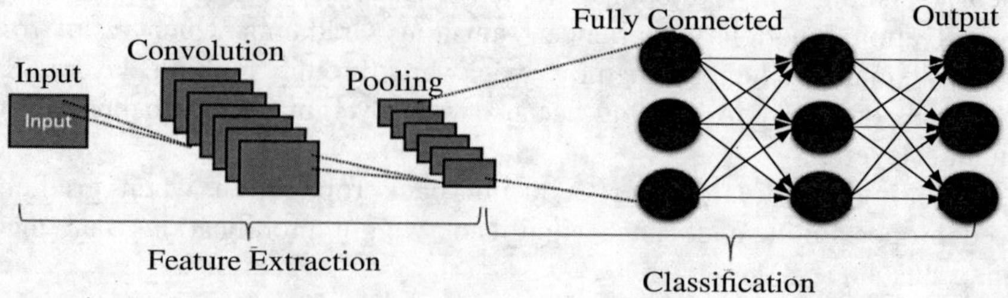

CNN is a specific type of deep learning model that is best suited for visual data analysis and processing, like images and videos. Compared to the traditional neural network, CNN is good at recognizing spatial relationship patterns and recognizing patterns in the case of visual data, since they closely resemble the human visual cortex structure. Convolutional Neural Networks (CNNs) are deep learning models created for the process and analysis of structured data like images and videos. Due to the capability of these models to automatically learn spatial hierarchies of features in an efficient way from raw input data, CNNs are now used as the building block for a variety of computer vision applications. CNNs are well suited to image processing since they exploit spatial relationships within data. In contrast, traditional neural networks treat every input feature as an independent value. CNNs capture patterns, such as edges, textures, and objects, through convolutional operations.

8.5.2 How CNN Works?

A CNN process images using layers that help point out important features such as edges, shapes, and textures.

The key constituents of a CNN are:

- **Convolution Layer:** This layer is used to filter the image based on features or patterns like colors, edges, or textures from the image; the result will be called the feature map.

- **Activation Function (ReLU):** It introduces non-linearity to help the network learn complex patterns in images.

- **Pooling Layer:** This decreases the spatial dimension of the feature maps and captures the key information. Among these, there are max pooling and average pooling techniques.

- **FC Layer:** Fully connected layer that acts like the conventional neural network once features have been extracted from images, as output is flattened, and is fed to make the final prediction.

- **Softmax/Output Layer:** This layer takes the final values and converts them into probabilities for classification, for example, dog, cat, or human.

8.5.3 Core Components

Activation Function

After every convolution layer, activation functions are used in the network for the introduction of non-linearity. The ReLU is most widely used among the activation functions used in the CNNs. The ReLU sets all the data to zero wherever the values appear negative and maintains positive values in the same. It is therefore capable of carrying out non-linear transformations that aid in learning diverse relationships and a wide range of distributions in the data.

Pooling Layers

Pooling decreases the spatial dimension of feature maps, hence the network becomes efficient in terms of time and is less likely to overfitting. Max-pooling just selects the maximum value in that area and uses it as a selection while average pooling uses the mean value. These layers of pooling allow a network to focus on what is salient for its data, thus keeping features where needed while bringing down the number of computations made.

Fully connected Layers

Fully connected layers appear closer to the tail of a CNN architecture, taking the high-level features that are extracted by convolutional and pooling layers in order to make decisions. The feature maps get flattened into one-dimensional vectors. So, all the features will connect to each output node in this layer. When it comes to classifying an object, fully connected layers are at the core, as they have a probability for assigning classes given the input image.

Output Layer

It is the last layer which provides the predictions by the CNN. In most classification problems, it uses the softmax function that transforms raw scores into probabilities. These probabilities represent how likely an image will belong to any class. The class with the highest probability is taken as the output of the network.

8.6 CONVOLUTION OPERATION

The part of the book focuses on explaining kernel operations and feature map processing within Convolutional Neural Networks.

Filters (Kernels)

Definition: Filters (also called kernels) are small matrices used in Convolutional Neural Networks (CNNs) to detect patterns like edges, textures, or specific features in input data (e.g., images). These filters are applied to the input through convolution operations.

- **Function:** Filters operate by moving across the input image through convolution to multiply elements together and add those products to generate a feature map.

Feature Maps

Definition: Feature maps are the outputs produced after applying filters to an input image. They represent the spatial arrangement of detected features across the image.

- **Function:** Feature maps highlight the presence of specific features (like edges or patterns) in different regions of the input. They provide a transformed, compact representation of the original data for further processing in the network.

8.6.1 Padding, Stride, and Receptive Field Concepts

Concept	Definition	Purpose
Padding	Adding extra pixels (usually zeros) around the image or feature map before applying a filter.	Ensures filters can be applied to edges and prevents the reduction of the spatial dimensions of the output.
Stride	The number of steps the filter moves across the input image during convolution.	Controls the spatial size of the output feature map; larger strides reduce output dimensions; smaller strides retain more spatial information.
Receptive Field	The area of the input that a neuron in the network is processing.	As the network deepens, the receptive field grows, enabling the model to capture larger and more complex features.

8.7 POOLING LAYERS

8.7.1 Max Pooling vs. Average Pooling

Aspect	Max Pooling	Average Pooling
Definition	A pooling operation that selects the maximum value from a region of the feature map covered by the filter.	A pooling operation that calculates the average value from a region of the feature map covered by the filter.
Operation	For each region in the input, the maximum value is selected, ignoring others.	For each region in the input, the average of all values in the region is calculated.
Advantages	Retains important features like edges and textures. Helps reduce overfitting by preserving prominent features.	More stable representation of features. Less sensitive to noise and outliers.

(Contd.)

Aspect	*Max Pooling*	*Average Pooling*
Disadvantages	Can be sensitive to noise and outliers. May lose finer details if the maximum is not representative.	Can blur important features. May result in a loss of key features in high-contrast images.
Use Cases	Object detection, image classification, and segmentation where key features matter.	Regression tasks, medical imaging, and scenarios where a smooth feature representation is needed.
Best for	Capturing sharp, high-contrast features such as edges or textures.	Preserving overall structure and general feature representation.
Effect on Spatial Resolution	Reduces spatial dimensions while retaining prominent features.	Reduces spatial dimensions but smoothens the overall feature map.

8.7.2 Role of Pooling in Dimensionality Reduction

In Convolutional Neural Networks (CNNs) pooling serves to reduce feature map spatial dimensions by consolidating data values. Pooling operations lead to dimensionality reduction by decreasing both the number of computations and network parameters which improves model efficiency.

Convolutional Neural Networks implement two major varieties of pooling operations known as max pooling and average pooling. A maximum value gets selected from feature map regions by max pooling whereas average pooling calculates the arithmetic mean. The combination of these methods enables the model to preserve essential input features while generating smaller data sets.

8.8 POPULAR CNN ARCHITECTURES

8.8.1 LeNet-5

Aspect	*Details*
Year	1998
Key Features	First successful CNN for handwritten digit recognition (MNIST) 7 layers: 2 convolutional layers, 2 subsampling (pooling) layers, 3 fully connected layers Uses sigmoid activation function
Significance	Pioneered CNNs for image classification tasks Demonstrated CNN viability for digit recognition Marked the beginning of deep learning for computer vision Simple architecture with only 60,000 parameters

8.8.2   AlexNet

Aspect	Details
Year	2012
Key Features	8 layers: 5 convolutional layers, 3 fully connected layers Uses ReLU activation function Introduced dropout for regularization Data augmentation GPU for training
Significance	Won 2012 ImageNet competition with a 16.4% top-5 error rate Popularized deep learning using GPUs for training Paved way for deeper networks in large-scale image classification Introduced dropout and data augmentation techniques for better generalization

8.8.3   VGGNet

Aspect	Details
Year	2014
Key Features	Small 3×3 convolution filters stacked in deeper layers Deep architecture, up to 19 layers Uses 2×2 max pooling layers consistently Fully connected layers at the end
Significance	Known for simplicity and modular design Achieved state-of-the-art results in ImageNet (2014) Popular for transfer learning due to its simple, well-understood structure Simplicity in design and use of small filters made it easy to understand and implement

8.8.4   ResNet

Aspect	Details
Year	2015
Key Features	Introduced residual (skip) connections to address vanishing gradient problem Deep architecture, up to 152 layers Uses batch normalization
Significance	Solved the vanishing gradient problem, enabling deeper networks Achieved top-5 error rate of 3.6% in ImageNet Revolutionized deep network design with residual learning Enabled the training of very deep networks with hundreds of layers, improving accuracy

8.9 RECURRENT NEURAL NETWORKS (RNNS) AND LSTMS

Sequential data represents information that becomes meaningful through the exact order of its individual components. The interpretation and understanding of sequence elements depend on the relationships between each current element and its preceding and succeeding parts. Text along with time-series data and speech and videos stand as common examples of sequences.

Key Characteristics:

- **Order Dependency:** The way data elements follow each other determines its meaning (e.g., "he is good" ≠ "good is he").
- **Contextual Relationship:** Every data element derives its meaning from the elements that precede it.
- **Variable Length:** Sequences exist in different sizes because of their contextual nature (e.g., sentence lengths, time durations).
- **Temporal or Spatial Nature:** The progression of data occurs over time like weather information and through position like DNA sequences.

Importance in Machine Learning

- Traditional machine learning models assume inputs are independent, which fails for sequential data.
- To learn from sequential data, researchers need to build models which include the following:
    - **Recurrent Neural Networks (RNNs):** Store information from preceding inputs.
    - **Long Short-Term Memory (LSTM)** and **GRU:** These models address long-term dependencies while preventing gradient vanishing.
    - **Transformers:** These state-of-the-art models utilize self-attention to analyses sequence connections.

These models make it possible to develop sophisticated systems that perform tasks like language translation, speech recognition, stock prediction and other advanced functions.

8.9.1 Applications of Sequential Modelling

Application Area	Tasks	Reason for Using Sequential Modeling
Natural Language Processing (NLP)	Text generation Machine translation Sentiment analysis Chatbots	Language depends on word order and context
Speech Recognition	Voice-to-text Voice assistants (e.g., Alexa, Siri)	Speech is a time-dependent signal where sequence affects meaning

(Contd.)

Application Area	Tasks	Reason for Using Sequential Modeling
Time Series Forecasting	Stock market prediction Weather forecasting Energy demand prediction	Future values depend on historical trends and patterns
Video Analysis	Action recognition Video captioning Surveillance	Frame sequences matter to understand motion and activities
Music & Audio Generation	Music composition Sound synthesis	Notes and sounds follow structured time-based patterns
Healthcare Monitoring	Patient vital tracking Disease trend prediction	Health data varies over time and reflects changes in condition
Anomaly Detection	Fraud detection Intrusion detection System fault identification	Anomalies are identified by deviations in normal sequential behavior
Robotics & Control Systems	Path planning Sensor data analysis	Movement and decisions depend on previous steps and inputs

8.9.2   Challenges with Standard Neural Networks for Sequences

Challenge	Explanation
Fixed Input Size	Standard neural networks (like feedforward networks) expect fixed-length inputs and outputs, which is unsuitable for variable-length sequences like text or speech.
No Memory of Previous Inputs	They treat each input independently, lacking any mechanism to remember earlier data points in a sequence.
Loss of Temporal/Sequential Context	Without context awareness, they can't capture the order or timing of inputs, which is crucial in tasks like language modeling or time series prediction.
Scalability Issues	Handling long sequences requires very large input vectors, leading to inefficiency and high computational costs.
Poor Performance on Time-Dependent Tasks	Standard networks struggle with tasks like translation or speech recognition, where understanding depends on past information.

8.10   BASICS OF RNNS

Recurrent Neural Networks (RNNs), a specific neural network model, is an essential baseline approach to algorithms that involve keeping input sequences in order. Standard neural network models do not have context about the input because the input is treated independently. RNNs build context in their algorithms through a built-in memory system that remembers previous elements of a sequence.

This memory capability of RNNs, which keeps track of elements in prior sequence data, makes RNNs effective for analyzing sequence data with dependent elements like language data, speech tapes, and predictions of future time series. RNNs process base sequences one step at a time dependent on an internal hidden layer called an internal state for each processing sequence, allowing the model to identify time-dependent associations between incoming observations per prior observation in a sequence. RNNs assume a fundamental role in sequence learning which deep learning approaches also leverage.

8.10.1   Vanishing Gradient Problem in RNNs

The Vanishing Gradient Problem presents a major difficulty in optimizing Recurrent Neural Networks especially with extended sequences. The problem arises when the gradients applied for weight updates in backpropagation reach extremely low values after passing through multiple layers or time steps. The learning process stops because of the minimal weight adjustments that result from this effect.

Why it Happens	The process of training RNNs moves gradients through the entire network from output to input during every time step. The process of gradient shrinking as they traverse the network leads to insignificant weight changes in the beginning time steps. The situation becomes worse when using activation functions that generate small gradients because their outputs range between 0 to 1.
Impact	• **Slow or Stalled Learning:** The small gradient updates prevent the model from understanding distant relationships in the data. • **Inefficient Training:** The network fails to understand sequential patterns effectively because it loses the required duration information during tasks such as speech and language modeling.

8.11 LONG SHORT-TERM MEMORY NETWORKS (LSTMS)

8.11.1 LSTM Cell Structure: Gates and Memory Cell

Long Short-Term Memory (LSTM) networks were designed to address the **vanishing gradient problem** in traditional RNNs and to enable models to capture long-term dependencies in sequential data. The key to LSTM's effectiveness lies in its **cell structure**, which includes special components known as **gates** and the **memory cell**.

8.11.2 Key Components of LSTM Cell

Memory Cell (c_t)	The memory cell serves as a storage unit for persistence which enables network knowledge retention between time periods. The memory cell forms the fundamental mechanism through which LSTM models learn dependencies that extend across distant time intervals by receiving updates during each time step.
Gates	The flow of information through LSTM cells is managed by three core gates: • **Forget Gate (f_t):** The gate makes decisions about which memory cell contents require elimination or "forgotten" status. This gate combines past hidden state h_{t-1} and current input x_t to produce a result between 0 and 1 which indicates complete deletion or complete preservation. • **Input Gate (i_t):** The gate determines which new information elements should enter the memory cell. The gate assesses the extent of new information to be saved in the memory cell through its evaluation of the former hidden state h_{t-1} and present **input x_t.** • **Output Gate (o_t):** The gate establishes the specific form of the upcoming hidden state h_t. The updated memory cell and the current input serve as the basis for calculating this hidden state which will be forwarded to the following time step and possible serve as the LSTM output.

8.11.3 Advantages of LSTM over Traditional RNNs

Advantage	*Explanation*
Handling Long-Term Dependencies	Traditional RNNs struggle to learn long-term dependencies due to the vanishing gradient problem, whereas LSTMs can retain long-term memory using memory cells and gates.
Mitigation of Vanishing Gradient	LSTMs have built-in mechanisms (forget, input, and output gates) that help prevent gradients from vanishing, allowing the model to learn over many time steps.
Selective Memory	LSTMs can decide what information to keep or discard through their gates, making them more efficient in processing sequences. RNNs lack this ability to control memory.

(Contd.)

Advantage	Explanation
Better Performance in Complex Tasks	LSTMs perform better than traditional RNNs in complex tasks like language translation, speech recognition, and time-series forecasting due to their ability to capture context over longer periods.
Improved Training Stability	LSTMs are more stable to train than RNNs because their architecture helps avoid issues like exploding or vanishing gradients, making them more robust during backpropagation.

8.11.4   Practical Applications of LSTMs

Application	Description
Natural Language Processing (NLP)	LSTMs are widely used in NLP tasks such as language modeling, text generation, machine translation, and sentiment analysis. They are capable of capturing complex dependencies in text.
Speech Recognition	LSTMs are effective in transcribing speech to text, as they can handle varying speech patterns and long-term dependencies between spoken words.
Time Series Forecasting	LSTMs are used in predicting future values based on past data in fields such as stock market prediction, weather forecasting, and sales forecasting.
Video Analysis and Captioning	LSTMs help in tasks like video classification, object tracking, and automatic video captioning by capturing temporal relationships between frames.
Anomaly Detection	LSTMs are used to detect unusual patterns in data, such as in fraud detection, network security, and health monitoring (e.g., identifying abnormal heart rates).
Music Generation	LSTMs can generate music by learning the structure of musical compositions and producing new melodies based on learned patterns.
Image Captioning	By combining CNNs for feature extraction and LSTMs for sequence generation, LSTMs are used to automatically generate captions for images.
Robot Control and Autonomous Systems	LSTMs are employed to control robots or autonomous systems, enabling them to learn from past experiences and predict future actions in dynamic environments.

Wrap-up

 Many of the most cutting-edge technologies of today, including autonomous systems, language generation, image classification, and speech recognition, are powered by deep learning. The foundations of neural networks, their learning process, and the reasons behind the rise in power of deep architectures are covered in this chapter. Important models like CNNs, RNNs, and LSTMs will be covered, along with the difficulties and training methods associated with them. By the end, you will comprehend the fundamental ideas that allow deep learning to find intricate patterns and resolve issues that conventional machine learning finds difficult.

QUESTIONS FOR PRACTICE

1. Define Deep Learning. How does it differ from traditional Machine Learning? *Anna University, 2022*

2. Explain the key characteristics and importance of Deep Learning in modern AI applications. *Vellore Institute of Technology, 2021*

3. What are Artificial Neural Networks (ANNs)? Describe the structure of an artificial neuron and how it differs from a biological neuron. *SRM Institute of Science and Technology, 2023*

4. Discuss activation functions. When and why are they used in neural networks? Give examples of common activation functions. *Amity University, 2022*

5. Explain the backpropagation algorithm, including the role of chain rule and gradient computation. *IIT Bombay, 2022*

6. Describe loss functions in neural networks. Give examples of loss functions used for regression and classification. *Manipal University, 2021*

7. Explain Convolutional Neural Networks (CNNs). Discuss convolution operation, padding, stride, and pooling layers. *BMS College of Engineering, 2023*

8. List and briefly describe popular CNN architectures such as LeNet-5, AlexNet, VGGNet, and ResNet. *Anna University, 2022*

9. Describe Recurrent Neural Networks (RNNs) and the vanishing gradient problem. How do LSTMs overcome this issue? *Amrita Vishwa Vidyapeetham, 2021*

10. Provide practical applications of LSTMs in sequential data modeling (e.g., NLP, time series forecasting). *IIT Delhi, 2023*

9

Natural Language Processing (NLP)

9.1 INTRODUCTION TO NATURAL LANGUAGE PROCESSING

Natural Language Processing (NLP) is a field of research that brings together computer science, artificial intelligence, and linguistics to analyze, process, and generate human language. It addresses computerized manipulation of natural language text and speech to enable machines to understand and make use of data created by human beings. With the growth of computer text data from sources such as social media, news, and customers' reviews, NLP has emerged as an essential tool to extract insights and automate language processing tasks. NLP involves a wide spectrum from basic text preprocessing to sophisticated uses such as translation, summarization, sentiment analysis, and dialogue systems.

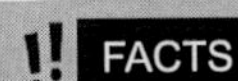

The term 'Natural Language Processing' dates back to the 1950s. Early NLP research began with machine translation projects, including attempts to automatically translate Russian into English during the Cold War.

9.1.1 What is NLP?

Definition and Scope

Natural Language Processing (NLP) is broadly defined as the automatic processing and understanding of human (natural) language by computers. In practice, NLP spans many tasks: it involves teaching machines to read, decipher, and generate language in a way that is useful. As one source notes, NLP "gives computers the ability to interpret, manipulate, and comprehend human language". It draws on computational linguistics, machine learning, and cognitive modeling. At a high level, NLP systems convert raw text or speech into structured representations (through tokenization, parsing, semantic analysis, etc.), extract meaning or intent, and often generate new text or responses. This broad scope includes tasks like language translation, speech recognition, information extraction, and question answering.

NLP's scope covers both written and spoken language. It applies to entire languages and specialized subsets (domain-specific jargon). For instance, NLP techniques process everything from simple commands ("turn on the lights") to complex documents (legal contracts, scientific articles). It may involve dealing with many languages and dialects—each with unique grammar and vocabulary —or analyzing short informal text (tweets, chat messages). As a subfield of AI, NLP interacts with areas like dialogue systems, text generation, and human-computer interaction. In sum, NLP's definition is broad: any computational method that enables machines to make sense of natural language falls under its domain.

Challenges in Understanding Human Language

- **Ambiguity:** In real-life language, words or phrases can carry two or more meanings. For example, "She's looking for a match" might mean she is looking for a romantic partner, a worthy adversary, or an item used to light a candle. The placement of the utterance in context could indicate what is intended.
- **Pragmatics and Context:** Meaning is context-dependent. Words like pronouns and idioms, sarcastic expressions, all need some form of context.
- **Vocabulary and Polysemy:** Words have many meanings. It becomes difficult to choose the correct one. New terms and slang keep on emerging, mostly through social media.
- **Linguistic Variation:** There are many languages and dialects, each with its separate rules. Even within a language, usage of words can change depending on formality and culture.

It is intriguing to think that factors can complicate simple tasks, such as part-of-speech tagging or determining sentiment. For example, rule-based systems generally perform well in a limited scope, yet they "struggle with the ambiguity and variability of natural language in totally open-ended applications." True understanding of language complicates understanding ambiguity, context, and variability—all of which statistical and neural algorithms that modern NLP is using to address and deal with, while ambiguity/context/variability remains active research in the field.

Significance of NLP in Contemporary Applications

NLP has emerged as a technology that cannot be lived without, allowing language analysis and interpretation automatically. Some of the most important areas it touches are:

Interaction between Humans and Machines	**Various Routine Processing**	**Global Development and Accessibility**	**Science and Medicine**
NLP powers voice-based personal assistants like Alexa and Siri and enhances the human experience when interacting with computers through natural dialogue	Document classification and translation are just two of a multitude of routine tasks processed through NLP	Speech technologies and translation processes facilitate communication and assist disabled users	NLP uses both published scientific information and medical research to enhance decision-making and literature review

9.1.2　Core Tasks in NLP

Natural Language Processing is the new deal in the manipulation of unstructured data. The otherwise unintelligible information about logs of customer services, legal documents, or even social media posts makes sense and not only that but also automatically generates text. What is impressive is that how much work has gone into NLP-from simple rule-based systems to deep learning models, which are capable of true language, contextual understanding, and meaning. The scope of the sector today applies to all—healthcare, finance, marketing and beyond. One can see all of it embedded in the toolset of a chatbot, a voice assistant, and recognize the significance it holds for all its uses.

Text Classification: One of the coolest things about NLP is that it can automatically sort huge amounts of text into categories.

 Sentiment analysis	Have you ever thought about how companies know what their actual customers think of them? In fact it is possible with NLP by analyzing text data. NLP can determine whether people are expressing a positive, negative, or neutral sentiment regarding something, and convey that to businesses regarding how customers feel.
 Named Entity Recognition (NER)	NER is like a detective for your data it looks through large bodies of text and pulls out critical names, places, dates, and organizations to identify who and what is important to you. The utilities in areas related to law are especially useful as monitoring the important entities in court documents can be a labor-intensive endeavor. NER minimizes the burden of managing this fundamental information.
 Text Summarization	Not one human has time to read each and every word in a 100-page report. NLP comes handy there, extracting lengthy documents, summarizing into small summaries to enable decision-makers to understand what's important rather than getting stuck in the weeds.

(Contd.)

Topic Modeling

NLP can help a company determine what is hot and what the prevailing topics are among the millions of texts. Envision feedback from customers, research papers, or social media noise. Using methods such as Latent Dirichlet Allocation, patterns and topics would jump off the page and make it so much easier to catch a new trend or perhaps an area in need of attention.

NLP, or Natural Language Processing, is a descriptive umbrella term for a very detailed variety of language-processing activities including the ability of machines to comprehend, interpret, and generate human language. NLP includes a range of tasks, from identifying the emotional intent of a sentence to translating text to languages. This section describes the most common NLP tasks and demonstrates their diversity of application and relevance across different fields.

This table categorizes the tasks, offering a well-organized and easy-to-understand overview of each NLP task.

NLP Task	Description	Application
Text Classification	This process assigns predefined categories or labels to text data, playing a crucial role in handling large volumes of text-based information.	Applied in spam email categorization, sentiment analysis of social media posts, news article classification, etc.
Named Entity Recognition (NER)	NER identifies and classifies entities like people, organizations, locations, and their relations within text.	Commonly used in tasks such as identifying company names in news articles or extracting dates and locations from legal documents.
Sentiment Analysis	This task detects the emotional tone behind text, categorizing it as positive, negative, or neutral to determine how people feel and think.	Applied in marketing, customer service, and social media monitoring for understanding consumer opinions and brand perception.
Machine Translation	Automatically translates text from one language to another, overcoming the complexities of language differences and facilitating cross-lingual communication.	Used in business, education, tourism, and global communication to break language barriers and foster understanding.
Text Summarization	This task condenses lengthy text into a concise, meaningful summary without losing the most important information.	Applied in areas like news aggregation, where concise summaries are essential, or in scholarly/legal settings to summarize long documents.

(Contd.)

NLP Task	Description	Application
Question Answering (QA)	QA systems answer natural language questions by retrieving relevant information, making information access more intuitive and efficient.	Used in virtual assistants, customer support tools, educational platforms, and more for answering user queries.
Text Generation	Generates coherent and relevant text based on an input prompt, requiring high-level creativity and contextual awareness.	Used for creative writing, chatbots, and automated content generation, including product descriptions and entire articles.

9.1.3 Foundational Techniques

NLP is a very rich area, and in order to successfully process and understand human language it makes use of a number of different techniques. A selection of the techniques commonly used in NLP technology is reviewed and defined below.

Natural Language Understanding (NLU)

Natural Language Understanding is one of the key concepts of Natural Language Processing, which enables machines to understand and interpret human language in a manner that is somewhat similar to human understanding. The problem in NLU is that it presents difficultly complex human language, namely in terms of ambiguity, variations in syntax, idioms, slang, and contextual dependencies.

Key Components of NLU

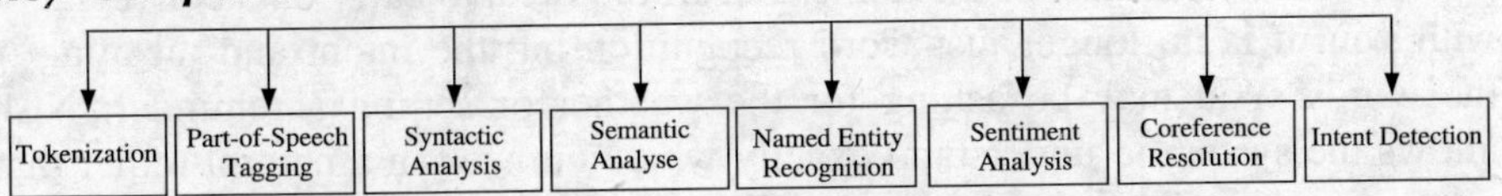

- **Tokenization:** The process of splitting a text into elementary tokens; this is in reference to breaking up a text into small units, which may include words, phrases, or symbols to analyze a sentence or even a document.
- **Part-of-Speech Tagging:** Part-of-Speech (POS) tagging involves identifying the grammatical category of each token, such as nouns, verbs, adjectives, etc. This component helps the system understand the role each word plays in a sentence, which is essential for grasping the overall meaning.
- **Syntactic Analysis:** It is defined as parsing, which involves the breaking down of sentences into their grammatical structure to understand how words are related to one another and in turn, how they link up for well-coherent phrases and sentences. Normally, constituency and dependency are used.

- **Semantic Analysis:** Here, meaning and relationship that words have toward each other in a phrase need to be identified. Here, whether the word functions as a subject, object, or action in the phrase need to be identified.

- **NER-Named Entity Recognition:** It is defined as identification and categorization of entities in text into predefined groups like names of people, groups, dates, or places. NER mainly encompasses understanding the context within the text.

- **Sentiment Analysis:** Identification based on an attitude or feeling that the text is saying: This can be founded with an attitude or feeling that a text expresses. It is capable of determining, for example, whether the text is talking about something with a neutral sensation, a negative feeling, or a good one. It enables understanding of the arbitrary tone of the language.

- **Coreference Resolution:** Coreference resolution is the process of determining, in a piece of text, when different words or phrases are references to the same thing. For example, in the sentence "Sourav said he would help," "he" refers to "Sourav."

- **Intent Detection:** Although a crucial feature in most applications, like chatbots, intent detection is about identifying what the user wants from his entry. For example, the user may say, "I want to book a flight," and then it emphasizes his intention about making a reservation.

NLU is a cognitive model of sorts for different NLP Components; it aids a variety of systems in understanding language the way that humans do, that is, by context, tone, and other aspects of communication.

For example, consider the ability of Siri or Alexa to carry on a conversation with you. It is no longer just word recognition but the intent and meaning of the words. You may be asking for the weather or setting a reminder; NLU allows the system to understand exactly what you need in a natural rather than robotic manner. These systems would have only been able to provide simple keyword-based responses in the absence of NLU. However, because of NLU, AI is able to engage users in a far more human-like way, so that interactions with technology can be intuitive and smooth.

Natural Language Generation (NLG)

Natural language generation, also known as NLG, is a subtopic of NLP, which pertains to using structured or unstructured data for creating human-like text. NLG systems, being developed within that continuum, produce coherent, contextually appropriate, and linguistically correct text, such that the information conveyed is understood by a human. The complexity of NLG therefore comes from needing to say something in the first place, but saying it in an engaging, contextually appropriate, and tone-and-style reflective way.

Key Components of NLG

Content Determination	This refers to the content that will make its way to the output text. A system must determine what is relevant to convey given the input data and what it is supposed to create.
Document Structuring	Once the content is ready, there is a need to logically structure it. In other words, provide a general structure outline for the document, in terms of identifying a reading order for the sentences and paragraphs to allow the reader to understand a smooth flow of information.
Sentence Aggregation	It is an important process that groups or aggregates a number of the information into one or a group of coherent sentences to avoid being repetitive and put the information in a concise reading format.
Lexicalization	The selection of a word or phrase that communicates the content of the document, with word choice that conveys messages while also flowing with and maintaining the intended tone and style.
Reference Generation	The process of how to mention the entities of the text. For instance, after the introduction of "the President," the following sentences may refer to "he" or "the leader" for example, or "the President," whatever best fits the context and clarity.

9.2   APPLICATIONS OF NLP

Natural Language Processing (NLP) is at the heart of many modern applications that allow computers to understand and process human language effectively. Below are some of its key areas of application:

Sentiment Analysis	Sentiment analysis evaluates the emotional tone suggested in a piece of text and classifies that emotion as positive, negative, or neutral. This can be especially helpful in: • Social media monitoring to evaluate public sentiment on various topics and trends. • Customer feedback analysis to determine satisfaction levels and improve offerings.
Machine Translation (MT)	Machine Translation allows the transfer of text from one language to another, removing language barriers. While the immediate methods of MT were rule-based or statistical approaches, current neural translations—specifically transformer-model-based translations—can provide translations of a quality that is similar and close to a human level across many world languages. For example: Google Translators, DeepL.
Chatbots and Virtual Assistants	Natural Language Processing (NLP) powers conversational systems that engage users in natural language. These bots interpret user input and generate natural, appropriate responses, transforming customer support and all kinds of everyday digital interactions. For example: customer service chatbots, Siri, Alexa, etc.

(Contd.)

Text Summarization	Text summarization condenses long documents into concise summaries, making information more digestible. It can be achieved in two ways: • **Extractive summarization:** Picks key sentences from the text. • **Abstractive summarization:** Generates new summaries using NLP models. Applications: **News article summarization, legal document condensation.**
Question Answering (QA) Systems	QA Systems either pull relevant answers directly out of a large text database or generate them with a natural language processing (NLP) models. QA systems can be either: • **Retrieval-based:** Answers will be pulled from existing documents. • **Generative based:** Answers will be generated by creating new documents. Examples: Search engines, AI assistants providing factual answers.
Text Classification	Text classification assigns categories or labels to text based on content. Common applications include: • Spam detection in emails. • Topic categorization in content management systems. • Intent recognition for chatbot interactions.
Speech Recognition and Synthesis	Speech technologies convert spoken language into written form (Speech-to-Text) and the other way (Text-to-Speech). These technologies combine natural language processing (NLP) with acoustic models, making it possible to communicate accurately. Examples are voice assistants and automated transcription systems.
Language Generation	NLP enables the automatic creation of natural-sounding text, useful in: • Auto-completion while typing. • Email and content generation. • Storytelling and chatbot responses.

9.3 TEXT PREPROCESSING AND FEATURE ENGINEERING

9.3.1 Text Preprocessing Techniques

Raw text data is messy. NLP pipelines begin with cleaning and transforming text data into a structured, organized form. Preprocessing usually consists of several steps including noise removal, normalization, tokenization and converting text into numbers, improving the chances of model performance in later steps. Each of these steps clean up the text while retaining meaning.

Text Cleaning and Normalization

Some of the techniques of Text cleaning and normalization as described below:

Text cleaning	Removes unwanted noise and standardizes format. Common steps include: Elimination of Punctuation and Special Characters: Punctuation signs, digits and special symbols (e.g., @, #, html tags), are frequently removed since without the punctuation the tokens do not have semantic content for many tasks. For instance, html tags are removed (e.g., using regex or a parser) with the intention to extract visible letters. Punctuation and other special characters reduced the size of the vocabulary and assisted the model with processing meaningful tokens.
Case normalization	Converting all the text to lowercase (case folding) helps treat "Apple" and "apple" as the same. It also simplifies the processing (e.g., IBM can be converted lower case to ibm depending on task).
Accent and Diacritic Removal	For languages that employ accented letters (e.g., é, ñ) the accents may be removed to Unicode normalize so that the various forms of letters conform to one base character. This step is beneficial especially when that distinction of accents does not matter or if the training data is less plentiful.
Whitespace and Noise	Additional whitespace, line breaks, or control characters, are generally trimmed. Occasionally, tokens that are too short to even matter or garbled strings are also removed.

Removing Noise: Punctuation, Special Characters, HTML Tags

In addition to punctuation, texts collected from the web or documents often contain markup (HTML, XML) and various symbols. Stripping HTML tags is crucial when processing web-scraped text, as tags are not part of natural language. For example, removing `<div>` or `<a href>` tags can be done via a regular expression or an HTML parser. Punctuation (commas, periods, quotes) is usually removed or separated from words so they don't form separate tokens. Special characters like URLs or numeric strings may also be removed if irrelevant. Cleaning noise reduces the dimensionality of the data and helps algorithms focus on actual words.

Code Example

```
import re
import unicodedata

text = "<p>Hello boys, How are you TODay! Welcome to Dib-
yendu's Café</p>"
text = re.sub(r'<[^>]+>', '', text)
text = re.sub(r'[^\w\s]', '', text)
```

```
text = ''.join(ch for ch in unicodedata.normalize('NFD',
text) if unicodedata.category(ch) != 'Mn')
text = text.lower().strip()
print(text)


OUTPUT
hello boys how are you today welcome to dibyendus cafe
```

This code removes HTML tags and punctuation, strips accents (e.g., "é" → "e"), and low-ercases the text. Such normalization helps ensure consistency before further processing.

Normalization and Accent Removal

A common step is case normalization, also known as lowercasing, which involves changing all capital letters to lowercase. This prevents words that have the same spelling but a different case from being treated as distinct (for example, "Apple" vs. "apple"). Diacritical stripping, also known as accent removal, changes accented characters back to their base (for example, "résumé" → "resume"). Specialized libraries or Unicode normalization can be used for this. Token matching and feature extraction are made easier by the uniform text form produced by these procedures.

Different tokenization strategies:

- **Word Tokenization**: Splitting on whitespace and punctuation to extract words. Most NLP tasks use word tokens as the basic unit. Example: "This is fun!"→ `"This"`, `"is"`, `"fun"`, `"!"]`
- **Sentence Tokenization**: Splitting text into sentences, useful for document-level tasks or generating sentence embeddings.
- **Subword/Byte-Pair Encoding (BPE)**: Splitting words into subword units (like "token", "ization") or even characters. This is used in modern neural models (e.g., BERT's WordPieces) to handle rare words and reduce vocabulary size.

Code Example

```
!pip install nltk
import nltk
nltk.download('punkt')


text = "Natural Language Processing (NLP) is amazing. Let's
tokenize!"
# Word tokenization
words = nltk.word_tokenize(text)
# Sentence tokenization
sentences = nltk.sent_tokenize(text)
print(words)
print(sentences)
```

```
OUTPUT
['Natural', 'Language', 'Processing', '(', 'NLP', ')', 'is',
'amazing', '.', 'Let', "'s", 'tokenize', '!']
['Natural Language Processing (NLP) is amazing.', "Let's to-
kenize!"]
```

9.3.2 Linguistic Structure Handling

Stemming and Lemmatization

Stemming and lemmatization both reduce words to their base or root forms. This process groups similar words together (e.g., "runs", "running", "ran" all reduce to "run"), reducing vocabulary size and improving feature consistency.

- **Stemming** applies heuristic rules to chop off word suffixes. For example, the Porter Stemmer removes "-ing" and "-ed" to convert "running" to "run" and "easily" to "easili" (not a dictionary word). Stemming is fast but can produce non-words.
- **Lemmatization** uses a dictionary (or morphological analysis) to convert a word to its valid lemma. For instance, "was" → "be", "cars"→ "car". Lemmatization is more accurate but requires part-of-speech information and computational resources.

Code Example

```python
# Step 1: Install and import NLTK tools
# !pip install nltk
import nltk
from nltk.stem import PorterStemmer, WordNetLemmatizer

# Step 2: Download required resources
nltk.download('wordnet')
nltk.download('omw-1.4')   # Optional: for better lemmatiza-
tion support

# Step 3: Initialize stemmer and lemmatizer
stemmer = PorterStemmer()
lemmatizer = WordNetLemmatizer()

# Step 4: Sample words for comparison
words = [
    "running", "ran", "runner", "easily", "fairly",
    "geese", "mice", "better", "best", "cats",
    "studies", "studying", "flies", "flying", "happier",
    "happiness", "wolves", "talked", "talking", "talks"
]
# Step 5: Apply stemming and lemmatization
stems = [stemmer.stem(w) for w in words]
lemmas = [lemmatizer.lemmatize(w) for w in words]
```

```
# Step 6: Display results side-by-side
print(f"{'Word':<12}{'Stem':<12}{'Lemma':<12}")
print("-" * 36)
for w, s, l in zip(words, stems, lemmas):
    print(f"{w:<12}{s:<12}{l:<12}")
```

```
OUTPUT

 Word       Stem        Lemma
------------------------------------
running    run         running
ran        ran         ran
runner     runner      runner
easily     easili      easily
fairly     fairli      fairly
geese      gees        goose
mice       mice        mouse
better     better      better
best       best        best
cats       cat         cat
studies    studi       study
studying   studi       studying
flies      fli         fly
flying     fli         flying
happier    happier     happier
happiness              happi       happiness
wolves     wolv        wolf
talked     talk        talked
talking    talk        talking
talks      talk        talk
```

The code is performing stemming and lemmatization—by processing 20 diverse words and printing their simplified forms

Stopword Removal

Stopwords are extremely common words (e.g., "and", "the", "is", "in") that carry little semantic weight in many analyses. Removing them can improve efficiency and focus models on meaningful words. The exact list of stopwords varies by language and task; standard lists exist in libraries like NLTK or spaCy.

Code Example

```
from nltk.corpus import stopwords
import nltk


# Step 1: Download stopword list
nltk.download('stopwords')
```

```
# Step 2: Define stopwords and sample text
stop_words = set(stopwords.words('english'))
text = "Natural language processing is a fascinating field
that enables machines to understand human language."

# Step 3: Tokenize and filter
tokens = text.split()  # Simple whitespace tokenizer
filtered = [word for word in tokens if word.lower() not in
stop_words]

# Step 4: Display results
print("Original Tokens:", tokens)
print("Filtered Tokens (without stopwords):", filtered)

OUTPUT

Original Tokens: ['Natural', 'language', 'processing', 'is',
'a', 'fascinating', 'field', 'that', 'enables', 'machines',
'to', 'understand', 'human', 'language.']
Filtered Tokens (without stopwords): ['Natural', 'language',
'processing', 'fascinating', 'field', 'enables', 'machines',
'understand', 'human', 'language.']
```

This code demonstrates stopword removal in NLP by filtering out common, non-informative words (like "is", "an", "to") from a tokenized sentence, helping retain only the meaningful content for downstream analysis.

In some NLP tasks (like sentiment or dialogue), even common words might carry cues, so removal is not always applied.

Part-of-Speech (POS) Tagging

Part-of-Speech tagging assigns each word a grammatical category (noun, verb, adjective, etc). For example, in the sentence "Time flies like an arrow", POS tagging would label Time (NOUN), lies (VERB), like (PREP), etc. POS tags help in downstream tasks.

Code Example

```
# Step 1: Install SpaCy and download English model
# !pip install spacy
# !python -m spacy download en_core_web_sm

import spacy

# Step 2: Load SpaCy English model
nlp = spacy.load("en_core_web_sm")

# Step 3: Define a rich sentence
text = "Dr. Banerjee quickly analyzed the complex NLP pipe-
line and proposed an elegant solution."
```

```
# Step 4: Process and display POS tags
doc = nlp(text)
print(f"{'Token':<15} → {'POS Tag':<10} | {'Explanation'}")
print("-" * 50)
for token in doc:
    print(f"{token.text:<15} → {token.pos_:<10} | {spacy.
explain(token.pos_)}")
```

OUTPUT

```
Token              POS Tag      Explanation
-----------------------------------------------------------
Dr.                PROPN        proper noun
Banerjee           PROPN        proper noun
quickly            ADV          adverb
analyzed           VERB         verb
the                DET          determiner
complex            ADJ          adjective
NLP                PROPN        proper noun
pipeline           NOUN         noun
and                CCONJ        coordinating conjunction
proposed           VERB         verb
an                 DET          determiner
elegant            ADJ          adjective
solution           NOUN         noun
.                  PUNCT        punctuation
```

9.3.3   Feature Extraction Techniques

Text must be transformed into numerical features that machine learning algorithms can use after it has been tokenized and cleaned. The three primary methods are Word Embeddings, TF-IDF, and Bag of Words.

Bag of Words Model

Each document is represented by a vector in the Bag of Words (BoW) model, which ignores word order and grammar and counts the number of times each vocabulary word appears in the document.

Example:

Documents: "I love NLP", "NLP is fun"

Vocabulary: ["fun", "i", "is", "love", "nlp"]

BoW vectors can be high-dimensional and sparse, which is addressed by TF-IDF and embeddings.

TF-IDF (Term Frequency-Inverse Document Frequency)

By multiplying term frequency (TF) by inverse document frequency (IDF), TF-IDF assigns a weight to each word based on its significance. Term Frequency

(TF) indicates how frequently a word occurs in a given sentence. Rare words (high IDF) are highlighted in contrast to common words (low IDF) using Inverse Document Frequency (IDF).

Formula:

```
TF-IDF(t, d) = TF(t, d) × IDF(t)
IDF(t) = log(N/(df_t))
```

Where:

- `TF(t, d)` is term frequency in document `d`
- `df_t` is number of documents containing term `t`
- `N` is total number of documents

Lets take an example, where we use TF-IDF to Detect Fake New.

Fake News Article	*Reliable Research Article*
"AI predicts the end of human doctors!"	"AI models improve disease diagnosis accuracy."
"AI will take over medical jobs overnight!"	"Medical AI assists doctors in better decision-making."
"Secret AI experiments are replacing surgeons!"	"AI supports personalized patient treatment plans."

Aspect	*Fake News Effect*	*Reliable News Effect*
Common Words (Low IDF)	"**AI**" appears in **every sentence**, making it **too generic** to prioritize.	Technical words like "**models**", "**accuracy**", "**diagnosis**" repeat across multiple sentences, confirming **credibility**.
Sensational Words (High IDF)	Words like "**takeover**", "**secret**", "**overnight**" appear **only in fake articles,** making them **unusual signals**.	Reliable news uses **fact-based words** like "diagnosis" and "decision-making," meaning **lower IDF and higher credibility**.
Search & Fact-Checking AI	AI **flags exaggerated headlines** using **high IDF values** on rare, misleading words.	AI **boosts balanced TF-IDF content,** ranking **factual articles higher**.

How TF-IDF Detects Fake News?

Spot Sensational Language: Fake news uses rare, attention-grabbing terms (high IDF), so AI flags them as potential misinformation.
Boost Reliable Sources: Trusted articles repeat important words (low IDF), meaning TF-IDF ranks them higher in search results.
Used in Journalism & AI Search Engines: Google and fact-checking tools prioritize articles with balanced TF-IDF scores, preventing misleading claims from trending.

Code Example

```python
from sklearn.feature_extraction.text import TfidfVectorizer
import pandas as pd

# Sample articles
fake_news = [
    "AI predicts the end of human doctors!",
    "AI will take over medical jobs overnight!",
    "Secret AI experiments are replacing surgeons!"
]

reliable_news = [
    "AI models improve disease diagnosis accuracy.",
    "Medical AI assists doctors in better decision-making.",
    "AI supports personalized patient treatment plans."
]

# Combine all articles
all_articles = fake_news + reliable_news

# Apply TF-IDF
vectorizer = TfidfVectorizer()
tfidf_matrix = vectorizer.fit_transform(all_articles)
feature_names = vectorizer.get_feature_names_out()

# Convert to DataFrame
df = pd.DataFrame(tfidf_matrix.toarray(), columns=feature_
names)

# Split back into fake and reliable
fake_df = df.iloc[:len(fake_news)]
reliable_df = df.iloc[len(fake_news):]

# Calculate average TF-IDF scores
fake_avg = fake_df.mean().sort_values(ascending=False)
reliable_avg = reliable_df.mean().sort_values(ascending=-
False)

# Display top TF-IDF words in each category
print("Top TF-IDF words in Fake News:\n")
print(fake_avg.head(10))

print("\n√ Top TF-IDF words in Reliable News:\n")
print(reliable_avg.head(10))

# Compare specific terms
terms_to_check = ["ai", "secret", "overnight", "take", "mod-
els", "accuracy", "diagnosis", "decision"]

print("\nTF-IDF Comparison for Key Terms:\n")
for term in terms_to_check:
    fake_score = fake_avg.get(term, 0)
    reliable_score = reliable_avg.get(term, 0)
    print(f"{term:<15} → Fake: {fake_score:.3f} | Reliable:
{reliable_score:.3f}")
```

```
OUTPUT

Top TF-IDF words in Fake News:

ai              0.187056
are             0.146218
surgeons        0.146218
secret          0.146218
replacing       0.146218
experiments     0.146218
will            0.137588
the             0.137588
take            0.137588
predicts        0.137588

√ Top TF-IDF words in Reliable News:

ai              0.187663
accuracy        0.146218
treatment       0.146218
diagnosis       0.146218
disease         0.146218
supports        0.146218
plans           0.146218
personalized    0.146218
patient         0.146218
improve         0.146218

√ TF-IDF Comparison for Key Terms:

ai          → Fake: 0.187 | Reliable: 0.188
secret      → Fake: 0.146 | Reliable: 0.000
overnight   → Fake: 0.138 | Reliable: 0.000
take        → Fake: 0.138 | Reliable: 0.000
models      → Fake: 0.000 | Reliable: 0.146
accuracy    → Fake: 0.000 | Reliable: 0.146
diagnosis   → Fake: 0.000 | Reliable: 0.146
decision    → Fake: 0.000 | Reliable: 0.130
```

"ai" appears in every sentence, so its TF-IDF is moderate—not too high, not too low. It's common across both fake and reliable news.

"secret", "experiments", "replacing", "predicts", and "take" are sensational or speculative terms. Their high TF-IDF scores mean they are rare overall but frequent in fake news, making them strong signals of exaggeration or misinformation.

These words are not shared with reliable news, which increases their IDF (inverse document frequency) and thus their TF-IDF score.

Word Embeddings (Word2Vec, GloVe)

Classic representations of the Bag of Words (BoW) and TF-IDF approaches do not incorporate any meaning of the words or context.

In contrast, word embeddings are dense vector representations of words that can represent the semantic relationships among the words. In an embedding space, similar words are represented by a similar vector. Common models include Word2Vec (Mikolov et al., 2013), and GloVe (Pennington et al., 2014). These methods can be considered fundamental to many state-of-the-art and modern methods in NLP because they allow models to generalize based on semantic similarity.

In practice, Word2Vec learns word vectors by training on large corpora using either the skip-gram or CBOW approach—predicting context words given a target word, or vice versa. After training, each word ww has a corresponding vector $v(w)v(w)$. For example:

$$v(\text{"king"}) - v(\text{"man"}) + v(\text{"woman"}) \approx v(\text{"queen"})$$

Pre-trained Word Embeddings

Word embeddings can be obtained in two ways: training on the task-specific data or utilizing **pre-trained embeddings**. Common pre-trained embeddings include Google's trained Word2Vec model and GloVe vectors built from large-scale datasets such as Common Crawl. These embeddings map each word into a lower-dimensional continuous space, typically ranging from 50 to 300 dimensions.

Implementing Word2Vec Using Gensim

Code Example

```python
# Install Gensim if needed
!pip install gensim

from gensim.models import Word2Vec
import numpy as np

# Imagine these are thoughts from a curious student exploring
NLP
sentences = [
    ["natural", "language", "processing", "is", "fun"],
    ["I", "love", "learning", "nlp", "and", "machine", "in-
telligence"],
    ["word", "embeddings", "capture", "meaning", "and",
"context"],
    ["algorithms", "learn", "semantic", "relationships",
"between", "words"],
    ["nlp", "helps", "computers", "understand", "human",
"language"]
]
```

```
# Train a Word2Vec model
model = Word2Vec(sentences, vector_size=50, window=3, min_
count=1, workers=2)

# Explore the vector for "nlp"
nlp_vector = model.wv["nlp"]
print("50-dimensional vector for 'nlp':\n")
print(np.round(nlp_vector, 3))

# Rounded for readability

# Bonus: Find words most similar to "nlp"
print("\nWords most similar to 'nlp':")
print(model.wv.most_similar("nlp"))

OUTPUT

50-dimensional vector for 'nlp':

[-0.016  0.009 -0.008  0.002  0.017 -0.009  0.009 -0.014 -0.007  0.019
 -0.003  0.001 -0.008 -0.015 -0.003  0.005 -0.002  0.011 -0.005  0.005
  0.011  0.017 -0.003 -0.018  0.009  0.001  0.015 -0.002 -0.005 -0.018
 -0.002  0.006  0.011  0.014 -0.011  0.004  0.012 -0.01  -0.006  0.014
  0.003  0.       0.007  0.       0.019  0.01  -0.018 -0.014  0.002  0.013]

Words most similar to 'nlp':
[('meaning', 0.22978785634040833), ('computers',
0.21908226609230042), ('learn', 0.16086997091770172),
('algorithms', 0.1487838625907898), ('word',
0.12486252188682556), ('intelligence', 0.08061248064041138),
('is', 0.07399575412273407), ('relationships',
0.05540495738387108), ('language', 0.04237734526395798),
('processing', 0.018277157098054886)]
```

This output shows how Word2Vec represents the word **"nlp"** as a 50-dimensional vector—a kind of numerical fingerprint capturing its meaning based on context. The values themselves aren't interpretable individually, but they allow the model to compare words mathematically. The similarity list reveals that **"nlp"** is most closely related to words like **"meaning"**, **"computers"**, and **"algorithms"**, suggesting that the model has learned NLP's association with language understanding and machine intelligence. This reflects how Word2Vec captures **semantic relationships** from co-occurrence patterns in text.

Word embeddings enable advanced NLP techniques, such as representing entire documents as averaged word vectors or using them as input to neural networks for contextual understanding.

9.4 SENTIMENT ANALYSIS

‼ FACTS

The first sentiment analysis was applied to movie reviews. In the early 2000s, researchers used NLP to classify film reviews as positive or negative, sparking the modern era of opinion mining.

Sentiment Analysis

Sentiment analysis, also referred to as opinion mining, is a sub-domain of NLP that deals with identifying the emotional tone or attitude represented in a text. It classifies whether an opinion expressed text is positive, negative or neutral. More broadly, it identifies subjective information, or attitudes, opinions and emotions.

Sentiment analysis, for instance, detects how a user feels about an item or topic in product reviews or social media posts. Two key concepts used in sentiment analysis are:

- **Subjectivity:** Determines whether a statement expresses personal feelings (subjective) or factual information (objective).
- **Sentiment Polarity:** Measures whether sentiment is **positive, negative, or neutral**.

Example:

"I love this phone" → **Positive polarity**

"This movie is terrible" → **Negative polarity**

Sentiment scores can be either **scalar values** (e.g., ranging from −1 to +1) or **discrete categories** (such as positive, neutral, and negative).

9.4.1 Approaches to Sentiment Analysis

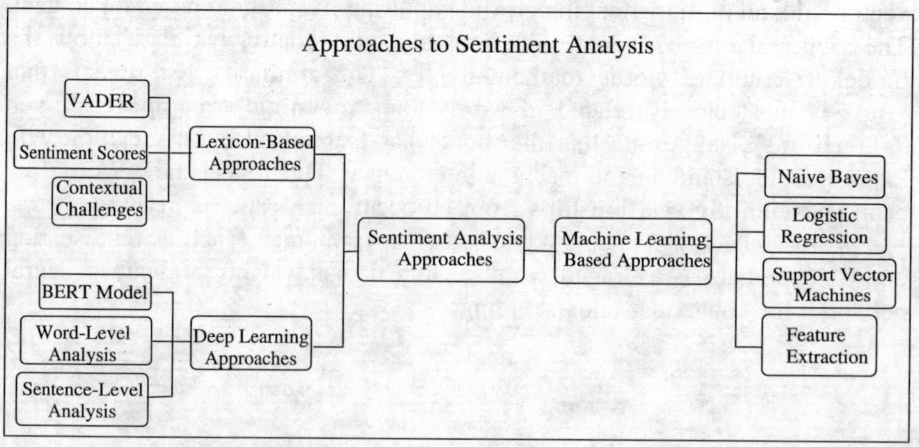

Lexicon-Based Approaches	Lexicon-based methods rely on predefined sentiment dictionaries where words are assigned **positive or negative sentiment scores**. The overall sentiment of a text is calculated by summing individual word scores. For example, in **VADER (Valence Aware Dictionary for Sentiment Reasoning)**, words like *"good"* carry positive scores, *"terrible"* has negative values, and *"the"* remains neutral. However, this approach struggles with **complex contexts**, such as: • **Negation Handling** (*"I do not love this phone"*) • **Intensity Modifiers** (*"very good"* vs. *"good"*) • **Sarcasm** (*"Great, another delay..."* may seem positive, but context is negative)
Machine Learning-Based Approaches	Machine learning models classify sentiment by learning patterns from labeled data. Common techniques include: • **Naive Bayes** • **Logistic Regression** • **Support Vector Machines (SVM)** These models **extract features** (such as TF-IDF or Bag-of-Words vectors) from training data and learn relationships between words and sentiment labels. Example workflow: 1. **Convert text into word vectors** 2. **Train a classifier on labeled sentiment examples** 3. **Use the trained model to predict sentiment on new data** Machine learning methods are **data-driven** and often outperform lexicon-based techniques when trained on large datasets.
Deep Learning Approaches	Deep learning models learn features automatically from the data itself and, at the same time, they model complex linguistic nuances. The models analyse sentiment at the word level and the sentence level, which allows it to discover long-range dependencies in the text. The BERT model, for example, is a pre-trained transformer model that can be fine-tuned for sentiment classification, thus achieving state-of-the-art performance.

Code Example

```python
# Lexicon-Based Approach (VADER)
from nltk.sentiment import SentimentIntensityAnalyzer
import nltk
nltk.download('vader_lexicon')

sid = SentimentIntensityAnalyzer()
print(sid.polarity_scores("I absolutely love this product!"))
print(sid.polarity_scores("This is the worst experience I have ever had."))
```

OUTPUT

```
{'neg': 0.0, 'neu': 0.385, 'pos': 0.615, 'compound': 0.6989}
{'neg': 0.369, 'neu': 0.631, 'pos': 0.0, 'compound': -0.6249}
```

"I absolutely love this product!"

- compound: +0.6989 → Strongly positive
- High pos score (0.615) confirms enthusiastic sentiment.

"This is the worst experience I have ever had."

- compound: −0.6249 → Strongly negative
- High neg score (0.369) reflects clear dissatisfaction.

```python
#Machine Learning-Based Approach (Naive Bayes Classifier)
from sklearn.feature_extraction.text import CountVectorizer
from sklearn.naive_bayes import MultinomialNB

# Step 1: Training data — short movie reviews
docs = [
    "I love this movie",          # Positive
    "This is a fantastic film",   # Positive
    "Terrible acting",            # Negative
    "I did not like the movie"    # Negative
]

# Labels: 1 = Positive sentiment, 0 = Negative sentiment
labels = [1, 1, 0, 0]

# Step 2: Convert text to numeric features using Bag-of-Words
vectorizer = CountVectorizer()
X_train = vectorizer.fit_transform(docs)

# Step 3: Train a Naive Bayes classifier
clf = MultinomialNB().fit(X_train, labels)
```

```
# Step 4: Test the model on new reviews
test_docs = [
    "what a great movie",    # Expected: Positive
    "the plot was awful"     # Expected: Negative
]

X_test = vectorizer.transform(test_docs)

# Step 5: Predict sentiment
predictions = clf.predict(X_test)
print("Sentiment Predictions:", predictions) # Output: [1 0]
```

OUTPUT

```
Sentiment Predictions:  [0 0]
```

The output Sentiment Predictions: [0 0] means that both test sentences were classified as negative by the Naive Bayes sentiment model.

** Note: There are other approach like Deep Learning Approach, where you can use pre-trained models.

9.5   TOPIC MODELING AND DOCUMENT CLUSTERING

9.5.1   Topic Modeling and Document Clustering

Introduction to Topic Modeling

Topic modeling is a non-supervised learning method that is used to discover abstract topics in a set of documents. The idea is that a document is made up of a mixture of topics where each topic has a distribution over words. This technique uncovers the latent thematic structure of a large collection of text.

Concept of Topics in Large Text Corpora

In topic modeling, a topic is a **cluster of semantically related words**. For example, in **news articles**, topics may include:

- **Sports:** game, team, score, coach
- **Economy:** market, stock, growth, inflation

A **topic modeling algorithm** analyzes a corpus and determines a set of topics, representing each document as a **distribution over topics**.

9.5.2   Applications of Topic Modeling

Topic modeling is used in various fields, including:

- **Document Organization:** Automatically clustering large sets of documents (news archives, research papers).

- **Recommendation Systems:** Tagging documents or products with topics to improve suggestions.
- **Trend Analysis:** Tracking topic evolution in social media and news.
- **Information Retrieval:** Enhancing search engines by matching documents based on topic relevance.
- **Content Analysis:** Identifying dominant themes in customer feedback, survey responses, or social media.

Topic models provide an **automated way** to **discover text structure**, offering insights into large datasets.

9.5.3 Techniques for Topic Modeling

Latent Dirichlet Allocation (LDA)

LDA is a **probabilistic generative model** for discovering topics in documents.

- It assumes **K topics** in advance.
- Each topic is represented by a **distribution over words**.
- Each document has a **distribution over topics**.

Generative Process:

1. Select a topic mixture for a document.
2. Choose a topic for each word based on the mixture.
3. Select a word from the chosen topic's distribution.

LDA infers topics by **analyzing word co-occurrences** across documents.

Example: Running LDA Using Gensim

Code Example

```
!pip install gensim

from gensim import corpora, models

# Sample documents
docs = [
    "Cats and dogs are common pets",
    "Many people have dogs and cats",
    "The stock market had a great year",
    "Investors in the market are optimistic"
]

# Preprocess: Tokenize and create dictionary
texts = [doc.lower().split() for doc in docs]
dictionary = corpora.Dictionary(texts)
corpus = [dictionary.doc2bow(text) for text in texts]
```

```python
# Run LDA
lda = models.LdaModel(corpus, num_topics=2, id2word=dictio-
nary, passes=20)

# Print topics
for idx, topic in lda.print_topics():
    print(f"Topic {idx}: {topic}")
```

OUTPUT

```
Topic 0: 0.067*"market" + 0.067*"the" + 0.067*"stock" +
0.067*"year" + 0.067*"a" + 0.067*"had" + 0.067*"great" +
0.066*"people" + 0.066*"many" + 0.066*"have"
Topic 1: 0.116*"are" + 0.070*"cats" + 0.070*"and" +
0.070*"dogs" + 0.070*"the" + 0.070*"market" + 0.069*"inves-
tors" + 0.069*"optimistic" + 0.069*"in" + 0.069*"common"
```

- Words like "market", "stock", "year", and "great" suggest this topic is about financial trends or market performance.
- The weights (e.g., 0.067) indicate how strongly each word contributes to this topic.
- Generic words like "the" and "a" appear due to their frequency but are less informative.
- Words like "cats", "dogs", and "common" suggest a topic about animals or shared traits.
- Interestingly, "market", "investors", and "optimistic" also appear, hinting at a metaphorical or mixed context—perhaps using animals to describe investor behavior (e.g., "bulls and bears").

Non-Negative Matrix Factorization (NMF)

NMF is a linear algebra-based method for topic modeling. It factorizes a **term-document matrix** VV into two smaller non-negative matrices:

- WW (terms × topics)
- HH (topics × documents)

NMF ensures each topic is represented **additively**, leading to **interpretable topics**.

Example: Running NMF Using Scikit-Learn

```python
from sklearn.decomposition import NMF
from sklearn.feature_extraction.text import TfidfVectorizer

# Step 1: Diverse sample documents — pets, finance, and real
estate
documents = [
    "Cats and dogs are beloved companions in many house-
holds.",
```

```
    "Pet ownership improves mental health and emotional
bonding.",
    "The stock market surged after a strong earnings season.",
    "Investors remain optimistic about tech and energy sec-
tors.",
    "Real estate is a stable long-term investment for many fam-
ilies.",
    "Housing prices in urban areas continue to rise.",
    "Dogs and cats require regular care and attention.",
    "Financial analysts predict growth in renewable energy
stocks."
]


# Step 2: Convert text to TF-IDF matrix
vectorizer = TfidfVectorizer(stop_words='english')
tfidf_matrix = vectorizer.fit_transform(documents)


# Step 3: Apply NMF to extract 3 latent topics
nmf_model = NMF(n_components=3, random_state=42)
W = nmf_model.fit_transform(tfidf_matrix)  # Document-topic
matrix
H = nmf_model.components_                   # Topic-word ma-
trix
# Step 4: Get feature names (words)
feature_names = vectorizer.get_feature_names_out()


# Step 5: Display top words for each topic
for topic_idx, topic_weights in enumerate(H):
    top_indices = topic_weights.argsort()[::-1][:6]
    top_words = [feature_names[i] for i in top_indices]
    print(f" Topic {topic_idx + 1}: {', '.join(top_words)}")
```

OUTPUT

Topic 1: dogs, cats, households, beloved, companions, care

Topic 2: energy, optimistic, tech, investors, sectors, remain

Topic 3: ownership, improves, bonding, mental, emotional, pet

NMF breaks down documents into hidden topics based on word patterns.

Each topic is a group of words that frequently co-occur across documents.

Your results show:

Topic 1: Focused on pets and companionship (e.g., "dogs", "cats", "households").

Topic 2: Related to finance and market sentiment (e.g., "energy", "investors", "tech").

Topic 3: Highlights emotional and mental benefits of pet ownership (e.g., "bonding", "mental", "emotional").

This shows how NMF can uncover meaningful themes from unstructured text—even with just a few documents. Let me know if you'd like to visualize these topics or map them back to specific documents!

9.6 TRANSFORMER MODELS AND ADVANCED ARCHITECTURES

Transformer-based models have revolutionized NLP, enabling powerful architectures such as **BERT** and **GPT**. This section explores the evolution from traditional sequence models to transformers, the core transformer architecture, and pre-trained models that have shaped modern NLP.

9.6.1 Evolution of NLP Architectures

From RNNs and LSTMs to Attention Mechanisms

- RNNs maintain a **hidden state** that stores past context while processing tokens one by one.
- LSTMs improved upon RNNs by addressing the **vanishing gradient problem** and capturing **long-range dependencies** more effectively.

These models enabled breakthroughs in **neural language modeling** and **sequence-to-sequence (seq2seq) tasks**, such as machine translation.

However, RNNs had inherent limitations:
- **Sequential Processing:** Prevents parallelization, leading to slower training.
- **Difficulty with Long Sequences:** Earlier tokens in long texts could be "forgotten" due to memory constraints.
- **Limited Bidirectional Context:** Many RNN-based models process input **one direction at a time**, making full-context representation challenging.

9.6.2 Transformer Architecture

Core Concepts: Self-Attention and Positional Encoding

The **Transformer** architecture, introduced in 2017, eliminates recurrence by relying entirely on **attention mechanisms**. It follows an **encoder-decoder framework**, where both components utilize **multi-head self-attention** and **feed-forward networks**.

Self-Attention Mechanism	Each token in the input sequence is mapped to three vectors: **Query (Q)** **Key (K)** **Value (V)** Attention scores are computed using dot products of **Q** and **K**, then normalized to form a weighted sum of **V**. This enables the model to adjust how words interact **based on learned relevance**.

Multi-Head Attention:	Multiple attention layers run in parallel to capture **different linguistic dependencies.** Enables transformers to analyze sentence relationships effectively.
Positional Encoding:	Since transformers **do not inherently encode word order**, positional encoding assigns numerical vectors that differentiate token positions. This allows models to recognize structured patterns, distinguishing phrases like: *"The cat sat"* vs. *"Sat the cat".*

Transformer Model Structure: Encoder-Decoder Framework

Transformers employ **stacked layers** for both encoding and decoding:

Encoder (Understanding Input Text)	1. **Self-attention:** Enables contextual relationships between words. 2. **Feed-forward network:** Processes token embeddings into meaningful representations.
Decoder (Generating Output Text)	1. **Masked self-attention:** Ensures the model does not see future tokens while predicting current ones. 2. **Encoder-decoder attention:** Allows the decoder to focus on specific parts of the input sentence while generating an output. 3. **Final feed-forward layer:** Produces probability distributions over vocabulary words.

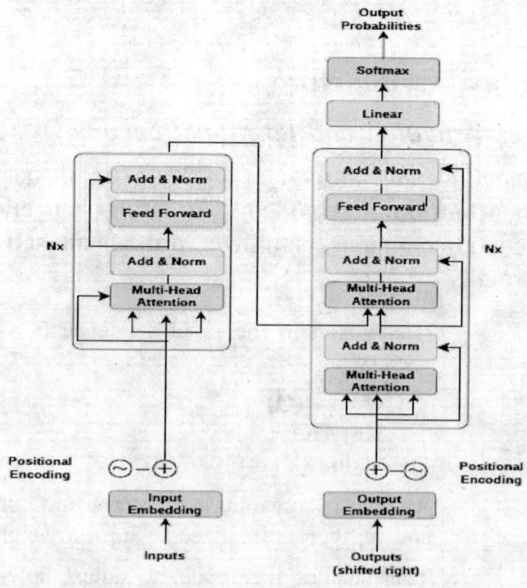

9.6.3 Pre-trained Language Models

Modern NLP relies heavily on **pre-trained models**, which are trained on large text datasets before being **fine-tuned** for specific tasks.

BERT (Bidirectional Encoder Representations from Transformers)	Only the encoder component is used in the transformer-based BERT model. Trained with Masked Language Modeling (MLM), which requires the model to predict missing words by masking some of the words in a sentence. Unlike conventional left-to-right models, it reads entire input sequences in both directions. It is helpful for a variety of NLP tasks because it captures context-rich representations.
Fine-tuning Applications	• **Question answering** • **Sentiment analysis** • **Named entity recognition (NER)**
GPT (Generative Pre-trained Transformer) Models	GPT models only use the transformer decoder component and concentrate on text generation. Using a causal language modeling (CLM) technique, it was trained to predict the following word based on a previous sequence. It works well for dialogue generation, summarization, and creative writing because it is optimized for natural-sounding text completion. With 175 billion parameters, the highly influential GPT-3 model exhibits robust zero-shot and few-shot learning capabilities on a variety of NLP tasks. Because GPT is optimized for generation rather than understanding, it is a good fit for AI-assisted writing, chatbot interactions, and storytelling.

Wrap-up

 Consider attempting to learn what people truly think about a product by reading thousands of customer reviews. Natural Language Processing, or NLP, can help with that. It enables computers to read and comprehend human language in the same way that humans do. NLP transforms jumbled text into insightful information, whether you're using it to categorize emails into spam, translate languages on your phone, or identify emotions in tweets. NLP enables data science to make sense of words at scale by fusing clever algorithms with grammar rules, which helps researchers, businesses, and even common apps make better decisions.

QUESTIONS FOR PRACTICE

1. Define Natural Language Processing (NLP). Explain its importance in Data Science.   *Anna University, 2022*

2. List the core tasks in NLP and give real-world examples for each.
                                     Vellore Institute of Technology, 2021

3. Explain text preprocessing techniques in NLP, including tokenization, stemming, and lemmatization.
                                     SRM Institute of Science and Technology, 2023

4. Discuss feature extraction methods for textual data, such as Bag-of-Words and TF-IDF.   *Amity University, 2022*

5. Explain sentiment analysis. What are the approaches to performing sentiment analysis on textual data?   *IIT Bombay, 2022*

6. Describe topic modeling and document clustering. Provide an example of how topic modeling can be used in customer feedback analysis.
                                     Manipal University, 2021

7. Explain the evolution of NLP architectures from traditional methods to transformers.   *BMS College of Engineering, 2023*

8. Describe the Transformer architecture and its key components.
                                     Anna University, 2022

9. Explain pre-trained language models and their significance in modern NLP applications.   *Amrita Vishwa Vidyapeetham, 2021*

10. Provide examples of practical applications of NLP, such as chatbots, machine translation, and information retrieval.   *IIT Delhi, 2023*

10

Time Series Analysis

10.1 TIME SERIES ANALYSIS

We call data as time series when we take a set of observations on a single variable based on equal spacing between the points. For example, daily temperatures, monthly sales figure, etc. Unlike individual data points, time series datasets expose how values evolve over time and can be used to both help identify patterns in the Time Series dataframe dataset as well assess general past behaviors or per-date relative trends from it. In data science, you absolutely must understand time series because so many real-world datasets are based on time (like for example stock prices, weather records and website traffic). Time series analysis and forecasting are among the most difficult but essential tools for predicting trends, behaviours or any activity based on historical data. It enables businesses to take better decisions, make optimal use of resources and mitigate risks by predicting market demand, sales trend patterns, stock prices, etc. Moreover, it is useful in forecasting and planning, such as finance/economics/health care/climate science/business management/resource optimization that lead to agility & edge over competition. In this chapter, the basic ideas of time series are introduced in an accessible and uncomplicated style.

10.1.1 Introduction to Time Series

Understanding Time Series Data and its Characteristics

What is Time Series Data?

Time series data means collecting numbers or information over time, like every day, month, or year. For example, tracking daily temperature, monthly phone bills, or yearly rainfall. What makes it special is that the order of the data matters—today's number comes before tomorrow's, and so on.

Definition: A time series is a sequence of data points gathered, collected, recorded or measured at successive, evenly-spaced time intervals.

Components of Time Series: Trend, Seasonality, Cycles, and Noise

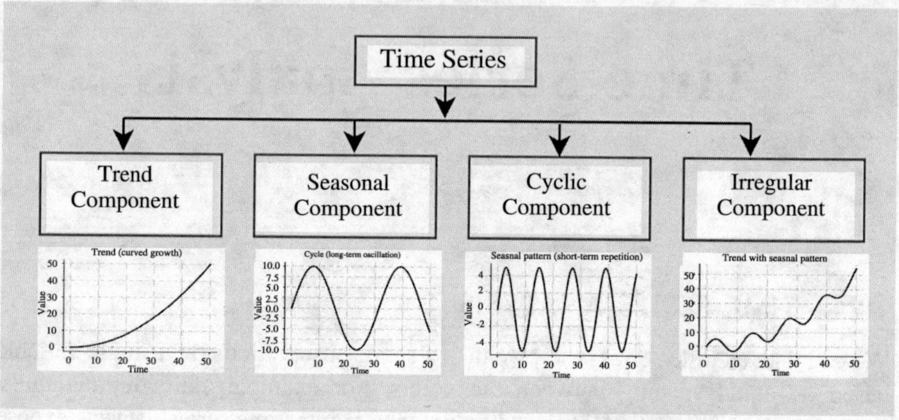

Real-world Applications

Here are a few examples of Time Series Analysis example in Data Science:

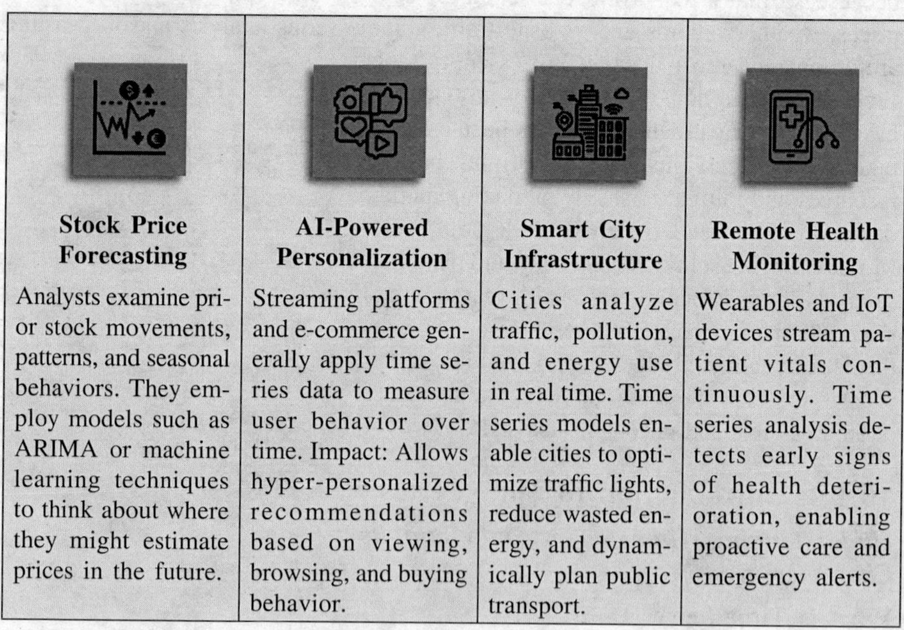

Stock Price Forecasting	AI-Powered Personalization	Smart City Infrastructure	Remote Health Monitoring
Analysts examine prior stock movements, patterns, and seasonal behaviors. They employ models such as ARIMA or machine learning techniques to think about where they might estimate prices in the future.	Streaming platforms and e-commerce generally apply time series data to measure user behavior over time. Impact: Allows hyper-personalized recommendations based on viewing, browsing, and buying behavior.	Cities analyze traffic, pollution, and energy use in real time. Time series models enable cities to optimize traffic lights, reduce wasted energy, and dynamically plan public transport.	Wearables and IoT devices stream patient vitals continuously. Time series analysis detects early signs of health deterioration, enabling proactive care and emergency alerts.

Genomic Time Series Analysis

Biomedical researchers track gene expression over time. Helps identify disease progression patterns and treatment responses in personalized medicine.

Real-Time Fraud Detection

Financial institutions monitor transaction streams. Time series models flag suspicious behavior instantly, improving fraud prevention without blocking legitimate activity.

Climate Risk Modeling

Governments and insurers analyze long-term environmental data. Time series analysis helps assess flood, drought, and wildfire risks, guiding policy and insurance pricing.

Satellite Data Streams

Earth observation satellites collect continuous data on land use, weather, and ocean currents. Time series models support disaster response, environmental monitoring, and global logistics.

10.1.2 Types of Time Series

The complexity of time series data can vary based upon how many variables are tracked over time. Before discussing how to analyze your time series data or forecast, you should understand that there are two types of time series:

- Univariate
- Multivariate

!! FACTS

Vector Auto Regression (VAR), introduced by Christopher Sims in 1980, revolutionized economics by showing how multiple variables—like interest rates, inflation, and GDP—dance together over time. It was a turning point in understanding interconnected systems.

10.1.3 Univariate Time Series

A univariate time series is a series of observations over time for one variable, or an observation that has been collected at regular intervals in time. Univariate time series is the most elementary yet most commonly used form of time series data.

Key Characteristics of Univariate Time Series
• Only **one variable** is measured.
• Observations are ordered by time.
• Analysis focuses on patterns like **trend**, **seasonality**, and **noise** in that one variable.

Mathematical Representation:

Let y_t represent the value of the variable at time t. Then a univariate time series looks like:

$y_1, y_2, y_3, ..., y_n$

Where:

y_t is the value at time t

n is the total number of time points

Real-Life Examples:

Daily Temperature of City	If you record the temperature at noon every day for Delhi. One number, a different one each day: the temperature. → 1 Variable (Temperature) → Univariate
Unit Sold	A company keeps track of how many units of its best-selling phone are sold each month. → One variable (units sold) → Univariate
Heart Rate	Tap your hourly heart rate from a smartwatch → 1 health metric: heart rate → univariate
Website Hits	A blog keeps record of his website visitors every week. → One metric (no. of visitors) → Univariate

Plotting a Univariate Time Series

Code Example

```python
import pandas as pd
import matplotlib.pyplot as plt

# Sample univariate time series: monthly sales
data = {'Month': pd.date_range(start='2023-01-01', periods=6,
freq='M'),
        'Sales': [120, 135, 150, 160, 145, 170]}
df = pd.DataFrame(data)

# Plotting the time series
plt.plot(df['Month'], df['Sales'], marker='o', color='blue')
plt.title('Monthly Sales Over Time')
plt.xlabel('Month')
plt.ylabel('Sales')
plt.grid(True)
plt.show()
```

OUTPUT

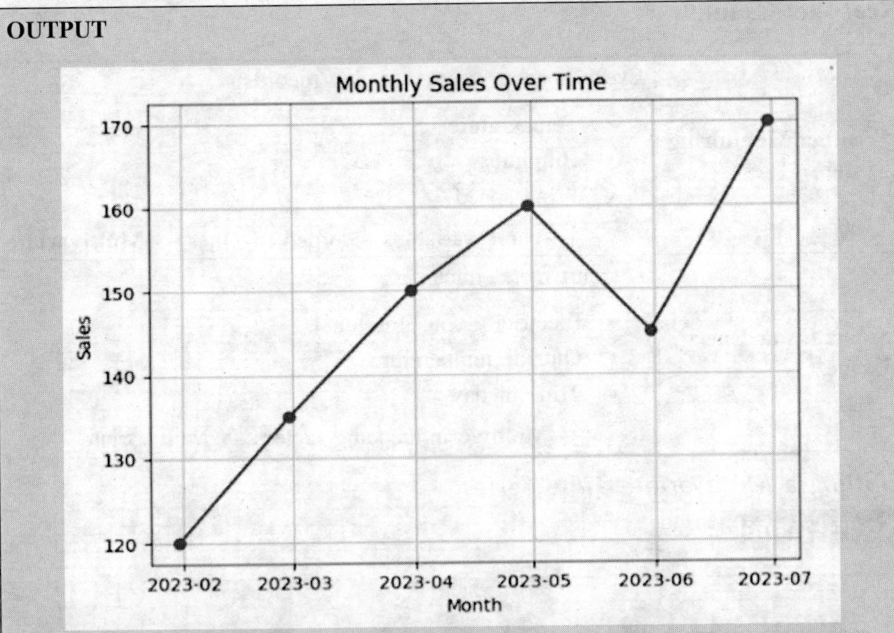

This example Python demonstrates how to create and visualize a simple univariate time series using pandas and matplotlib. It begins by importing the necessary libraries, pandas for data handling and matplotlib.pyplot for plotting. Next, a dataset is created that includes two columns: "Month", which identifies six consecutive months beginning in January 2023 (created using pd.date_range), and "Sales", which identifies the corresponding sales amount for each month. This data is placed in a pandas DataFrame, called df. After that, the "Sales" values are plotted against "Month" using plt.plot() with circular markers (marker='o') and a blue line. Labels and titles are added to the graph to ensure clarity, and a grid is added to improve visibility. Finally, the line chart is shown using plt.show(), illustrating how sales amounts increase and decrease over this time period.

10.1.4 Multivariate Time Series

A **multivariate time series** involves recording **two or more variables** at the same time intervals. These variables may be related and often influence each other.

Key Characteristics of Multivariate Time Series
• Multiple variables are measured at each time point.
• Variables may be interdependent.
• Analysis can reveal relationships between variables over time.

Real-Life Examples:

Weather Monitoring System	Every hour, a weather station records: • Temperature • Humidity • Wind speed → Three variables recorded together → **Multivariate**
Smart Home Energy Usage	A smart meter tracks: • Electricity consumption • Outside temperature • Time of day → Multiple influencing factors → Multivariate

Plotting a Multivariate Time Series

Code Example

```python
import pandas as pd
import matplotlib.pyplot as plt

# Create a sample multivariate time series dataset
data = {
    'Date': pd.date_range(start='2023-01-01', periods=10, freq='D'),
    'Sales': [200, 220, 250, 270, 300, 310, 290, 330, 360, 380],
    'Ad_Spend': [50, 60, 65, 70, 80, 85, 75, 90, 95, 100],
    'Customers': [40, 45, 50, 55, 60, 62, 58, 65, 70, 72]
}

df = pd.DataFrame(data)

# Plotting all three variables
plt.figure(figsize=(10, 6))
plt.plot(df['Date'], df['Sales'], label='Sales', marker='o')
plt.plot(df['Date'], df['Ad_Spend'], label='Advertising Spend',
marker='s')
plt.plot(df['Date'], df['Customers'], label='Number of Customers',
marker='^')

plt.title('Retail Store Performance Over Time')
plt.xlabel('Date')
plt.ylabel('Values')
plt.legend()
plt.grid(True)
plt.tight_layout()
plt.show()
```

OUTPUT

The code demonstrates a multivariate time series, in which many variables of interest, that are related, will be examined over time. The values recorded include Sales, Advertising Spend, and Number of Customers, all tracked for a 10-day period from January 1, 2023. The data is then organized into a pandas DataFrame and then visualized with matplotlib, plotting all 3 variables in the same plot, marked with different markers, and with a legend. The resulting line chart will show how all three variables change together, and allow trends, patterns, and relationships, such as whether more advertising spending correlates with sales or customer counts to be determined. The chart is able to visualize how each variable interacts with the others over a time period, using a single time series plot.

Choosing between Univariate and Multivariate Time Series

Univariate Time Series	*Multivariate Time Series*
• You only have one variable available. • The variable is self-contained and shows meaningful patterns over time. • You're learning time series for the first time. 	• You have multiple variables that may influence each other. • You want to understand relationships between variables. • You're solving a complex problem where one variable alone isn't enough.

Example Scenarios

Scenario	Type	Explanation
Forecasting monthly sales of a product	Univariate	Past sales alone may be enough to predict future sales.
Predicting electricity usage based on temperature and time of day	Multivariate	Usage depends on weather and time — multiple variables needed.
Monitoring heart rate over time	Univariate	Only one health metric is tracked.
Studying how weather affects crop yield	Multivariate	Temperature, rainfall, and humidity all impact crops.
Analyzing website traffic based on ad spend and social media activity	Multivariate	Traffic is influenced by multiple marketing channels.

Exploring Time Series Patterns

More than just a list of numbers over time, a time series includes patterns that provide insight into how things change over time. Whether it's stock prices, daily temperatures, website traffic, or monthly sales, the patterns we find in data give analysts and data scientists information and value that improves their comprehension of behavior, their forecasts of future trends, or their data-driven decision-making.

We must break down these patterns and comprehend the underlying factors that drive them in order to analyze and forecast effectively. This process, which we call time series decomposition, entails breaking the series down into significant elements like trend, seasonality, cycle, and noise.

10.2 COMPONENTS OF TIME SERIES: TREND, SEASONALITY, CYCLES, NOISE

Every time series is a mixture of several hidden patterns. In the below section we will be exploreing each one with a simple explanation using Python Code.

10.2.1 Trend

A **trend** represents the *long-term direction* of data movement—upward, downward, or stable. It reflects general growth or decline over time, ignoring short-term fluctuations.

Example: A company's sales may steadily increase over several years due to business expansion.

Code Example

```python
import numpy as np
import pandas as pd
import matplotlib.pyplot as plt

#Create a simple upward trend
np.random.seed(0)
time = pd.date_range(start='2023-01-01', periods=24, freq='M')
trend = 100 + np.arange(24) * 5  # steadily increasing
noise = np.random.normal(0, 5, 24)
data = trend + noise

plt.figure(figsize=(8,4))
plt.plot(time, data, marker='o', label='Observed Data')
plt.plot(time, trend, color='red', linewidth=2, label='Trend')
plt.title("Trend Component in Time Series")
plt.xlabel("Month")
plt.ylabel("Sales")
plt.legend()
plt.grid(True)
plt.show()
```

OUTPUT

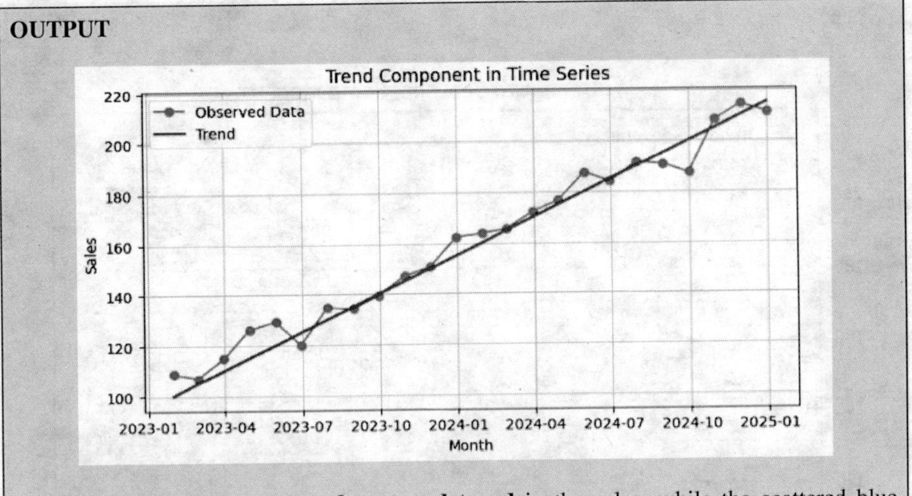

The red line showing the **steady upward trend** in the sales, while the scattered blue pointing to (observed data) include small random variations around that trend.

10.2.2 Seasonality

Seasonality is a repeating pattern at regular intervals—daily, weekly, monthly, or yearly.It often results from predictable events such as holidays, weather, or human habits.

 **FACTS**

Seasonality was first studied in economics. Early economists noticed recurring seasonal patterns in agricultural yields and trade, which later shaped forecasting models.

Example: Ice cream sales peak every summer and drop during winter.

Code Example

```python
seasonal_pattern = 10 * np.sin(np.linspace(0, 3*np.pi, 24))
seasonal_data = trend + seasonal_pattern + noise

plt.figure(figsize=(8,4))
plt.plot(time, seasonal_data, marker='o', label='Trend +
Seasonality')
plt.title("Trend with Seasonal Component")
plt.xlabel("Month")
plt.ylabel("Sales")
plt.legend()
plt.grid(True)
plt.show()
```

OUTPUT

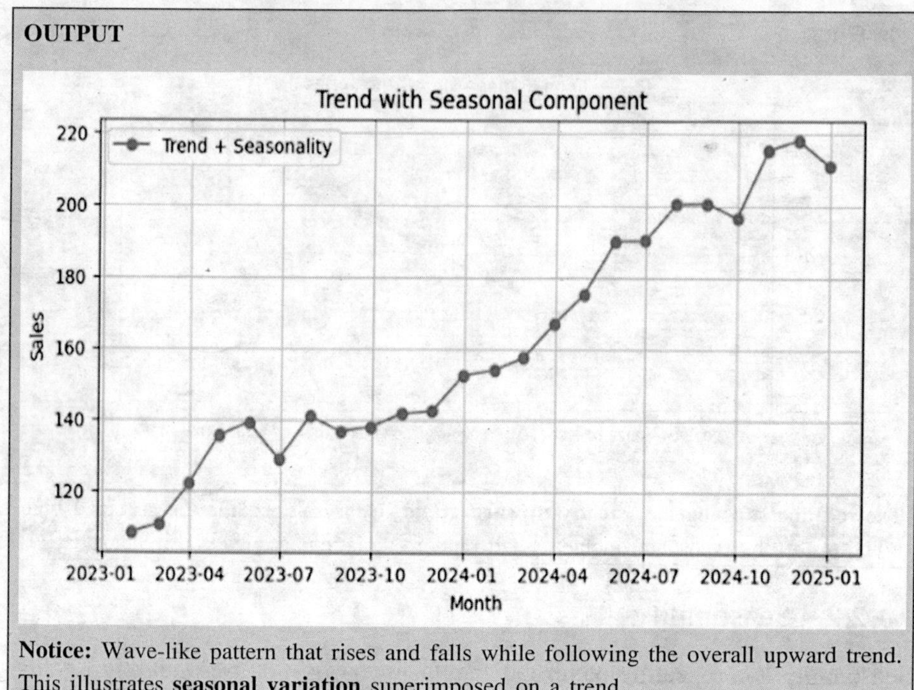

Notice: Wave-like pattern that rises and falls while following the overall upward trend. This illustrates **seasonal variation** superimposed on a trend.

10.2.3   Cycles

Cyclical patterns are long-term oscillations that occur over irregular periods, often influenced by external economic or business conditions—not by the calendar like seasonality.

Example: The economy follows boom and recession cycles that repeat but not at fixed intervals.

Code Example

```python
cycle = 15 * np.sin(np.linspace(0, 1.5*np.pi, 24))
cyclic_data = trend + cycle + noise
plt.figure(figsize=(8,4))
plt.plot(time, cyclic_data, marker='o', label='Trend + Cyclic Pattern')
plt.title("Cyclical Component in Time Series")
plt.xlabel("Month")
plt.ylabel("Sales")
plt.legend()
plt.grid(True)
plt.show()
```

OUTPUT

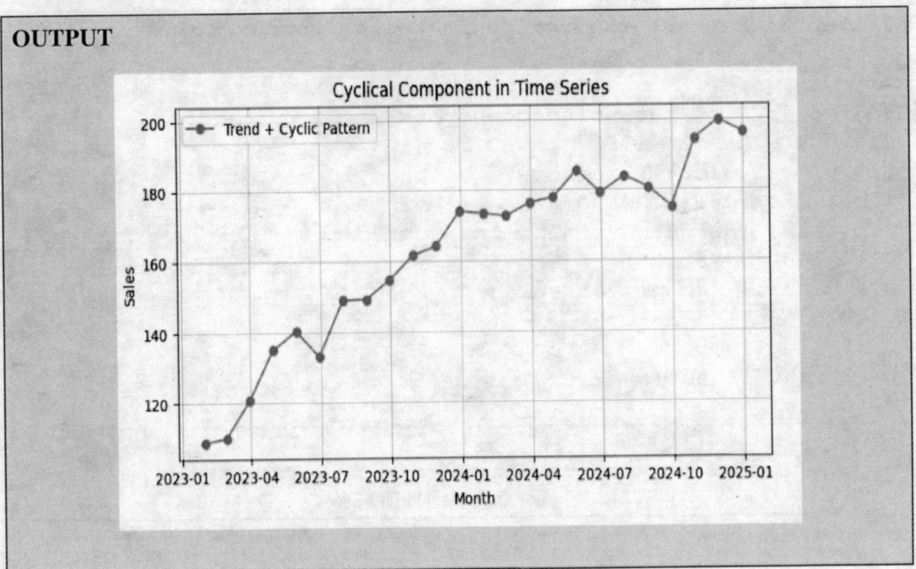

10.2.4 Noise (Irregular Component)

The noise or residual reflects random fluctuations not explained by trend, seasonality or cycle.

It arises from factors that are not amenable to forecasting such as unforeseen developments in the market, imperfections in the data, or pure chance.

Visualizing Random Noise

```python
import pandas as pd
import numpy as np
import matplotlib.pyplot as plt
from statsmodels.tsa.seasonal import seasonal_decompose

# Step 1: Load a realistic time series dataset
# Example: Monthly airline passengers (built-in dataset)
url = 'https://raw.githubusercontent.com/jbrownlee/Datasets/
master/airline-passengers.csv'
df = pd.read_csv(url, parse_dates=['Month'], index_
col='Month')

# Step 2: Decompose the time series
result = seasonal_decompose(df['Passengers'], model='addi-
tive', period=12)
```

```python
# Step 3: Extract the residual (noise) component
residual = result.resid

# Step 4: Plot the noise component
plt.figure(figsize=(10, 4))
plt.plot(residual, marker='o', linestyle='-', color='black',
label='Residual (Noise)')
plt.title("Noise Component in Time Series")
plt.xlabel("Month")
plt.ylabel("Random Variation")
plt.legend()
plt.grid(True)
plt.tight_layout()
plt.show()
```

OUTPUT

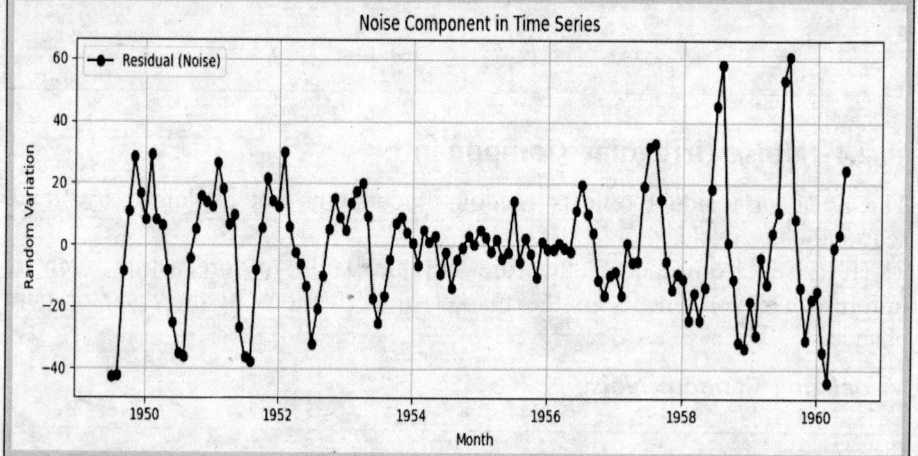

Summary of Components

Component	Description	Example
Trend	Long-term direction (growth/decline)	Increasing annual sales
Seasonality	Repeating short-term pattern	Monthly peak in summer
Cycle	Irregular long-term fluctuation	Economic boom and bust
Noise	Random unpredictable variation	Sudden sales dip due to strike

Seasonal Decomposition: Breaking Down Patterns

Different components of real-world time series data—trend, seasonality, cycles, and noise—overlap and can make identification of patterns, even via visual inspection, very difficult.

To separate significant signals from a deluge of time-mixed signals, we employ a statistical technique known as seasonal decomposition.

For forecasting and model building, this method makes it clear how various elements contribute to the overall pattern.

Using a synthetic dataset that contains all of the primary time series components, the code is applied step-by-step.

Code Example

```python
# Import required libraries
import numpy as np
import pandas as pd
import matplotlib.pyplot as plt
from statsmodels.tsa.seasonal import seasonal_decompose

# Step 1: Create synthetic time series data
np.random.seed(42)
time = pd.date_range(start='2022-01-01', periods=36, freq='M')

# Components
trend = 50 + np.arange(36) * 2  # upward trend
seasonal = 10 * np.sin(2 * np.pi * np.arange(36)/12) #
12-month seasonality
noise = np.random.normal(0, 3, 36)  # random noise

# Combine components
sales = trend + seasonal + noise

# Create DataFrame
df = pd.DataFrame({'Month': time, 'Sales': sales})
df.set_index('Month', inplace=True)

# Step 2: Plot the overall time series
plt.figure(figsize=(10,5))
plt.plot(df.index, df['Sales'], marker='o', color='blue')
plt.title('Observed Time Series: Monthly Sales')
plt.xlabel('Month')
plt.ylabel('Sales')
plt.grid(True)
plt.show()

# Step 3: Perform seasonal decomposition
decomposition = seasonal_decompose(df['Sales'], model='addi-
tive', period=12)

# Step 4: Plot decomposition results
decomposition.plot()
plt.suptitle('Seasonal Decomposition of Time Series', fon-
tsize=14)
plt.subplots_adjust(top=0.88)
plt.show()
```

OUTPUT

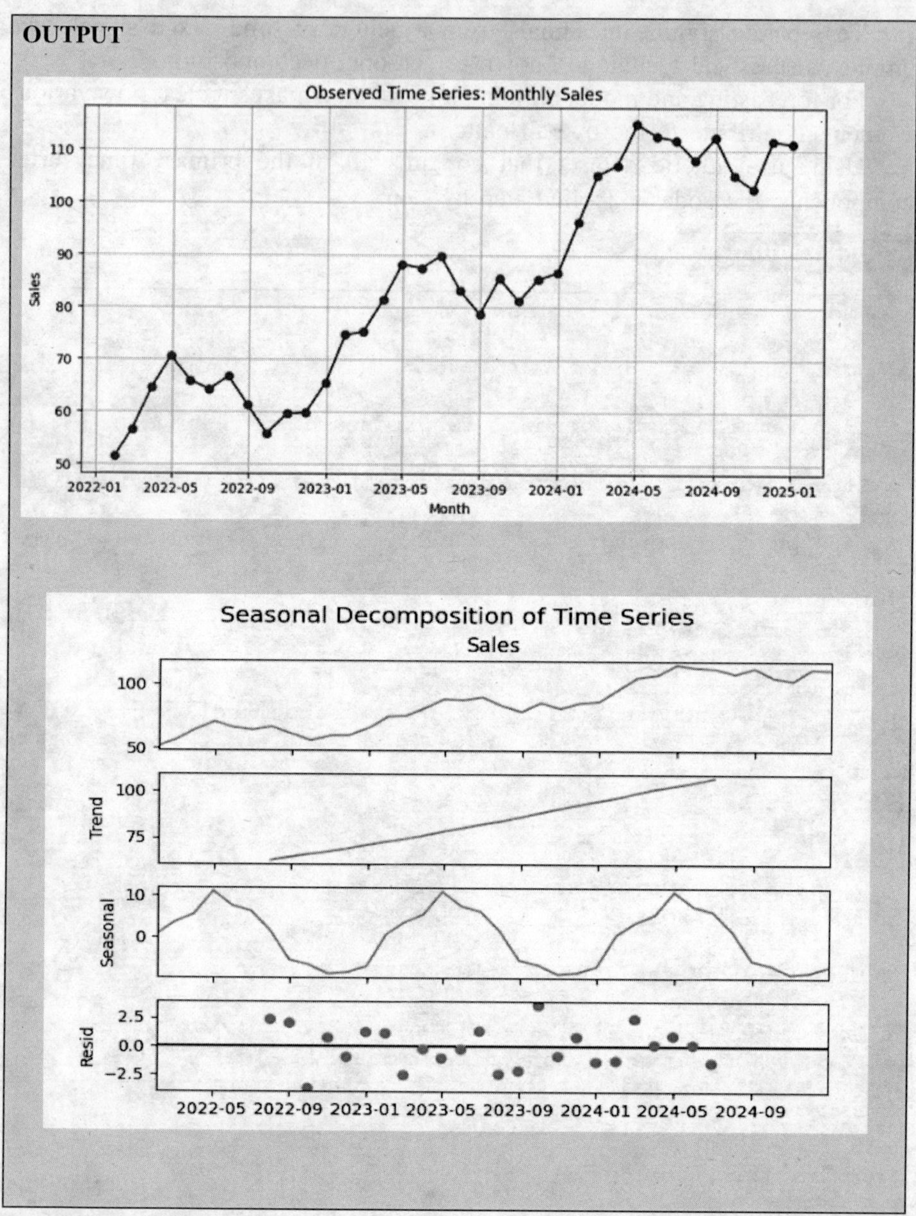

Additive vs. Multiplicative Decomposition

Type	Additive	Multiplicative
Formula	Y = Trend + Seasonal + Noise	Y = Trend × Seasonal × Noise
Use When	Seasonal variation is constant	Seasonal variation grows with level of data
Examples	If summer sales always rise by a fixed amount (e.g., +20 units)	If summer sales rise by a percentage (e.g., +20%)

Visual and Statistical Tests for Patterns

After decomposing a time series the next step is to validate and quantify the patterns that we see.

Visual plots provide great intuition but on the other hand, statistical tests help verify if a pattern is really there for instance if data has an important trend, repeating seasonal effects or autocorrelation.

This section is devoted to both visual and statistical approaches in time series pattern detection with Python code and simple interpretations for beginners.

Method	Type	Purpose	Interpretation
Line Plot	Visual	Detect trend and cycles	Upward/downward slope = trend; waves = seasonality
Histogram	Visual	See data distribution	Skewed or irregular = instability
ACF Plot	Visual	Detect correlation with past values	Repeated spikes = seasonality
ADF Test	Statistical	Check for stationarity	$p > 0.05 \rightarrow$ non-stationary
Ljung–Box Test	Statistical	Test autocorrelation	$p < 0.05 \rightarrow$ pattern exists
Seasonal Strength	Statistical	Quantify seasonal impact	Closer to 1 $\rightarrow$ strong seasonality

10.2.5 Understanding Stationarity and Why it Matters

Visualizing Non-Stationarity

Code Example

```python
import pandas as pd
import numpy as np
import matplotlib.pyplot as plt

time = pd.date_range(start='2023-01-01', periods=36, freq='M')
trend = 50 + np.arange(36) * 1.5
noise = np.random.normal(0, 3, 36)
sales = trend + noise

df = pd.DataFrame({'Month': time, 'Sales': sales}).set_index('Month')
plt.plot(df.index, df['Sales'], marker='o')
plt.title("Non-Stationary Time Series (Trend Present)")
plt.show()
```

OUTPUT

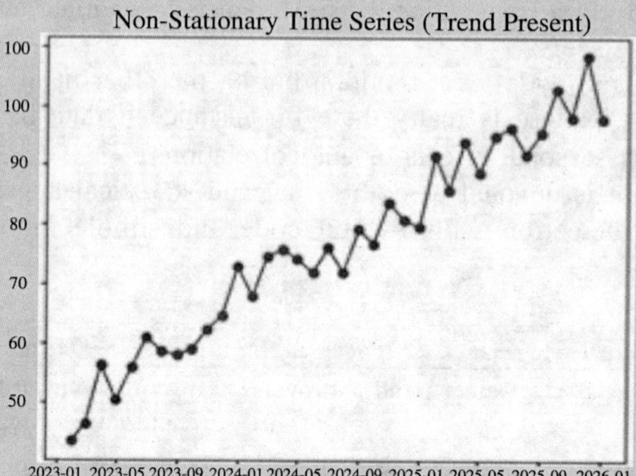


```
df['Sales_diff'] = df['Sales'].diff()
df['Sales_diff'].dropna().plot(marker='o', title="Differenced
(Stationary) Series")
plt.show()
```

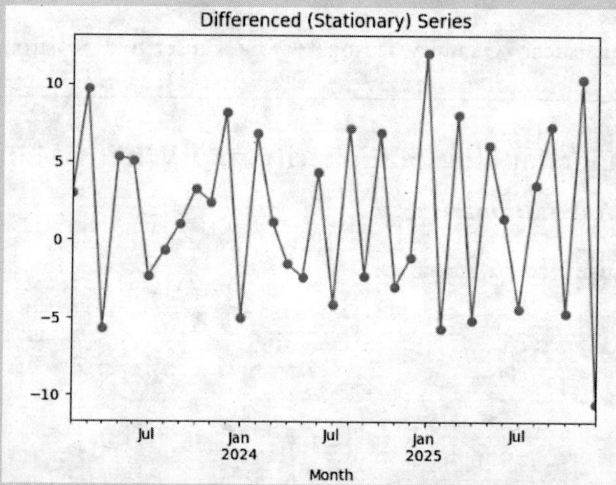

Making Data Stationary: Differencing and Transformation, there are two options

To stabilize the mean and variance:

- **Differencing:** Subtract previous values from the current value to remove trend.
- **Transformation:** Apply log or square root to reduce variability.

```
from statsmodels.graphics.tsaplots import plot_acf, plot_pacf

plot_acf(df['Sales_diff'].dropna(), lags=12)
plot_pacf(df['Sales_diff'].dropna(), lags=12)
plt.show()
```

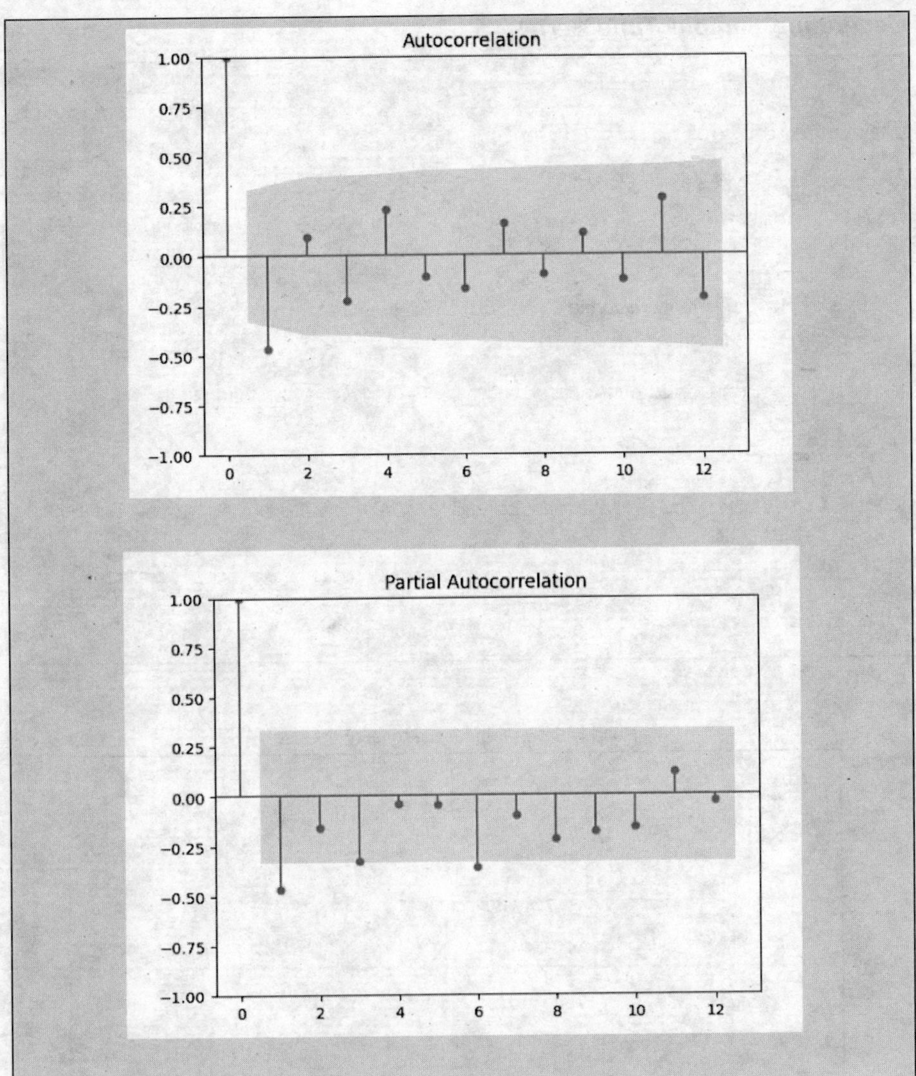

Time Series Analysis and Forecasting Example

The province of time series analysis looks at how variables change over time. Understanding this type of pattern is important for forecasting and making planning and management decisions. This section introduces beginners to the time series patterns/structures, the preparation of data and the forecasting methods with Python examples and ways to visualize with figures and practical stories.

Generating Sample Time Series

```python
import pandas as pd
import numpy as np
import matplotlib.pyplot as plt

np.random.seed(42)
time = pd.date_range(start='2022-01-01', periods=36, freq='M')
trend = 50 + np.arange(36) * 1.5
seasonality = 8 * np.sin(2 * np.pi * np.arange(36)/12)
noise = np.random.normal(0, 3, 36)
sales = trend + seasonality + noise

df = pd.DataFrame({'Month': time, 'Sales': sales}).set_index('Month')

plt.figure(figsize=(10,4))
plt.plot(df.index, df['Sales'], marker='o', linestyle='-')
plt.title("Monthly Sales: Trend + Seasonality + Noise")
plt.xlabel("Month")
plt.ylabel("Sales")
plt.grid(True)
plt.show()
```

OUTPUT

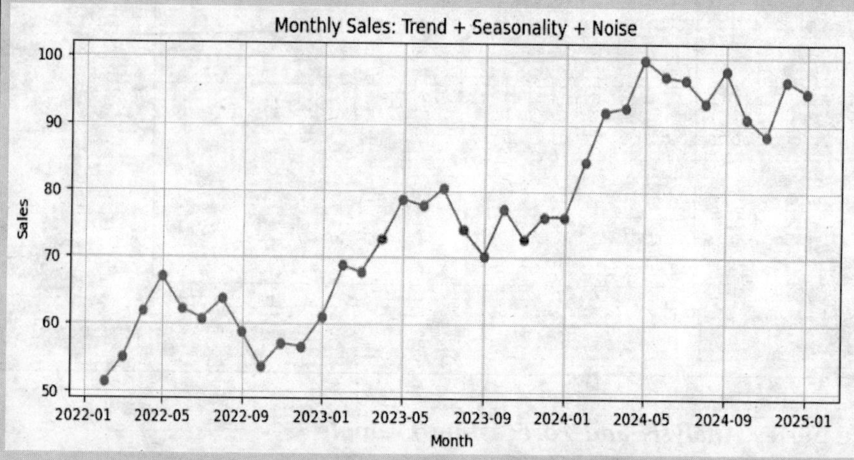

Seasonal Decomposition

```python
from statsmodels.tsa.seasonal import seasonal_decompose

decomp = seasonal_decompose(df['Sales'], model='additive',
period=12)
decomp.plot()
plt.show()
```

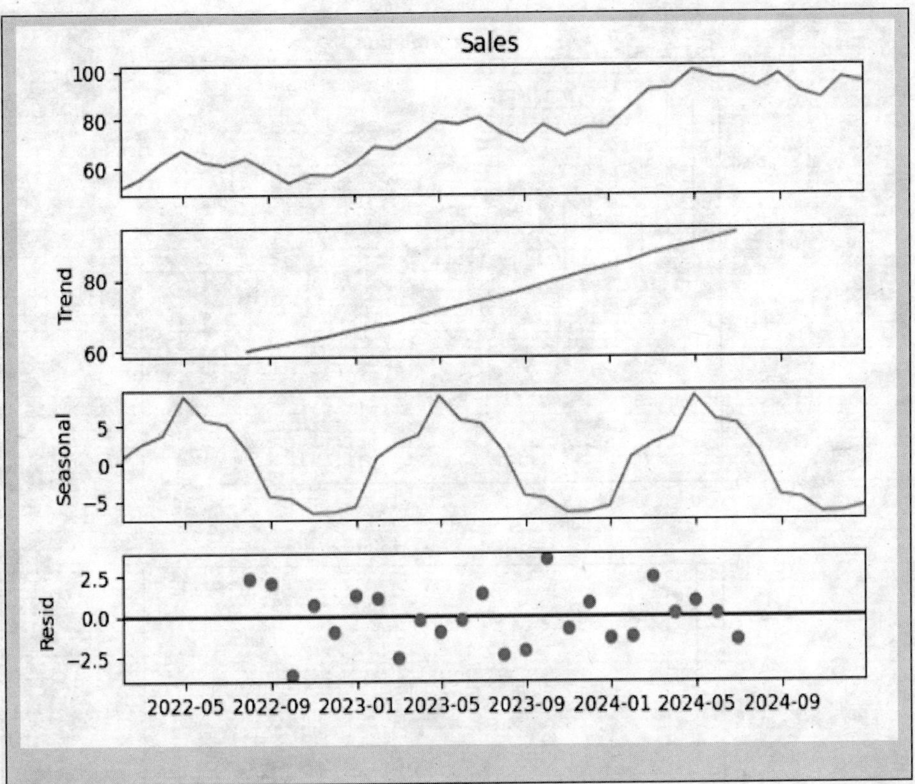

Visual and Statistical Tests for Patterns

```python
from statsmodels.graphics.tsaplots import plot_acf, plot_pacf
from statsmodels.tsa.stattools import adfuller
from statsmodels.stats.diagnostic import acorr_ljungbox
import matplotlib.pyplot as plt

# Plot ACF and PACF
plot_acf(df['Sales'], lags=20)
plot_pacf(df['Sales'], lags=17)  # Must be < 18 for 36 data
points
plt.show()

# Augmented Dickey-Fuller Test
adf_result = adfuller(df['Sales'])
print("ADF p-value:", adf_result[1])

# Ljung-Box Test for autocorrelation
lb_test = acorr_ljungbox(df['Sales'], lags=[12], return_
df=True)
print(lb_test)
```

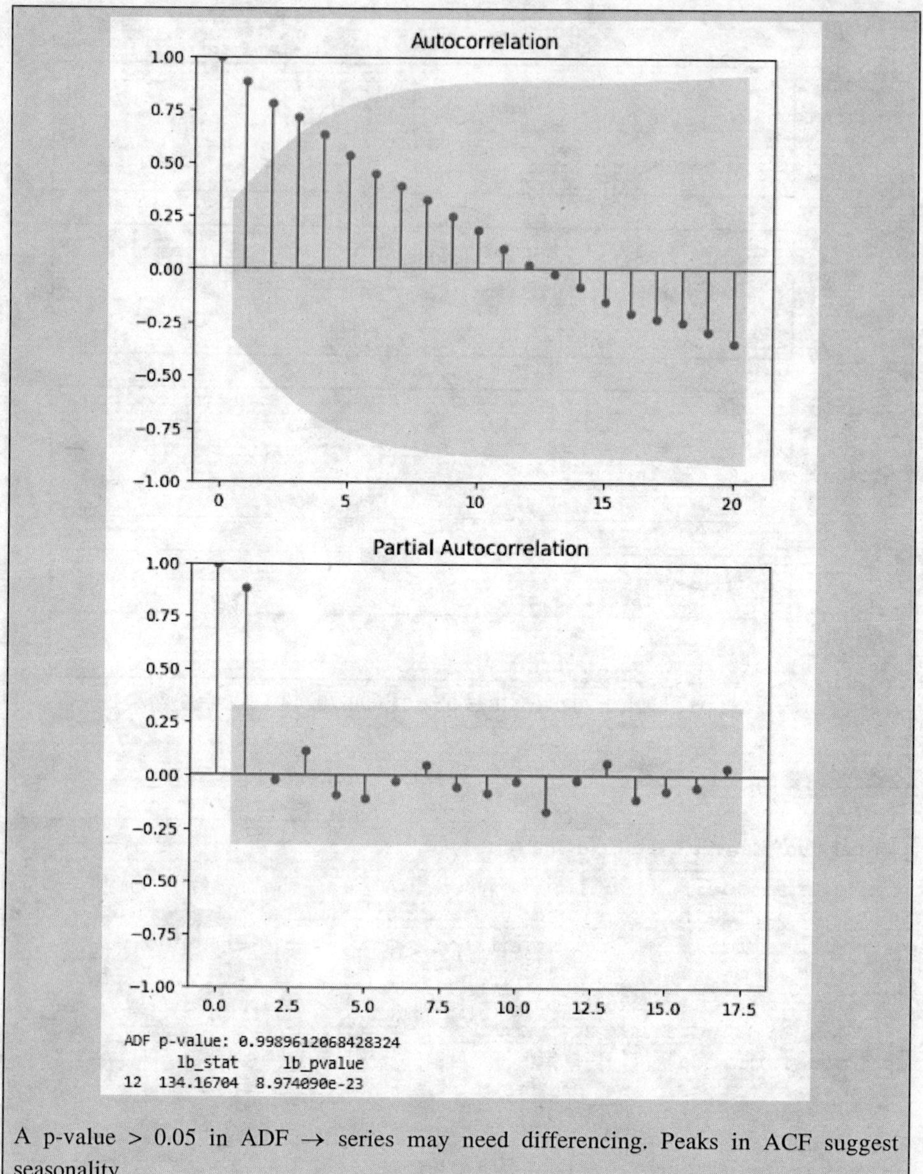

A p-value > 0.05 in ADF → series may need differencing. Peaks in ACF suggest seasonality.

10.2.6   ARIMA Models and Exponential Smoothing (Holt-Winters)

1. ARIMA Forecasting

```
from statsmodels.tsa.arima.model import ARIMA
arima_model = ARIMA(df['Sales'], order=(1,1,1))
fit_arima = arima_model.fit()
forecast_arima = fit_arima.forecast(steps=6)
```

```
order=(1,1,1) means:
      1 autoregressive term (AR)
      1 differencing to make the series stationary (I)
      1 moving average term (MA)
```

2. Plotting ARIMA Forecast

```python
plt.figure(figsize=(10,4))
plt.plot(df.index, df['Sales'], marker='o', linestyle='-',
label='Actual')
plt.plot(pd.date_range(df.index[-1]+pd.Timedelta(days=1),
periods=6, freq='M'),
         forecast_arima, marker='x', linestyle='--', la-
bel='ARIMA Forecast')
plt.title("ARIMA Forecast vs Actual Sales")
plt.xlabel("Month")
plt.ylabel("Sales")
plt.legend()
plt.grid(True)
plt.show()
```

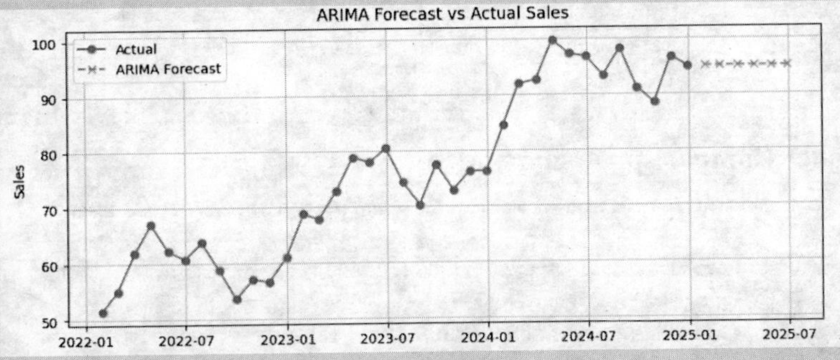

3. Holt-Winters Forecasting

```python
from statsmodels.tsa.holtwinters import ExponentialSmoothing

hw_model = ExponentialSmoothing(df['Sales'], seasonal='add',
seasonal_periods=12).fit()
forecast_hw = hw_model.forecast(6)
```

> Goal: Forecast using Holt-Winters, which captures trend +
> seasonality.
> seasonal='add' assumes additive seasonal effects.
> seasonal_periods=12 means yearly seasonality (monthly
> data).

4. Plotting Holt-Winters Forecast

```python
plt.plot(pd.date_range(df.index[-1]+pd.Timedelta(days=1),
periods=6, freq='M'),
         forecast_hw, marker='s', linestyle='-.', la-
bel='Holt-Winters Forecast')
```

```
plt.title("Holt-Winters Forecast vs Actual Sales")
plt.xlabel("Month")
plt.ylabel("Sales")
plt.legend()
plt.grid(True)
plt.show()
```

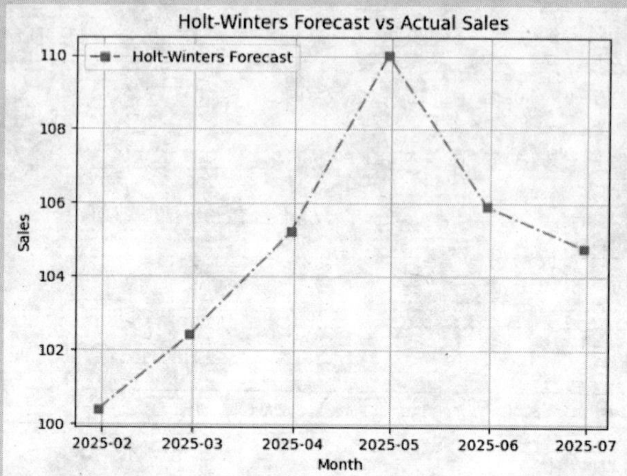

5. Model Comparison Using RMSE

```
from statsmodels.tsa.holtwinters import ExponentialSmoothing

hw_model = ExponentialSmoothing(df['Sales'], seasonal='add',
seasonal_periods=12).fit()
forecast_hw = hw_model.forecast(6)

from sklearn.metrics import mean_squared_error
import numpy as np

rmse_arima = np.sqrt(mean_squared_error(df['Sales'][-6:],
forecast_arima))
rmse_hw = np.sqrt(mean_squared_error(df['Sales'][-6:], fore-
cast_hw))

print(f"ARIMA RMSE: {rmse_arima:.2f}")
print(f"Holt-Winters RMSE: {rmse_hw:.2f}")
```

OUTPUT

```
ARIMA RMSE: 3.50
Holt-Winters RMSE: 12.45
```

Wrap-up

Time series analysis is an advantageous statistical methodology. Time series analysis examines a collection of data points over a period of time, enabling modeling and forecasting to better understand the dynamic process. An important aspect of time series modeling and forecasting is to achieve the characteristic of stationarity, which means that in a stochastic process the probability distribution isn't changing over time, so that a forecast is more likely to be reliable. Issues such as non-stationarity and noise still make time series analysis invaluable in analyzing time-ordered data.

QUESTIONS FOR PRACTICE

1. Define a time series. What are the key differences between univariate and multivariate time series?   *Anna University, 2022*

2. Explain the concepts of seasonality, trend, cycle, and noise in time series data with examples.   *Vellore Institute of Technology, 2021*

3. What is stationarity in time series? Why is it important for modeling?
                                SRM Institute of Science and Technology, 2023

4. Describe the Autoregressive Integrated Moving Average (ARIMA) model. Explain each component with an example.
                                                        Amity University, 2022

5. Explain exponential smoothing methods, including simple, double, and Holt-Winters methods.   *IIT Bombay, 2022*

6. How can you detect and handle seasonality and trend in a time series dataset?   *Manipal University, 2021*

7. Describe the difference between additive and multiplicative time series models. Provide examples of when to use each.
                                                BMS College of Engineering, 2023

8. Explain the process of forecasting using ARIMA and how model parameters are selected.   *Anna University, 2022*

9. Discuss common evaluation metrics for time series forecasting models, such as MAE, MSE, and RMSE.   *Amrita Vishwa Vidyapeetham, 2021*

10. Provide a practical application of time series analysis in finance or retail, illustrating the use of forecasts for decision making.   *IIT Delhi, 2023*

11

Data Privacy, Ethics, and Responsible AI

11.1 DATA PRIVACY AND SECURITY

11.1.1 Importance of Data Privacy in the Digital Age

The digital age has seen the generation and collection of huge quantities of data. Data is being generated everywhere, from browsing history to health records, every second we are in the middle of a huge data flow.

Data Science is the tool that not only extracts valuable information from this data but also has to bear the ethical consequences like when it comes to privacy.

The first question that must be answered before any consideration is— *What is Data Privacy?*

Data Privacy is essentially the right of individuals to control the use of their personal data. Hence, in data science respecting privacy is one of the very few things that can be considered mandatory.

Data scientists are working with a great variety of personally identifiable information (PII), which include not only names and email addresses but also medical records. If the handling of such data goes wrong, very dire consequences may result, such as legal actions, loss of reputation, and even harm to the individuals concerned.

In data science, bias refers to systematic errors that lead to unfair or inaccurate outcomes. It can instigate from varies source like:

- The data itself
- The way data is collected
- The algorithms used
- Human assumptions

We should also try to understand—Why it Matters or rather why it is critical? Facts are highlighted below:

- **Personal Harm:** Leaked personal data (like financial or medical info) can lead to identity theft or discrimination.
- **Trust:** Users are more likely to share data with organizations they trust.
- **Compliance:** Mishandling data can lead to legal consequences under regulations like GDPR.

11.1.2 Key Data Protection Laws

With the rise of the digital data particularly now it is a digital economy age, data privacy regulations have become a critical subject matter worldwide. The below table depicts few of the most popular. These types of data protection laws provide a framework for the ethically acquiring data, processing it, and how it is stored, etc.

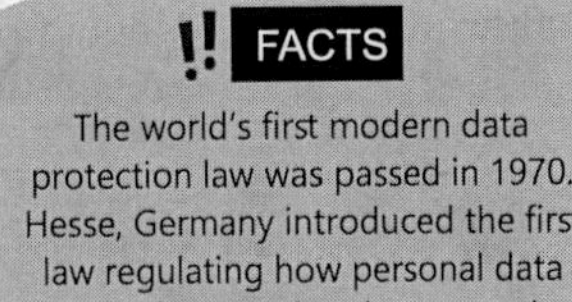

Law	Region	Focus
GDPR	European Union	Consent, right to erasure, data minimization, purpose limitation
HIPAA	USA (Health)	Confidentiality of personal health information (PHI)
CCPA	California, USA	Right to know, delete, opt-out of data sale

11.2 BIAS AND FAIRNESS IN ALGORITHMS

Nowadays, Artificial Intelligence (AI) and Machine Learning (ML) enables systems increasingly are used in decision-making for certain cases that for example—job recommendations, healthcare treatments, loan approvals, or say criminal sentencing. But have you ever though what if these systems inherit or even amplify human prejudices? This will lead to the whole system to be malfunctioning. This is where understanding *bias and fairness* becomes critical.

11.2.1 Algorithmic Bias and its Impact

Actually Algorithmic bias occurs when AI systems favor one group over another unfairly. This usually occurs not because the machine is "intentionally unfair" but because the data and methods we use show the inequalities present in society.

We have to understand the fact that, Bias isn't always intentional—but its effects can be deeply harmful. How about we dive into a real-world case?

Domain	Biased Outcome	Consequences
Hiring Tools	Favoring male resumes over female ones	Gender discrimination in employment
Predictive Policing	Over-targeting minority neighbourhoods	Reinforcement of systemic racism
Credit Scoring	Penalizing applicants from certain zip codes	Socio-economic exclusion
Healthcare	Undiagnosing diseases in certain demographics	Health disparities

11.2.2 Sources of Bias

AI systems are only as good as the data and assumptions they are built on. Let's explore the most common origins of bias.

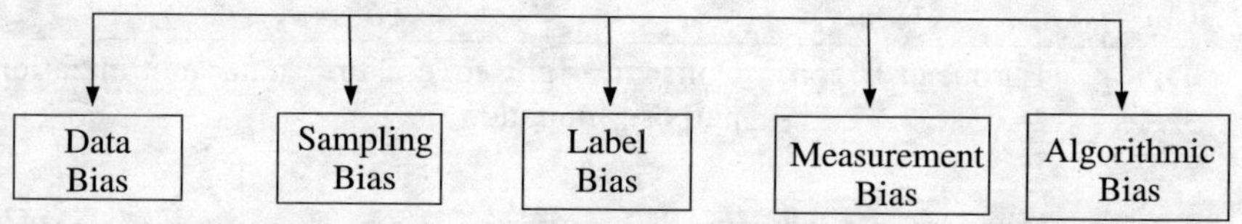

Source	Description	Example
Data Bias	Historical data reflects past discrimination	Using biased police records for future crime prediction
Sampling Bias	Non-representative training data	Using only urban data to train a model for rural healthcare
Label Bias	Human-labeled data reflects subjective judgments	Judges' biases reflected in criminal risk scores
Measurement Bias	Inaccurate proxies used for complex outcomes	Using income as a proxy for intelligence
Algorithmic Bias	Bias introduced by model assumptions or design	Optimizing only for accuracy, ignoring fairness

11.2.3 Bias Detection and Mitigation

If you need to build fair and ethical AI systems, we understand how to find and fix bias. Here are some pointers which ideally should be followed at different phases of a Data Science Project Life Cycle.

Bias Detection Techniques in AI

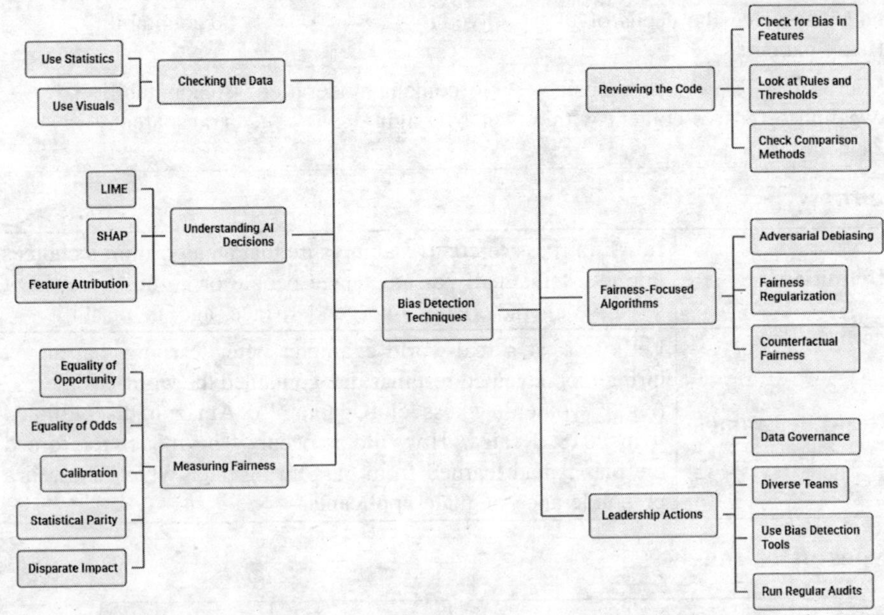

Bias Detection is important and it is a shared responsibility across the whole team. We should note:

- Making fair AI is not just the job of the computer folks.
- Everyone in the team—coders, testers, and bosses—must help make sure the system treats people equally.
- They check the data to see if it's fair and doesn't favor one group over another.

11.3 RESPONSIBLE AND ETHICAL AI

11.3.1 Principles of Fairness, Accountability, and Transparency

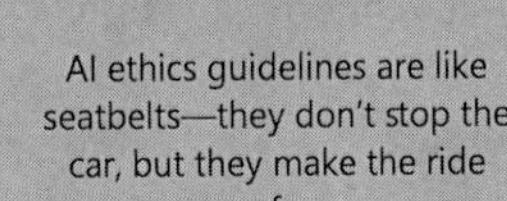

Scenario	What Went Wrong	Violated Principle
Apple Card offered lower credit limits to women than men with similar financial profiles	Gender bias in algorithmic credit scoring	Fairness
COMPAS recidivism tool predicted higher reoffending risk for Black defendants	Racial bias in criminal justice algorithms	Fairness, Transparency

(Contd.)

Scenario	What Went Wrong	Violated Principle
A healthcare algorithm underestimated the needs of Black patients	Training data lacked diversity	Fairness, Accountability
Microsoft's Tay chatbot began tweeting offensive content within 24 hours	No content moderation or oversight	Accountability, Transparency

Fairness

Definition	In AI, fairness refers to making sure that an algorithm's choices don't systematically disadvantage people or groups because of sensitive characteristics like gender, race, age, or disability.
Real-Life Example	Let's look at a real-world example. After learning that an AI hiring tool devalued resumes that contained the word "women's" (e.g., "women's chess club captain"), Amazon discontinued it in 2018. Really? How did it occur? The model reinforced the bias it had learned from past hiring data, which showed a preponderance of male applicants.

Types of Fairness

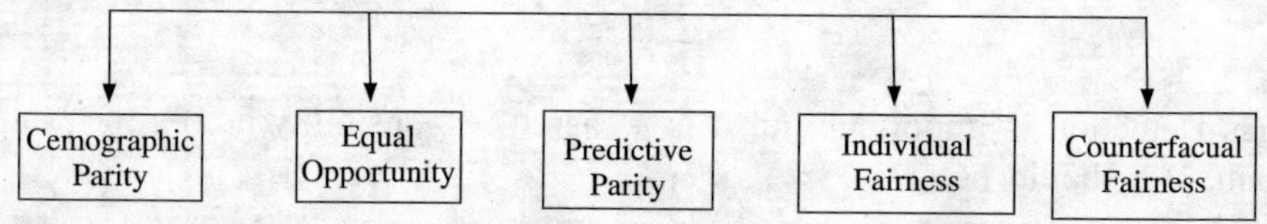

Type	Description	Real-Life Analogy
Demographic Parity	Equal selection rates across groups	Equal loan approval rates for men and women
Equal Opportunity	Equal true positive rates across groups	Same cancer detection rate for all ethnicities
Predictive Parity	Equal precision across groups	Same fraud detection accuracy for all income levels
Individual Fairness	Similar individuals receive similar outcomes	Two similar resumes get the same interview score
Counterfactual Fairness	Changing a sensitive attribute shouldn't change the outcome	A qualified candidate shouldn't be rejected just for being female

Demographic Parity

Code Example

```
from fairlearn.metrics import MetricFrame, selection_rate
from sklearn.metrics import accuracy_score
import pandas as pd
```

```
# Dummy data
y_true = [1, 0, 1, 1, 0]
y_pred = [1, 0, 0, 1, 1]
sensitive_features = pd.Series(['Male', 'Female', 'Female',
'Male', 'Female'])

# MetricFrame
metric_frame = MetricFrame(
    metrics={"accuracy": accuracy_score, "selection_rate":
selection_rate},
    y_true=y_true,
    y_pred=y_pred,
    sensitive_features=sensitive_features
)

print(metric_frame.by_group)
```

```
OUTPUT
                     accuracy        selection_rate
sensitive_feature_0
Female               0.333333        0.333333
Male                 1.000000        1.000000
```

Accountability

Definition	In AI, accountability refers to holding people or institutions accountable for the results produced by AI systems. This entails having the ability to track down decisions, examine systems, and assign blame when something goes wrong.
Real-Life Example	We'll relate it to a real-life situation once more. Due to a flawed model that gave school performance precedence over individual merit, a UK government algorithm downgraded thousands of students' grades in 2020. The government was forced to return to teacher-assigned grades due to public outcry and the lack of clear accountability for the decision.

Key Components

Component	Description	Real-Life Analogy
Traceability	Track how a model was trained and how it makes decisions	Like a flight recorder for AI
Auditability	Enable independent review of data and models	Like a financial audit for algorithms
Responsibility	Assign clear ownership of AI systems	Someone must answer for a faulty medical diagnosis
Governance	Establish policies and oversight for ethical AI use	Ethics board reviews high-risk AI deployments

Logging Model Decisions

Code Example

```python
import logging
import pandas as pd
import random

# Setup logging to both file and console
logger = logging.getLogger()
logger.setLevel(logging.INFO)

# Clear existing handlers
for handler in logger.handlers[:]:
    logger.removeHandler(handler)

# File handler
file_handler = logging.FileHandler('model_decisions.log')
file_handler.setFormatter(logging.Formatter('%(asctime)s - 
%(levelname)s - %(message)s'))
logger.addHandler(file_handler)

# Console handler
console_handler = logging.StreamHandler()
console_handler.setFormatter(logging.Formatter('%(asctime)s 
- %(levelname)s - %(message)s'))
logger:addHandler(console_handler)

# Simulated model function
def mock_model(features):
    # Simple rule-based prediction for demo
    return int(features['Income'] > 50000 and fea-
tures['Age'] < 40)

# Logging function
def log_decision(input_data, prediction, model_name="Risk-
ModelV1", reviewer="Dibyendu"):
    logger.info(
        f"Model: {model_name}, Reviewer: {reviewer}, Input: 
{input_data}, Prediction: {prediction}"
    )

# Sample test data
X_test = pd.DataFrame({
    'Gender': ['Male', 'Female', 'Female'],
    'Age': [35, 45, 28],
    'Income': [60000, 40000, 52000]
})

# Run predictions and log
for i in range(len(X_test)):
```

```
    features = X_test.iloc[i].to_dict()
    prediction = mock_model(features)
    log_decision(features, prediction)
```

OUTPUT

```
2025-10-26 03:39:56,965 - INFO - Model: RiskModelV1, Review-
er: Dibyendu, Input: {'Gender': 'Male', 'Age': 35, 'Income':
60000}, Prediction: 1
2025-10-26 03:39:56,967 - INFO - Model: RiskModelV1, Review-
er: Dibyendu, Input: {'Gender': 'Female', 'Age': 45, 'In-
come': 40000}, Prediction: 0
2025-10-26 03:39:56,968 - INFO - Model: RiskModelV1, Review-
er: Dibyendu, Input: {'Gender': 'Female', 'Age': 28, 'In-
come': 52000}, Prediction: 1
```

Each log entry records the model name, reviewer, input features, and prediction — enabling traceability and auditability for every decision made.

This creates a traceable log of model decisions for future audits or investigations.

Transparency

Definition	Transparency in AI means making the system's behavior, logic, and data sources understandable to humans. It includes explainability, documentation, and communication.
Real-Life Example	This time our example is from Google. In 2015, Google Photos mistakenly labeled Black people as "gorillas."—Image? Google apologized and retagged the label, but the lack of transparency about how the image recognition system worked made it difficult to understand or fix the root cause.

Key Dimensions

Dimension	Description	Real-Life Analogy
Explainability	Understand how the model makes decisions	Like a teacher explaining a grade
Data Provenance	Know where the data came from and how it was processed	Like a food label showing ingredients
Algorithmic Transparency	Disclose model architecture and training methods	Like open-source software documentation
Communication	Clearly explain AI behavior to stakeholders	Like a doctor explaining a diagnosis

Summary Table

Principle	Real-World Failure Example	Goal	Tools & Techniques
Fairness	Amazon's biased hiring tool	Prevent discrimination	Fairlearn, AIF360, reweighing
Accountability	UK exam grading algorithm	Assign responsibility and enable audits	Logging, model cards, governance
Transparency	Google Photos mislabeling	Make decisions understandable	SHAP, LIME, documentation

11.4 TOWARDS ETHICAL AND TRUSTWORTHY AI

Transparency, accountability, and fairness are more than just moral principles. The data scientist who created a model is not the only person responsible for creating fair AI. Every team member must ensure that the system treats everyone equally, whether they are writing code or making important decisions. To determine whether the machine is acting unfairly, they examine the data, the rules, and specialized tools. Bosses must also bring in individuals from various backgrounds, maintain clean data, and repeatedly check the system. Only then will everyone, regardless of identity, be treated fairly by the machine.

Wrap-up

Fairness and privacy protection are becoming necessities as AI becomes more and more integrated into daily life. This chapter examines the ethical risks associated with biased algorithms, responsible data handling, and the guiding principles of reliable AI systems. The fundamentals of justice, accountability, and transparency will be covered, along with important privacy laws and strategies for identifying and reducing bias. These concepts serve as the foundation for developing trustworthy AI technologies.

QUESTIONS FOR PRACTICE

1. Explain the importance of data privacy and security in the digital age. Provide examples of breaches and their consequences.

    Anna University, 2022

2. Discuss key data protection laws in India and their relevance to Data Science projects. *Vellore Institute of Technology, 2021*

3. Define algorithmic bias. What are the common sources of bias in AI systems? *SRM Institute of Science and Technology, 2023*

4. Explain the impact of biased algorithms in real-world applications. Give an example from finance or healthcare. *Amity University, 2022*

5. Describe techniques to detect and mitigate bias in machine learning models.
   IIT Bombay, 2022

6. What are the principles of Fairness, Accountability, and Transparency (FAT) in AI? Explain each principle with examples.
   Manipal University, 2021

7. Discuss the concept of ethical AI. How can organizations ensure their AI systems are trustworthy? *BMS College of Engineering, 2023*

8. Explain different types of fairness in AI, such as demographic parity and equal opportunity. *Anna University, 2022*

9. What is accountability in AI systems? Discuss the responsibilities of developers and organizations. *Amrita Vishwa Vidyapeetham, 2021*

10. Suggest best practices for building responsible and ethical AI applications in industries like healthcare, finance, and education.
    IIT Delhi, 2023

Appendix A
Python Quick Reference for Data Scientist

STATISTICS AND PROBABILITY	
Mean	`np.mean(data)`
Median	`np.median(data)`
Mode	`statistics.mode(data)`
Standard Deviation	`np.std(data)`
Variance	`np.var(data)`
Correlation	`np.corrcoef(x, y)[0,1]`
Covariance	`np.cov(x, y)[0,1]`
Percentile	`np.percentile(data, 75)`
Interquartile Range	`np.percentile(data, 75) - np.percentile(data, 25)`
Z-score	`(x - np.mean(data)/np.std(data)`
Probability	`P(A) = favorable/total`
Binomial Distribution	`np.random.binomial(n=10, p=0.5)`
Normal Distribution	`np.random.normal(mean=0, std=1)`
Poisson Distribution	`np.random.poisson(lam=5)`
Exponential Distribution	`np.random.exponential(scale=1)`
Uniform Distribution	`np.random.uniform(low=0, high=1)`
Central Limit Theorem	`means = [np.mean(np.random.choice(data, 30)) for_in range(1000)]`
Confidence Interval	`mean ± z * (std/sqrt(n))`
Hypothesis Testing	`from scipy import stats; t_stat, p_value = stats.ttest_ind(group1, group2)`

DATA IMPORT AND LOADING

Load only specific columns	`pd.read_csv('data.csv', usecols=['col1','col2'])`
Read compressed files	`pd.read_csv('data.csv.gz')`
Read from SQL with filter	`pd.read_sql("SELECT * FROM table WHERE date > '2023-01-01'", con)`
Load specific Excel sheet	`pd.read_excel('file.xlsx', sheet_name='Sheet2')`
Read in chunks	`for chunk in pd.read_csv('large.csv', chunksize=10000):`
Specify data types	`pd.read_csv('data.csv', dtype={'id': 'int32', 'amount': 'float32'})`
Parse dates during load	`pd.read_csv('data.csv', parse_dates=['date_col'])`
Handle missing values	`pd.read_csv('data.csv', na_values=['NA', 'null', ''])`
Skip rows	`pd.read_csv('data.csv', skiprows=range(1,100))`
Read sample rows	`pd.read_csv('data.csv', nrows=1000)`
Use Dask for big data	`import dask.dataframe as dd; ddf = dd.read_csv('*.csv')`

EXPLORATORY DATA ANALYSIS (EDA)

Quick data overview	`df.info()`
Statistical summary	`df.describe(include='all')`
Check missing values	`df.isnull().sum()`
Correlation matrix	`df.corr()`
Value counts	`df['category'].value_counts()`
Memory usage	`df.memory_usage(deep=True).sum()/1e6`
Duplicate check	`df.duplicated().sum()`
Unique values count	`df['col'].nunique()`
Data type conversion	`df['col'] = pd.to_numeric(df['col'], errors='coerce')`
Quick visualization	`df.hist(bins=50, figsize=(12,8))`
Group statistics	`df.groupby('category')['value'].agg(['mean','std','count'])`
Cross tabulation	`pd.crosstab(df['col1'], df['col2'])`
Check for constant columns	`[col for col in df.columns if df[col].nunique() == 1]`

DATA CLEANING AND PREPROCESSING	
Convert to category	`df['cat_col'] = df['cat_col'].astype('cat-egory')`
Remove duplicates	`df.drop_duplicates(subset=['id'], in-place=True)`
Fill missing values	`df['col'].fillna(df['col'].median(), in-place=True)`
Create missing indicator	`df['col_missing'] = df['col'].isnull().astype(int)`
Remove outliers (IQR)	`Q1, Q3 = df['col'].quantile([0.25, 0.75]); IQR = Q3 - Q1; df = df[~((df['col'] < (Q1 - 1.5*IQR))	(df['col'] > (Q3 + 1.5*IQR)))]`
Standardize column names	`df.columns = df.columns.str.lower().str.re-place(' ', '_')`
Extract datetime features	`df['year'] = df['date'].dt.year; df['month'] = df['date'].dt.month`
One-hot encoding	`pd.get_dummies(df, columns=['category'], drop_first=True)`
Label encoding	`from sklearn.preprocessing import Label-Encoder; df['encoded'] = LabelEncoder().fit_transform(df['col'])`
Scaling features	`from sklearn.preprocessing import Stan-dardScaler; scaler = StandardScaler(); df_scaled = scaler.fit_transform(df)`
Create interaction terms	`df['feat1_x_feat2'] = df['feat1'] * df['feat2']`
Binning continuous variables	`df['age_group'] = pd.cut(d-f['age'], bins=[0,18,35,60,100], la-bels=['child','adult','middle','senior'])`

DATA VISUALIZATION	
Quick histogram	`df['col'].hist(bins=30)`
Scatter plot	`plt.scatter(df['x'], df['y'], alpha=0.5)`
Box plot	`df.boxplot(column='value', by='category')`
Correlation heatmap	`sns.heatmap(df.corr(), annot=True, cmap='coolwarm')`
Pair plot	`sns.pairplot(df[['col1','col2','col3']])`
Count plot	`sns.countplot(data=df, x='category')`
Distribution plot	`sns.histplot(data=df, x='value', kde=True)`
Time series plot	`df.set_index('date')['value'].plot()`
Bar plot with error	`df.groupby('category')['value'].mean().plot(kind='bar', yerr=df.groupby('catego-ry')['value'].std())`

(Contd.)

DATA VISUALIZATION	
Save high-res plot	`plt.savefig('plot.png', dpi=300, bbox_inches='tight')`
Subplots grid	`fig, axes = plt.subplots(2, 2, figsize=(12,8))`
Customize style	`plt.style.use('seaborn-v0_8-darkgrid')`
Interactive plot (Plotly)	`import plotly.express as px; fig = px.scatter(df, x='x', y='y', color='category'); fig.show()`

MODEL TRAINING AND BUILDING	
Train-test split	`from sklearn.model_selection import train_test_split; X_train, X_test, y_train, y_test = train_test_split(X, y, test_size=0.2, random_state=42)`
Logistic Regression	`from sklearn.linear_model import LogisticRegression; model = LogisticRegression(max_iter=1000); model.fit(X_train, y_train)`
Random Forest	`from sklearn.ensemble import RandomForestClassifier; model = RandomForestClassifier(n_estimators=100, random_state=42); model.fit(X_train, y_train)`
Gradient Boosting	`from sklearn.ensemble import GradientBoostingClassifier; model = GradientBoostingClassifier(n_estimators=100); model.fit(X_train, y_train)`
Cross-validation	`from sklearn.model_selection import cross_val_score; scores = cross_val_score(model, X, y, cv=5)`
Pipeline creation	`from sklearn.pipeline import Pipeline; pipe = Pipeline([('scaler', StandardScaler()), ('model', LogisticRegression())])`
Make predictions	`y_pred = model.predict(X_test)`
Predict probabilities	`y_proba = model.predict_proba(X_test)[:, 1]`

NATURAL LANGUAGE PROCESSING	
Lowercase text	`text.lower()`
Remove HTML tags	`re.sub(r'<.*?>', '', text)`
Remove extra spaces	`' '.join(text.split())`
Text length	`len(text)`
Word count	`len(text.split())`
Spell checking	`TextBlob(text).correct()`
Text similarity (Jaccard)	`len(set1 & set2)/len(set1|set2)`
Text classification (Naive Bayes)	`MultinomialNB().fit(X_train, y_train)`

(Contd.)

NATURAL LANGUAGE PROCESSING	
Text generation (GPT-2)	`model.generate(input_ids, max_length=50)`
Remove emojis	`re.sub(r'[^\x00-\x7F]+', '', text)`
Extract hashtags	`re.findall(r'#\w+', text)`
Extract mentions	`re.findall(r'@\w+', text)`
String starts with	`text.startswith('prefix')`
String ends with	`text.endswith('suffix')`
String contains	`'word' in text`
String strip whitespace	`text.strip()`
UTF-8 encoding	`text.encode('utf-8')`
UTF-8 decoding	`bytes_data.decode('utf-8')`
String formatting	`f'Hello {name}'`
String find index	`text.find('substring')`
String count occurrences	`text.count('word')`
String reverse	`text[::-1]`
String title case	`text.title()`
String swap case	`text.swapcase()`
String is space	`text.isspace()`
String is lower	`text.islower()`
String is upper	`text.isupper()`

MODEL EVALUATION	
Accuracy score	`from sklearn.metrics import accuracy_score; accuracy_score(y_test, y_pred)`
Classification report	`from sklearn.metrics import classification_report; print(classification_report(y_test, y_pred))`
Confusion matrix	`from sklearn.metrics import confusion_matrix; cm = confusion_matrix(y_test, y_pred)`
ROC-AUC score	`from sklearn.metrics import roc_auc_score; roc_auc_score(y_test, y_proba)`
Precision-Recall	`from sklearn.metrics import precision_recall_curve; precision, recall, _ = precision_recall_curve(y_test, y_proba)`
MSE/RMSE	`from sklearn.metrics import mean_squared_error; mse = mean_squared_error(y_test, y_pred); rmse = np.sqrt(mse)`
R-squared	`from sklearn.metrics import r2_score; r2 = r2_score(y_test, y_pred)`
MAE	`from sklearn.metrics import mean_absolute_error; mae = mean_absolute_error(y_test, y_pred)`

(Contd.)

MODEL EVALUATION	
Cross-val metrics	`from sklearn.model_selection import cross_validate; cv_results = cross_validate(model, X, y, cv=5, scoring=['accuracy','f1','roc_auc'])`
Plot ROC curve	`from sklearn.metrics import RocCurveDisplay; RocCurveDisplay.from_estimator(model, X_test, y_test)`
Plot confusion matrix	`from sklearn.metrics import ConfusionMatrixDisplay; ConfusionMatrixDisplay.from_estimator(model, X_test, y_test)`

Appendix B
Reference Datasets in Python Libraries

Dataset Name	How to Import (Code)	About the Dataset	Best For
Iris Dataset	`from sklearn.datasets import load_iris` `iris = load_iris()`	Classic dataset with 3 iris species, 4 features (sepal/petal dimensions), 150 samples	Classification, EDA, ML Basics
Boston Housing	`from sklearn.datasets import fetch_openml` `boston = fetch_openml(name='boston', version=1)`	506 samples, 13 features (crime rate, rooms, age, etc.), house prices	Regression, Feature importance
Diabetes Dataset	`from sklearn.datasets import load_diabetes` `diabetes = load_diabetes()`	442 patients, 10 baseline variables (age, sex, BMI, etc.), disease progression	Regression, Medical data analysis
Wine Dataset	`from sklearn.datasets import load_wine` `wine = load_wine()`	3 wine types, 13 chemical features, 178 samples	Classification, Clustering
Breast Cancer	`from sklearn.datasets import load_breast_cancer` `cancer = load_breast_cancer()`	569 samples, 30 features, malignant/benign classification	Classification, Healthcare ML

(Contd.)

Dataset Name	How to Import (Code)	About the Dataset	Best For
Digits Dataset	```from sklearn.datasets import load_digits digits = load_digits()```	1797 handwritten digits (0-9), 8x8 pixel images	Image classification, MNIST alternative
Titanic Dataset	```import seaborn as sns titanic = sns.load_dataset('titanic')```	891 passengers, survival data with age, class, sex, fare	Classification, Feature engineering
Tips Dataset	```import seaborn as sns tips = sns.load_dataset('tips')```	244 restaurant bills with tip amounts, gender, day, time	EDA, Visualization practice
Penguins Dataset	```import seaborn as sns penguins = sns.load_dataset('penguins')```	344 penguins, species, island, bill dimensions, body mass	EDA, Classification, Missing values
California Housing	```from sklearn.datasets import fetch_california_housing housing = fetch_california_housing()```	20,640 samples, 8 features, median house value	Regression, Large dataset practice
20 Newsgroups	```from sklearn.datasets import fetch_20newsgroups news = fetch_20newsgroups()```	18,846 documents across 20 topics	NLP, Text classification
Fashion MNIST	```from tensorflow.keras.datasets import fashion_mnist (train_X, train_y), (test_X, test_y) = fashion_mnist.load_data()```	70,000 fashion items, 10 categories	Deep Learning, CNN practice
CIFAR-10	```from tensorflow.keras.datasets import cifar10 (train_X, train_y), (test_X, test_y) = cifar10.load_data()```	60,000 color images, 10 classes	Computer Vision, Color images

Index